The New Teacher Book

Finding purpose, balance, and hope
during your first years in the classroom

**Edited by Linda Christensen, Stan Karp,
Bob Peterson, and Moé Yonamine**

A RETHINKING SCHOOLS PUBLICATION · THIRD EDITION

The New Teacher Book: Finding purpose, balance, and hope during your first years in the classroom
Third Edition
Edited by Linda Christensen, Stan Karp, Bob Peterson, and Moé Yonamine

A Rethinking Schools Publication

Rethinking Schools, Ltd., is a nonprofit publisher and advocacy organization dedicated to sustaining and strengthening public education through social justice teaching and education activism. Our magazine, books, and other resources promote equity and racial justice in the classroom.

To request additional copies of this book or a catalog of other publications, or to subscribe to *Rethinking Schools* magazine, contact:

6737 W. Washington St.
Suite 3249
Milwaukee, WI 53214
800-669-4192
rethinkingschools.org

Follow @RethinkSchools

© 2019 Rethinking Schools, Ltd.

Third edition

Cover and Book Design: Nancy Zucker
Cover Illustration: Rafael López
Production Editor: Elizabeth Barbian
Proofreading: Lawrence Sanfilippo
Indexing: Carol Roberts

ISBN: 978-0-942961-03-4

Library of Congress Control Number: 2019930823

The Library of Congress categorized the second edition as follows:
The new teacher book : finding purpose, balance, and hope during your first years in the classroom / edited by Terry Burant ... [et al.]. -- 2nd ed.
p. cm.
Includes index.
ISBN 978-0-942961-47-8
1. First year teachers. 2. First year teachers--In-service training--Handbooks, manuals, etc. 3. Effective teaching. 4. Teaching. I. Burant, Terry, 1958-
LB2844.1.N4N476 2010 371.1--dc22
2010035979

Contents

CHAPTER 1: Starting Strong

CHAPTER 3: Challenges and Opportunities

CHAPTER 4: Measuring What Matters

CHAPTER 5: Beyond the Classroom

Preface

Why We Re-Wrote This Book

This third edition of *The New Teacher Book* began, appropriately enough, with new teachers. In the summer of 2017, with grant support from the National Education Association, Rethinking Schools convened two groups of early career educators for three-day retreats in Portland, Oregon, and Milwaukee, Wisconsin.

The gatherings had two goals: 1) to deepen our collective understanding of the practice of critical teaching for social and racial justice, and 2) to critically review the second edition of Rethinking Schools' *The New Teacher Book* with a view toward producing a significantly revised and updated new edition.

About 40 early career teachers came from seven states. More than two-thirds were women; more than two-thirds teachers of color. Some were from the LGBTQ communities. They taught across all grade levels and content areas in high-poverty schools, middle-class schools, and high-income schools. For three days they worked with Rethinking Schools editors, dissecting the second edition and discussing the elements needed to fill classrooms with learning, community, and justice. The work continued through the 2017–18 school year with writing groups in Oregon, Wisconsin, and New Jersey. The new teachers we worked with made invaluable contributions to this book, and it includes many of their voices and insights. More than half of this volume is new. It also reflects nearly a decade of sweeping change in education since our last edition was published in 2010.

The first three chapters of this third edition focus on what we believe are the keys to sustaining a successful career as a social justice educator: creating compassionate classroom communities, building a powerful curriculum rooted in students' lives and challenging real-world content, and mastering the craft of teaching. The fourth and fifth chapters include new sections on the crucial, but contentious issues of assessment and evaluation and on the polarized politics of education reform. The book ends with a list of resources and contacts for turning the ideas in it into advocacy and action.

At the end of our retreats in the summer of 2017, one participant wrote, "This was a powerful and transformative experience at this stage in my teaching career. I wish I had this wealth of resources, and community of social justice educator-activists sooner." We hope this book can similarly provide resources and promote community for new generations of educators.

Public education — like nearly every democratic value and institution in our society — is currently under attack from the forces of racism, misogyny, and greed. For democracy and public education to thrive we will need many new generations of teachers committed to social justice. This book is offered in hope and thanks to them.

Introduction to the Second Edition

Why We Wrote This Book

When the editors of Rethinking Schools first conceived of this book, we thought back to our days as new teachers. We hoped to create the book we needed in those sometimes exhilarating, sometimes lonely, often hard first days of our teaching careers. This book is meant as a conversation among colleagues. We hope it is a conversation that helps you keep your vision and values intact as you struggle in institutions that may or may not be those citadels of idealism where you imagined yourself teaching.

We wrote this book because it's important for the profession that new teachers with social justice ideals stay in the classroom. Our communities need teachers who see the beauty and intelligence of every student who walks through their doors and who are willing to keep trying to reach those who have already been told they aren't worthy. Our students need teachers who value students' home languages and who know how to build academic strength from those roots.

We need teachers who learn how to develop curriculum that ties students' lives, history, and academic disciplines together to demonstrate their expertise when top-down curriculum mandates explode across a district. Our school districts need teachers who can advocate against the dumbing-down of curriculum, against testing mania, and against turning our classrooms over to corporate-created curriculum. Our country needs teachers who understand the connections between race, class, and tracking. How else do we make a lasting change?

We wrote this book because we want you to hold on to those impulses that brought you to teaching: a deep caring for students, the opportunity to be the one who sparks student growth and change, as well as the desire to be involved in work that matters. We need teachers who want to work in a place where human connections matter more than profit.

We wrote this book because we have had days — many days — where our teaching aspirations did not meet the reality of the chaos we encountered. We have experienced those late afternoons crying-alone-in-the-classroom kind of days when a lesson failed or we felt like our students hosted a party in the room and we were the uninvited guests. We wrote this book hoping it might offer solace and comfort on those long days when you wonder if you are cut out to be a teacher after all.

We also wrote this book because we understand the connection between what happens behind the classroom door and what happens outside of it. A key skill for new teachers is to see ourselves as defenders of public schools — getting involved in our local and national education unions, connecting with allies among parents, community groups, other unions, everyone who has a stake in fighting privatization and corporate rule.

Given the full-court press against public schools, we need to remind all teachers to not be so classroom-focused that we don't pay attention to the larger political context that is shaping our lives in the classroom. The other reason to open the classroom door and peer outside is that new teachers' survival often depends on connecting with other teachers for support and assistance for social, political, and pedagogical reasons. Isolated new teachers are bound to burn out.

There is a huge difference between having lots of book knowledge about a given area — literature, history, math, science — and knowing how to translate that knowledge into lessons that help students learn. All teachers — new and veteran — need skills to develop curriculum that celebrates the delightful aspects of our students' lives. And we need strategies that address the tragedy of some students' lives and the tragedy that the world delivers — misogyny, racism, homophobia, poverty, war. We need to discover ways to weave these into our curriculum. That takes time.

Rethinking Schools editors have assembled numerous books that focus on creating social justice curriculum: from *Rethinking Columbus* to *Rethinking Mathematics* to *Teaching for Black Lives* to *Rethinking Sexism, Gender, and Sexuality*. We hope you will look to them for curricular help. In all of our books, and in our quarterly *Rethinking Schools* magazine, we celebrate the lessons and units and strategies that worked for our students, that created days when we walked out of the building celebrating the joy of teaching.

And what we know from our years in the classroom is that we only get good at it when we do it year after year. So we wrote this book to assure you that you will get better as the years move on if you continue to study your classroom, hone your craft, read professional literature, keep up with news, and connect with your colleagues and communities. Teaching is an art. Keep practicing.

Acknowledgements

The *New Teacher Book* started out in our classrooms and became animated when we worked with colleagues in our schools, districts, unions, and teacher action groups. This edition came to life after two rousing summer institutes with early career teachers, which were funded by National Education Association (NEA), and yearlong writing sessions across multiple states with many teachers.

We would like to thank the NEA for generously sponsoring the two Rethinking Schools summer institutes and for supporting a vision of teachers as social justice workers. The NEA's subsequent financial assistance helped cover the production costs of this 3rd edition.

The early career teachers who came to our retreats not only made us rethink what we brought to the book, but also challenged us to see education and our work with renewed commitment to justice across intersectional issues of race, gender, sexuality, class, and language. We were inspired by the work and words of:

Katy Alexander, Madeleine Allen, Camila Arze Torres Goitia, Emily Black, Jayme Causey, Zanovia Clark, Juan Córdova, Mykhiel Deych, Stephanie Gallardo, Gregory Gallet, Chelsea Hallam, Angela Harris, Shawnté Hines, Nushrat Hoque, Josh Jackson, Jaydra Johnson, Julia Kirkpatrick, Natalie Labossiere, Anders Miller, Jasman Myers, Marcelia Nicholson, Ikechukwu Onyema, Turquoise LeJeune Parker, Hannah Pawlak, Ivelis Perez, Rose Peterson, Marilyn Pinto, Matt Reed, Katy Resop Benway, Melany Reyes-Cruz, Danielle Robinson, Christopher

Rodriguez, Cristiana Sardo, Meshele L. Scipio, Jessica Stein, Gabriel A. Tanglao, John Terry, Zellie Thomas, Ian Twiss, and Christopher Werner.

Although this book brings the wisdom of new teachers, the foundational ideas of previous editors still run through its pages. We'd like to thank Terry Burant, Kelly Dawson Salas, Rita Tenorio, Stephanie Walters, and Dale Weiss for their work. Many of these articles first found print in *Rethinking Schools* magazine. Rethinking Schools editors Wayne Au, Bill Bigelow, Ari Bloomekatz, Grace Cornell Gonzales, Jesse Hagopian, David Levine, Larry Miller, Adam Sanchez, Dyan Watson, and Ursula Wolfe-Rocca continually pushed us to make each article clear, concise, and useful to new teachers. Gina Palazzari and Lindsay Stevens anchored our Milwaukee office, overseeing printing, marketing, and distribution efforts needed to put this book into new teachers' hands.

In order for this book to move from idea to article to print, the editorial team relied on the talents of two people: Nancy Zucker and Elizabeth Barbian. Nancy Zucker, who oversees the design and layout of our magazine as well as many of our books, brought an artist's eye to *The New Teacher Book*. As production editor, Elizabeth's insights as an elementary bilingual teacher, her extraordinary skills as an editor, and her fastidious work in organizing unruly editors made this book possible.

We also want to thank the many talented, dedicated, and social justice-minded people who continue to enter the teaching profession. We dedicate this book to you.

—Linda Christensen, Stan Karp, Bob Peterson, and Moé Yonamine

Starting Strong

When we named this chapter "Starting Strong," we didn't mean the "Don't smile until Christmas," be tough, let them know who is boss misrepresentation of strength. Nor did we mean the "Starting strong" of laying down rules, distributing forms, reciting litanies of what students must learn, or passing out lists of standards they must rise to during the year.

We mean starting strong by building community so that students feel safe enough to take intellectual risks and ask tough questions, develop empathy by listening to their classmates' stories, gain knowledge by engaging in a curriculum that puts their lives at the center, and embrace their own and others' cultures, histories, and languages. We mean starting strong by considering the ways everything in our classrooms tells students whether or not they belong — from what's on the walls to how the desks are arranged to the way the teacher greets them as they walk in the room. Are they precious and welcome? Is their language an asset or a liability as Moé Yonamine discusses in "Uchinaaguchi: The language of my heart"? Is their name cradled as Hiwot Adilow demands in her poem "Name"?

In "A Message from a Black Mom to Her Son," Dyan Watson writes a letter to her son,

Caleb, remembering her experiences as a student and reminding teachers what she wants for her child.

> Caleb, I want your teachers to help you love being in your skin. I want them to make space for you in their curricula, so that you see yourself as integral to this country's history, to your classroom's community, to your peers' learning. I want your teachers to select materials where Blacks are portrayed in ordinary and extraordinary ways that actively challenge stereotypes and biases. Most of all, Caleb, I want your teachers to know you so they can help you grow.

In fact, if our society supported schools so that teachers taught every student who walked through the door as if they were a beloved family member and a cherished member of our communities, our schools would become the kind of democratic spaces where students could cultivate their skills and knowledge about the world and learn to count the gifts they bring. When we start strong we ground teaching in social justice ideals, believing in all students' capacities to learn and change their world.

Creating Community Out of Chaos

BY LINDA CHRISTENSEN

O nce, during 4th-period English, I came dangerously close to becoming the teacher who pushes students out of class into the halls, into the arms of the school dean, and out into the streets. I understand the thin line teachers tread between creating safe classrooms and creating push-out zones.

It started harmlessly enough. I had returned to the school where I taught for decades to co-teach junior English with a fabulous teacher, Dianne Leahy. Forty students were stuffed into our classroom. The school district instituted another new schedule to save money, so we only saw our students every other day for 90 minutes. A few weeks into the school year, I was still confusing Ana and Maria, Deven and Terrell, and Melissa and Erika. It took so long to settle the students down every day that Dianne and I were exasperated by how little real work students completed. We competed with cell phones and side-talking, as well as frequent interruptions due to students strolling in and out of the classroom or plugging in their cell phones while we attempted to demonstrate a writing strategy or initiate a discussion about the play we were studying. In addition to the lack of forward movement on reading and writing during the day, students did not complete their homework. Embarrassed by their behavior and their skimpy work, I hoped that no one would walk in and see us totally at the mercy of these 16- and 17-year-olds.

We tried to build relationships. Dianne found out who played what sport, who danced, who was a cheerleader, who loved skateboarding. I watched her kneel in front of kids as she passed out folders with a word of praise or a question that demonstrated she cared about them as individuals. Daily we attempted to connect names to faces and faces to aspirations.

While out on a hike after a particularly frustrating day where the struggle over cell phones, side-talk, and unkindness interrupted our work once again, I remembered a former student, Sekou, who returned from Morehouse College with a story about a ritual that he participated in during the early days of his freshman year and how it made him feel part of the scholarly brotherhood. I thought perhaps Dianne and I needed a ritual to help students remember that the classroom is a sacred place of learning. Eager to create community out of the chaos, I prepared a document for students to sign that promised they would complete their work, refrain from using cell phones, and participate fully in class by respectfully listening to others. Now, even as I write this list, it doesn't sound too far-fetched. In fact, it sounds like what school is about.

I brought the document to class and distributed it to students. They accepted the first bullet — do your work — but when we got to cell phones, Sierra said, "I'm not signing. I text during class, and it doesn't interfere with my work."

Her voice brought a flood of others. Melanie said, "I'm not signing. I already do my work." Ursula seconded that. Vince agreed. Then Jasmine said, "I only pledge with God." Kevin gave her a high five, and several others laughed and wadded up the paper. I'm not sure if it was Jason or Victor who said, "Let's all not sign. What can they do? They can't kick all of us out of class."

I had a moment of pure panic. Ten minutes into a 90-minute period, and I had a revolt on my hands. Part of me was horrified as I watched the class coalesce into one angry swarm, and part of me thought, "Hot damn. We have a class of activists."

This is the point at which my 30-plus years in the classroom and my memory of other hard years helped me weather the moment. I could have sent Victor, Sierra, and others to the dean's office with referrals for insubordination, beginning an out-of-control relationship that would teeter between their defiance and my desire to control the classroom. When the class chaos tips teachers to institute measures that tighten the reins by moving defiant students out of class and sending them to the disciplinarian (which moves them one step closer to the streets), they have lost the class.

As classroom teachers, we wield an enormous amount of power to control students' destiny. Dianne and I were determined to keep all of these students in junior English, but it is conceivable that a teacher with

40 students might want to cut a few, especially those who resist. Because we have taught for many years, we knew that we would win most students over, but this experience made me wonder about the new teacher down the hall — one who doesn't have that history of a beautiful June classroom community to recall.

The tide turned when one of the football players said, "I want to play Grant on Friday night, so I'm signing." A number of other students followed suit. They even walked out of the classroom and returned saying, "I am a scholar." They didn't go through the arch of hands I had envisioned, nor did they say it like they believed it, but we did make it through the class, although students looked at me like I was a skunk for the rest of the day.

This incredibly misguided move on my part reminded me that students need to be engaged in meaningful curriculum and to develop relationships with their teachers and each other. They need a learning community where they feel safe to risk and dare and even fail. There is no shortcut to making that happen.

Each September I have this optimistic misconception that I'm going to create a compassionate, warm, safe place for students in the first days of class — often because my recollection is based on the final quarter of the previous year. In the past, that atmosphere did emerge in a shorter time span. But we were living in what seemed like a more secure and less violent time.

Classroom community isn't always synonymous with warmth and harmony. Real community is forged out of struggle.

While students shared the tragedies of divorce and loss of friendships, their class talk was less often disrupted by the pressure cooker of society — and I was more naive and rarely explored those areas. We were polite to each other as we kept uncomfortable truths at bay. Classroom community isn't always synonymous with warmth and harmony.

Building Community Out of Chaos

Politeness is often a veneer mistaken for understanding, when in reality it masks uncomfortable territory, the unspeakable pit that we turn from because we know the anger and pain that dwell there. During my years at Jefferson High School in Portland, Oregon — where the interplay of race, class, sexual orientation, and gender created a constant background static — it was important to remind myself that real community is forged out of struggle. Students won't always agree on issues; the arguments, tears, laughter, joy, and anger are the crucible from which a real community starts.

Still, I hate discord. When I was growing up, I typically gave up the fight and agreed with my sister or mother so that a reconciliation could be reached. I can remember running to my "safe" spot under my father's overturned rowboat, which hung over two sawhorses in the backyard, whenever anger ran loose in our house. As a teacher, I learned to understand that discord — when paired with a social justice curriculum — can give birth to community.

Too often these days I'm in the middle of that anger, and there's no safe spot. My first impulse is to make everyone sit down, be polite, and listen to each other — a great goal that I've come to realize doesn't happen easily. Topics like gentrification, racism, and homophobia seethe like festering wounds. When there is an opening for discussion, years of anger and pain surface because most students haven't been taught how to talk with each other about these painful matters.

I can't say that I've found definitive answers, but over the years I have come to understand some of the mistakes I have made. I also found a few constants: To become a community, students need more than an upbeat, supportive teacher. They need to understand the parallels of hurt, struggle, and joy across race, class, gender, and cultural lines; they need to uncover the roots of inequality in our society and to work together for change.

Writing and Sharing Personal Stories

Building community begins when students explore their own lives and engage with their classmates. Dianne and I chose the first book, Sherman Alexie's screenplay *Smoke Signals*, to create links to students' lives since the play focuses on relationships between children and their parents. In the beginning, students weren't connecting to the play. That changed when we started discussing the alcoholism and the father/son relationship in the book. Terrell talked about how Arnold, the father, was an alcoholic asshole. His frank assessment broke the ice. Others jumped in. They hated it when Arnold hit Victor, his son, just because he dropped his father's beer. Uriah talked about how Arnold used alcohol to wash away his guilt for burning Thomas' parents in a house fire.

Although the discussion was short and some students still side-talked, the class conversation marked the first movement toward compelling work. But the turning point came when we asked students to write a forgiveness poem (see Resources). In this lesson, students read Lucille Clifton's "forgiving my father" and two student samples — one by a student who forgives her mother for moving so much and creating disruptions in her life, and one by a student who doesn't forgive his father's absence from his life. Our students actually stopped talking and listened to the poems. Then we said, "Write a list of who you want to forgive or not forgive. Then choose one to write about. If you don't want to write about your life, you can write a poem from Victor's point of view in the book."

Students wrote silently, mostly. They wrote in the classroom, on the stairs in the hallway, sprawled against the lockers in front of our class. They wrote furiously. At times, they crept close to a friend and handed their paper over. At the end of the period, students got up on the stage Dianne built for her room and shared their poems. Students cried together as they shared their poetry written to absent fathers, to dead grandparents, to themselves. That was a Thursday. The following Monday, they returned to class and wanted to share more. Trevon caught me in the hall: "Are we going to share our poems in class? I want to hear everyone's."

That's what curriculum that puts students' lives at the center does. It tells students that they matter; that the pain and the joy in their lives can be part of the curriculum.

Although Dianne and I still struggled, that poem cracked the class. That's what curriculum that puts students' lives at the center does. It tells students that they matter; that the pain and the joy in their lives can be part of the curriculum.

The "Forgiveness Poem" lesson signaled the importance of this work in bringing students' lives into our classroom. Micere Mugo, a Kenyan poet, said, "Writing can be a lifeline, especially when your existence has been denied, especially when you have been left on the margins, especially when your life and process of growth have been subjected to attempts at strangulation."

Students need to learn about each other's lives as well as reflect on their own. When they hear personal stories, classmates become real instead of cardboard stereotypes. Once they've seen how people can hurt, once they've shared pain and laughter, they can't treat people as objects to be kicked or beaten or called names as easily. When students' lives are taken off the margins and placed in the curriculum, they don't feel the same need to put down someone else.

In order to create an authentic community in my classroom, I develop lessons that help students see the humanity of their classmates. At Jefferson in the age of gentrification, students are both gentrified and gentrifiers — their distrust of each is based on historic and contemporary evictions (see "Rethinking Research: Reading and Writing About the Roots of Gentrification" in Resources). But the class also harbors neighborhood kids who share a past history, including a long-established pecking order from their previous schools.

Students find someone whom they think is weak and attack them. In my fourth-block class, the victim was Jim. He'd been in my class the year before. I'd watched him progress as a writer and thinker. In his end-of-year evaluation, he drew a picture of himself as a chef; his writing was the dough. In an essay, he explained how writing was like making bread. He was proud of his achievements as a writer.

Jim was going blind because of a hereditary disease. It didn't happen overnight, but he struggled with terror at his oncoming blindness. Because he was steadily losing his eyesight, he was clumsy in the classroom. He couldn't see where he was going. He knocked into people and desks. He accidentally overturned piles of books. Students responded with laughter or anger. Some days he cried silently into the fold of his arms. He told me, "I know the darkness is coming." Several male students in the class made fun of him for crying as well. One day, Amber was in a typically bad mood, hunched inside her too-big coat and snarling at anyone who came near. When Jim bumped her desk on the way to the pencil sharpener and her books and papers tumbled on the floor, she blew up at him for bumbling around the room. Jim apologized profusely and retreated into his shell after her attack.

A few days later I gave an assignment for students to write about their ancestors, their people. First, they read Margaret Walker's poems "For My People" and "Lineage," and others. I told them they could imagine their people as their immediate ancestors, their race, their nationality, or gender. Jim wrote:

To My People with Retinitis Pigmentosa
Sometimes I hate you
like the disease

I have been plagued with.
I despise the "sight" of you
seeing myself in your eyes.
I see you as if it were you
who intentionally
damned me to darkness.
I sometimes wish
I was not your brother;
that I could stop
the setting of the sun
and wash my hands of you forever
and never look back
except with pity,
but I cannot.
So I embrace you,
the sun continues to set
as I walk into darkness
holding your hand.

Students were silenced. Tears rolled. Kevin said, "Damn, man. That's hard."

Amber apologized to Jim in front of the class. At the end of the year she told me that her encounter with Jim was one of the events that changed her. She learned to stop and think about why someone else might be doing what they're doing, instead of immediately jumping to the conclusion that they were trying to annoy her.

My experience is that given a chance, students will share amazing stories. Students have told me that my willingness to share stories about my life with them opened the way for them to tell their stories. Students have written hard stories about divorce, drug and alcohol abuse, imprisoned family members, sexual abuse. They've also written stories about finding joy in becoming a camp counselor or spending time with a grandparent. Through their sharing, they make openings to each other. Sometimes it's just a small break. A crack. A passage from one world to another. And these openings allow the class to become a community.

Building Social Imagination

Building community in the classroom also means getting students to enter the lives of characters in literature, history, or real life they might otherwise dismiss or misunderstand. I don't want their first reaction to difference to be laughter or withdrawal. Empathy is key in community building.

I choose literature that intentionally makes students look beyond their own world. In a class I co-taught with social studies teacher Bill Bigelow, we used an excerpt from Ronald Takaki's *Strangers from a Different Shore* (1990) about Filipino writer Carlos Bulosan. Bulosan wrote, "I am an exile in America." He described the treatment he received, good and bad. He wrote of being cheated out of wages at a fish cannery in Alaska, being refused housing because he was Filipino, being tarred and feathered and driven from town.

We asked students to respond to the reading by keeping a dialogue journal. Dirk wrote, "He's not the only one who feels like an exile in America. Some of us who were born here feel that way, too." As he continued reading, he was surprised that some of the acts of violence Bulosan encountered were similar to those endured by African Americans. In his essay on immigration, Dirk chose to write about the parallels between Bulosan's life and the experiences he's encountered:

> When I was growing up I thought African Americans were the only ones who went through oppression. In the reading 'In the Heart of Filipino America,' I found that Filipinos had to go through a lot when coming to America. I can relate with the stuff they went through because my ancestors went through sort of the same thing.

Dirk went on to describe the parallels in housing discrimination, lynching, name-calling, and being cheated out of wages that both Filipinos and African Americans lived through.

Besides reading and studying about "others," Bill and I wanted students to come face to face with people they usually don't meet as a way of breaking down their preconceived ideas about people from other cultures. During this unit we continued to hear students classify all Asians as "Chinese." In the halls, we heard students mimic the way Vietnamese students spoke. When writing about discrimination, another student confessed that she discriminated against the Mexican students at our school. We paired our members of our class with ELL students who had come from other countries — Vietnam, Laos, Cambodia, Eritrea, Mexico, Guatemala, Ghana. They each interviewed their partner and wrote a profile of the student to share in class. Students were moved by their partners' stories. One student whose brother had been killed at the beginning of the year was paired with a girl whose sister was killed during the war in Eritrea. He connected to her loss and was amazed at her strength. Others were appalled at how these students had been mistreated at Jefferson. Many students later wrote about the lives of their partners in their essays on immigration.

Besides making immigration a contemporary rather than a historical topic, students heard the sorrow their fellow students felt at leaving home. In our "curriculum of empathy," we wanted our class to see these students as individuals rather than ELL students, "Chinese" students, or an undifferentiated mass of Mexicans.

A curriculum of empathy puts students inside the lives of others.

A curriculum of empathy puts students inside the lives of others. By writing interior monologues, acting out improvisations, taking part in role plays, and creating fictional stories about historical events, students learn to develop understanding about people whose culture, race, gender, or sexual orientation differs from theirs. This is imperfect and potentially dangerous, of course, because sometimes students call forth stereotypes that need to be unpacked.

In his end-of-year evaluation, Tyrelle wrote, "I learned a lot about my own culture as an African American but also about other people's cultures. I never knew Asians suffered. When we wrote from different characters in movies and stories, I learned how it felt to be like them."

Students as Intellectual Activists

Community is also created when students struggle together to achieve a common goal. Sometimes the opportunity spontaneously arises out of the conditions or content of the class, school, or community. During the first year Bill Bigelow and I taught together, we exchanged the large student desks in our room with another teacher's smaller desks without consulting our students. We had 40 students in the class, and not all of the big desks fit in the circle. They staged a "stand in" until we returned the original desks. We had emphasized Frederick Douglass' admonition that power concedes nothing without a demand — and they took it to heart.

One year, our students responded to a negative newspaper article about how parents feared to send their children to our school by organizing a march and rally to "tell the truth about Jefferson to the press." Of course, these "spontaneous uprisings" only work if teachers are willing to give over class time for the students to organize and if they've highlighted times when people in history resisted injustice, making it clear that solidarity and courage are values to be prized in daily life, not just praised in the abstract and put on the shelf.

But most often I have to create situations for students to work outside the classroom. I want them to connect our work in class and action in tangible ways. Sometimes I do this by asking students to take what they have learned and create a project to teach at nearby elementary or middle schools. After students critique the media (see "Unlearning the Myths that Bind Us" in Resources), they are usually upset by the negative messages children receive, so I have them write and illustrate books

Community and activism: These are the goals in every course I teach.

for elementary students. They brainstorm positive values they want children to receive, read traditional and contemporary children's books, critique the stories, and write their own. They develop lesson plans to go with their books. For example, before Bev read her book about John Brown she asked, "Has anyone here ever tried to change something they thought was wrong?" After students shared their experiences, she read her book. Students also created writing assignments to go with their books so they could model the writing process.

Students were nervous prior to their first teaching engagements. As they practiced lesson plans and received feedback from their peers, there was much laughter and anticipation. They mimicked "bad" students and asked improper questions that had nothing to do with the children's book: Is she your girlfriend? Why does your hair look like that? When they returned from the other schools, there were stories to share: children who hugged their knees and begged them to come back, kids who wouldn't settle down and listen, kids who said they couldn't write. My students proudly read the writings that came out of "their" class. They responded thoughtfully to each student's paper.

The seriousness the students showed was in sharp contrast to the seeming apathy they had displayed at the beginning of the year.

Through the years, I've come to understand that the key to reaching my students and building community is helping students excavate and reflect on their personal experiences, and connecting them to the world of language, literature, and society. We move from ideas to action, perhaps the most elusive objective in any classroom. Community and activism: These are the goals in every course I teach. The steps we take to reach them are not often in a straight path. We stagger, sidestep, stumble, and then rise to stride ahead again. ✳

RESOURCES

Christensen, Linda. 2015. "Forgiveness Poems." *Rhythm and Resistance: Teaching Poetry for Social Justice*. Rethinking Schools.

Christensen, Linda. 2017. "Rethinking Research: Reading and Writing About the Roots of Gentrification." *Reading, Writing, and Rising Up: Teaching About Social Justice and the Power of the Written Word (2nd Edition)*. Rethinking Schools.

Christensen, Linda. 2017. "Unlearning the Myths that Bind Us: Critiquing Cartoons and Society." *Reading, Writing, and Rising Up: Teaching About Social Justice and the Power of the Written Word (2nd Edition)*. Rethinking Schools.

A Message from a Black Mom to Her Son

BY DYAN WATSON

Dear Caleb,

When you were almost 2, we would drop off your cousin, Sydney, at her K–8 elementary school. The ritual went something like this:

"OK, Syd, have a good day."

"OK," she'd groan as she grabbed her backpack. "Bye, Caleb."

"Bye," you'd wave and grin with your entire body.

"Bye," Sydney would say one last time as she shut the door. I'd roll down the car window.

"Byeeeee," you'd sing.

"Bye," Sydney would laugh as she caught up with friends.

I'd roll up the window as you said "bye" a few more times, then start to whimper. "It's OK, sweetie, she'll be back before you know it. And you'll be off joining her before I know it."

And it's true. Before I know it, Caleb, you will be throwing your backpack on and waving goodbye as you run off across the playground. I think about that moment often and wonder about the condition of schools you'll enter. I worry about sending you, my Black son, to schools that over-enroll Black boys into special education, criminalize them at younger and younger ages, and view them as negative statistics on the dark side of the achievement gap.

Son, my hope for you is that your schooling experiences will be better than this, that they'll be better than most of mine.

For three years of my K–8 schooling, from 7:40 a.m. until 3:05 p.m.,

I was Black and invisible. I was bused across town to integrate a white school in southeast Portland, Oregon. We arrived at school promptly at 7:30 a.m. and had 10 full minutes before the white children arrived. We spent that time roaming the halls — happy, free, normal. Once the white children arrived, we became Black and invisible. We were separated, so that no more than two of us were in a class at a time. I never saw Black people in our textbooks unless they were in shackles or standing with Martin Luther King Jr. Most of us rarely interacted with a Black adult outside of the aide who rode the bus with us. I liked school and I loved learning. But I never quite felt right or good. I felt very Black and obvious because I knew that my experience was different from that of my peers. But I also felt invisible because this was never acknowledged in any meaningful way. I became visible again at 3:05 p.m. when I got back on the bus with the other brown faces to make our journey home.

Caleb, I want your teachers to help you love being in your skin. I want them to make space for you in their curricula, so that you see yourself as integral to this country's history, to your classroom's community, to your peers' learning. I want your teachers to select materials where Blacks are portrayed in ordinary and extraordinary ways that actively challenge stereotypes and biases. Most of all, Caleb, I want your teachers to know you so they can help you grow.

One day a teacher was trying to figure out why I was so angry since I was generally a calm, fun-loving kid. She said to me: "I know you, Dyan. You come from a good family." But did she know me? She knew that I lived on the other side of town and was bused in as part of the distorted way that Portland school

I worry about sending you, my Black son, to schools that over-enroll Black boys into special education, criminalize them at younger and younger ages, and view them as negative statistics on the dark side of the achievement gap.

authorities decided to "integrate" the schools. But did she know what that meant? My mom — your grandma — got us up at 6 a.m. in order for me to wash up, boil an egg just right, fix my toast the way I liked it, and watch the pan of milk so that it didn't boil over, so I could have something hot in my stomach before going to school. You know Grandma, she doesn't play. We had to eat a healthy breakfast before going to school, and we had to fix it ourselves. Maybe that's what that teacher meant by "good family." My teacher didn't know that we had to walk, by ourselves, four blocks to the bus stop and wait for the yellow bus to come pick us up and take us to school. It took us a half hour to get to school. Once there, I had to constantly code-switch, learn how not to be overly Black, and be better than my white counterparts.

Caleb, I want your teachers to know your journey to school — metaphorically and physically. I want them to see you and all of your peers as children from good families. I don't want you to have to earn credit because of whom you're related to or what your parents do for a living. And I don't want your teachers to think that you're special because you're Black and have a family that cares about you and is involved in your life. I want them to know that all children are part of families — traditional or not — that help shape and form who they are.

The summer before beginning 4th grade, I started teaching myself how to play the clarinet. It was the family instrument in that both of my older sisters played it when they were younger. For years I wanted to be a musician. It was in my blood. My grandfather was a musician, all of my uncles can sing very well, and my dad — your grandfather — was a DJ in Jamaica once upon a time. At the end of 5th grade, my band director took each member aside to provide feedback on whether or not she or he should continue music in middle school. My teacher told me that I just didn't have it and should quit. I was devastated. I had dreams of becoming a conductor and I loved playing music. I learned to read music and text at the same time before entering kindergarten, so I couldn't understand what my teacher saw or heard that made him think that I, at the tender age of 11, didn't have what it took to pursue playing in a middle school band. He knew nothing about me and had never asked any questions about me, our family, my aspirations. He didn't seek to make me a better musician.

I want your teachers to make space for you in their curricula, so that you see yourself as integral to this country's history, to your classroom's community, to your peers' learning.

Caleb, I hope that you will have teachers who realize they are gatekeepers. I hope they understand the power they hold and work to discover your talents, seek out your dreams and fan them, rather than smother them. I hope they will see you as part of a family, with gifts and rich histories that have been passed down to you. I hope they will strive to know you even when they think they already know you. I hope your teachers will approach you with humility and stay curious about who you are.

When I was in 4th grade, my elementary school held a back-to-school night that featured student work and allowed families to walk the halls and speak with teachers. In each classroom was a student leader, chosen by teachers. I was not sure what my role was supposed to be. But at one point, a couple came in, desiring to speak with Mrs. S. She was busy, so I thought I'd chat with them while they waited. As I approached them, they recoiled in fear and, with panicked looks, turned away from me and said, "Mrs. S.?" My teacher looked away from the folks she was working with and said, "It's OK, she's not like the rest." I don't remember what happened next. All I remember is that this seemed to be one of the first in a long line of reassurances that I was special and not like other Black boys and girls. For many years afterward, I was told on more than one occasion, "You're not like other Blacks." This was supposed to be a compliment.

Caleb, I pray that your teachers will not look at you through hurtful racial preconceptions. I pray that they will do the work necessary to eliminate racist practices in themselves and in those around them. I pray that they stand up for you in ways that leave you feeling strong and capable. I pray that they will nurture your spirit, and that you, in turn, will desire to be a better you.

Son, I end this letter by sharing a story that Grandma has told me many times, that I hope will one day resonate with you. On the first day of kindergarten, many of the kids were crying and clinging to their parents. But not me. I was ready! I wanted to be like my three older siblings and go to school. So I gave my mom a hug, let go of her hand, waved goodbye, and found my teacher. And remember how I told you that my oldest sister taught me how to read before I went to school? The teacher found this out and used this skill, along with my desire to be at school, to teach the other kids the alphabet and help them learn how to read. I believe, in part, that is why I became a teacher. She saw something in me and encouraged me to develop my passion — even at this young, sweet age.

That, my son, is my hope for you. I hope your teachers will love you for who you are and the promise of what you'll be.

Love,
Mama

Honor Their Names

BY LINDA CHRISTENSEN

At a sports bar in British Columbia, a gracious and gregarious young woman seated us. As we slid across the bench in the booth, I asked her name. "Carol," she said.

"Carol," I repeated. "My name is Linda. We have names from a different generation."

She laughed. "Oh, my real name is Chichima. Carol is my white name. My family is from Nigeria, so when we immigrated, I changed my name at school. It's easier for the teachers. We all have white names."

"Why is that?" I asked.

"Some of the teachers don't like to say our long names. So on the first day of school, they say, 'What's your white name?' All of my friends have white names."

Of course, this doesn't just happen in British Columbia. It happens in Portland, Oregon, where I live. It happens wherever multiple cultures and languages, one dominant and the others marginalized, bump up against each other. But it's a problem whether it happens in Bozeman, Montana; Reno, Nevada; or Montclair, New Jersey.

Students' names are the first thing teachers know about the young people who enter our classrooms; they can signal country of origin, gender, language. Students' names provide the first moment when a teacher can demonstrate their warmth and humanity, their commitment to seeing and welcoming students' languages and cultures into the classroom. The poet Alejandro Jimenez wrote about this moment in his poem "Mexican Education":

When my mother registered me for the 3rd grade
In January of '96
My ESL teacher
Had trouble with the multiple syllables in my name
She said — "Alejandro is too long, let's call him Alex."

My mother looked at the floor and said, "OK."

To give students nicknames or to refuse to pronounce student names is to reject them from their families, languages, and cultures. To devalue something as intimate and personal as the names their parents bestowed at birth, to whitewash them, to rub out their faces, skins, and vocal cords is akin to saying, "You don't belong" on the first day of school. So we say their names.

In her fiery poem "Name" (see p. 21), Hiwot Adilow talks back to people who attempt to abbreviate her name or give her a nickname:

> i'm tired of people asking me to smooth my name out for
>   them,
> they want me to bury it in the english so they can understand.
> I will not accommodate the word for mouth,
> I will not break my name so your lazy english can sleep its
>   tongue on top,
> fix your lips around it.
> no, you can't give me a stupid nickname to replace this gift of
>   five letters
>
> . . .
>
> my name is a poem,
> my father wrote it over and over again.
> it is the lullaby that sends his homesickness to bed

Although I love the study of linguistics, my tongue is a fat slug that tortures every language equally. I took years of French without learning pronunciation; now, in my 60s I struggle through Spanish lessons, still torturing vowels and consonants. So when I take roll on the first day of class, I create a phonemic translation above each student's name to remind myself how to pronounce it. As Adilow wrote:

> take two syllables of your time to pronounce this song of mine,

it means life,
you shouldn't treat a breath as carelessly as this.
cradle my name between your lips as delicately as it
    deserves —

Every year on the first day of school, I have the opportunity to affirm my students as members of our classroom by cradling their names between lips and trying to sing the songs of their homes. ✳

RESOURCE

Christensen, Linda. 2017. "Name Poem: To Say the Name Is to Begin the Story." *Reading, Writing, and Rising Up: Teaching About Social Justice and the Power of the Written Word (2nd Edition)*. Rethinking Schools.

Name

BY HIWOT ADILOW

i'm tired of people asking me to smooth my name out for them,
they want me to bury it in the english so they can understand.
i will not accommodate the word for mouth,
i will not break my name so your lazy english can sleep its tongue
      on top,
fix your lips around it.
no, you can't give me a stupid nickname to replace this gift of five
      letters.
try to pronounce it before you write me off as
lil one,
afro,
the ethiopian jawn,
or any other poor excuse of a name you've baptized me with in
      your weakness.
my name is insulted that you won't speak it.
my name is a jealous god
i kneel my english down every day and offer my begging and broken
      amharic
to be accepted by this lord from my parents' country.
this is my religion.
you are tainting it.
every time you call me something else you break it and kick it
you think you're being clever by turning my name into a cackle?
hewhat? hewhy? he when how he what who?
he did whaaaat?
my name is not a joke.
this is more than wind and the clack of a consonant.

my father handed me this heavy burden of five letters decades before
    i was born.
with letters, he tried to snatch his ethiopia back from the middle of
    a red terror.
he tried to overthrow a fascist.
he was thrown into prison,
ran out of his home
my name is a frantic attempt to save a country.
it is a preserved connection,
the only line i have leading me to a place i've never been.
it is a boat,
a plane,
a vessel carrying me to earth i've never felt.
i speak myself closer and closer to ethiopia by wrapping myself in
    this name.
this is my country in ink.
my name is the signature at the end of the last letter before the
    army comes,
it is the only music left in the midst of torture and fear,
it is the air that filled my father's lungs when he was released from prison,
the inhale that ushers in beginning.
my name is a poem,
my father wrote it over and over again.
it is the lullaby that sends his homesickness to bed
i refuse to break myself into dust for people too weak to carry my name
    in their mouths.
take two syllables of your time to pronounce this song of mine,
it means life,
you shouldn't treat a breath as carelessly as this.
cradle my name between your lips as delicately as it deserves
it's Hiwot,
say it right.

Hiwot Adilow is an Ethiopian American poet from Philadelphia. She received her BA from the University of Wisconsin–Madison, where she was a First Wave Urban Arts Scholar. Hiwot is one of the 2018 recipients of the Brunel International African Poetry Prize and author of the chapbook In the House of My Father *(Two Sylvias Press, 2018). Her writing appears or is forthcoming in* Winter Tangerine, Callaloo, The Offing, *and elsewhere and has been anthologized in* The BreakBeat Poets Vol 2.0: Black Girl Magic *(Haymarket Books, 2018). This poem was first published in* Apiary Magazine, *Issue 6.*

Uchinaaguchi
The language of my heart

BY MOÉ YONAMINE

"**D**on't you talk that dirty language," my teacher shouted at me after he punched me in the head. I got up off of the floor, dusted off the navy skirt of my school uniform, and put my chin up. I walked away as he continued to shout at me in Japanese with that unmistakable island accent. As I walked down the 8th-grade hall, I could still hear him. I walked straight out of the school building and out of the gates of our school.

I took a pledge that day: No one will ever stop me from speaking Uchinaaguchi, the Indigenous language of my homeland, Okinawa. I came to the United States as an immigrant when I was a small child. I returned to Okinawa as a 13-year-old with the hope of learning about our culture, language, and history. This was the lesson of my first week of school back on my home island.

In 1972, the Japanese government re-annexed the Ryukyu Islands — my beloved Kingdom of Dragons. Okinawa is the largest of the islands. My mother was 19, just starting college. She had grown up during the "American generation," when the U.S. military occupied all 55 of our islands. As students, my mother and father were taught both Japanese and English, as our Uchinaaguchi diminished — kept out of the schools even back then. So when I got home that day, my head still hurting, my father wasn't surprised by what had happened. He said: "It's a Japanese school. You're supposed to speak Japanese." I felt a flood of tears begin.

But my grandfather sat on the floor across the room and began to teach me the story: In 1945, our country was caught in the crossfire and destroyed. Occupied by Japan, we were the island that the Allies wanted as a stepping-stone to invade Japan. The two military forces staged their fight without regard for Okinawa's sovereignty. As many as 150,000 Okinawan civilians, many of them children, died over the three-month battle. My grandfather watched. He saw his own best friends killed by Japanese and U.S. soldiers during the bombings and battles. Yet he promised himself that war would never bully him into forgetting who he was. He said he needed me to remember: "Don't let anyone make you forget who you are." I told him I had walked away from my teacher and walked out of the school. "We all have to stand up," he said. "When it's wrong, we have to stand up."

Under Japanese government control, the public school system in Okinawa enforces the sole use of the Japanese language in curriculum and teaching. All of the textbooks and content emphasize the centrality of Japanese language and culture. Every teacher I had from early elementary and middle school upheld this in their teaching practices and classroom interactions. Being a good student meant assimilating, following the rule that Uchinanchu students of Okinawa speak Japanese at all times. My grandparents' generation proudly spoke Uchinaaguchi. Now, 70 years after the Battle of Okinawa, UNESCO has declared Uchinaaguchi a "severely endangered" language.

Today, most speakers of Uchinaaguchi are past the age of 50. My generation can't understand the elders who speak to us at the markets. The *minyō* lyrics and hummable melodies instantly bring me to tears, yet I'm unable to translate the words for my children. I wish they could feel the *kanasasoulmn* — that's a word that doesn't exist in English. It expresses the emotion that you love something so much that it brings you sadness. The aunties and uncles who animate their conversations with tone changes and arms swaying gather at our homes, maintaining our Indigenous oral storytelling ways. But our youth are deaf to this language.

I have friends who say they wish their skin were lighter, that their last name didn't make their island roots so obvious, that they will make sure their children speak without a hint of island accent.

They have forgotten. They have forgotten that we are the result of Indigenous beauty thousands of years old, the specific age unknown because we are a people of oral language, not written language. They have forgotten that our island dancers tell the stories of ocean waves with their hands, our resilience with their stomping, our friendliness in their eyes, and our humor in the way the lips curve to display sarcasm. *Tii*, the firm hand strikes of our Okinawan karate, reveal the powerful resistance developed long ago to fight against Japanese feudal occupation. And they have forgotten the respect given to the oldest woman of the family leading the *ūtōtō* of Indigenous prayer, connecting this world with loved ones in the spirit world. But I will not forget.

I will tell my children and my students about the day when my little sister, Aki, at the age of 6, danced in front of thousands of island people, mostly elderly grandparents, in a festival to honor our culture. Smiles of pride could be seen stretching to the very back row. Their shouts in our native tongue cued to rhythm so perfectly that it sent vibrations through my spine. Mesmerized by the taiko drumming and the red and gold streaming down the dancers' backs, one elder after another wiped their tears. When Aki and her friends finished their dances and walked off stage, one grandmother raised her wrinkled hand, beckoning Aki to come as I stood nearby waiting to greet her. Aki looked at me, unsure, and I gestured for her to go ahead. The grandmother took Aki's hand, rubbed it gently, and thanked her in Uchinaaguchi, saying *nihe-debiru* over and over as she wept. The grandmother's daughter draped a lei of candy around Aki's neck. The grandmother said to Aki, "Don't forget who you are. Don't ever forget" as she walked slowly away.

> **Schools must be places where our youth are empowered to learn and nourish heritage languages.**

No Indigenous people should have to fight having their language taken away from the youth, because the youth are our future. *Mirukuyuu* is another word that doesn't exist in Japanese or English. Both languages translate it as "youth." But when we Uchinanchu hear *mirukuyuu*, it means "peaceful generation" at the same time as we visualize calm ocean waves. If our *mirukuyuu* lose their language, they will lose their culture and their identity. Schools must be places where our youth are empowered to learn and nourish heritage languages, to use them and spread them to the next generation. And this must begin today. My language is not dirty. My language is powerful. *Kanasasoulmn*, Uchinaaguchi, the language of my heart. ✳

Uncovering the Lessons of Classroom Furniture

You are where you sit

BY TOM McKENNA

Imagine the following scenario: Students enter a classroom with the desk and chairs neatly arranged in straight rows. They hesitate at the door, make a quick assessment of the room and choose a place to sit. They work their way down narrow rows of chairs, careful not to disturb the tight arrangement of furniture. They sit quietly, deposit backpacks under their seats, place a notebook on the desk, and look straight ahead to the front of the room and the much larger teacher desk that stares back at them.

Shortly before the class is scheduled to start, an adult figure enters the room, writes their name on the front board along with the name of the class, and assumes a seat at the big desk or the podium standing by its side. School is in session.

Welcome to day one of lessons about power, pedagogy, and relationships to physical and symbolic capital.

I watched students file into my classroom for 35 years. Never have I witnessed students attempt to change the arranged furniture, nor ask to do so. Instead, they arrange themselves according to the teacher's prearranged design.

I normally conduct my classes at Portland Youth Builders, the high school completion/GED school where I teach in one of Portland's poorest neighborhoods, with chairs arranged in a large circle. This day, I arrange the chairs in rows. Students walk in the door, stop suddenly, look at me and ask, "What's this all about?"

I simply ask them to take a seat and offer no explanation for our newly arranged room. I take attendance and ask if anyone has any thoughts they want to share before we start class.

Deavon says: "I don't like this. I have to turn around to see who's talking. Can we change the chairs back to the way they usually are, please?"

I ask how other students feel about sitting in rows. Darren says: "I don't like it either. It feels like school."

A chorus of "Yeah, I don't like it" affirms Deavon and Darren's comments.

"OK, let's do this." I offer a compromise to my grumbling students. "Let's change the chairs around, but I want you to talk about various classroom seating arrangements when we make the change." I hold up architectural drawings of five different classroom arrangements to illustrate what I want them to discuss. "We are going to divide into small groups, each group is going to get one of these drawings, and I am going to ask you to talk about some of the implications of classroom furniture arrangements."

"Tom, you're going deep on us today," says Robert.

"Yeah, what are you up to?" asks Alexxis.

What I'm up to is this: I'm trying to provide students with an opportunity to think about ordinary things in their lives, like classroom furniture arrangements, and push them to find connections between how they sit in a classroom and how they learn to view themselves in a larger political world. I want them to think about what other than math or English is being taught in a classroom divided into rows. What "hidden lessons" are being imparted about power, learning, and equality, what lessons do students learn about who they are from the material shaping of their space?

I ask the students to count off — "one, two, three, four, five" — and put them into five small groups. Then I give each group an architectural drawing of a different classroom design. I give group one a drawing of chairs in rows; group two, chairs in a circle; group three, chairs in a forum arrangement; group four, small groups of four students per group; and group five, chairs facing the wall as one might find in a computer lab.

I ask each group to answer the following questions about its respective classroom arrangement:

- What does your arrangement suggest about student-student relationships in the classroom?

- What does it suggest about teacher-student relations?
- What does it suggest about how learning occurs?
- What does it suggest about power?
- How do you feel when you find yourself seated in your respective arrangement?

At first, students give me quizzical looks. I walk them through the first question about a classroom arranged in rows. "When you were sitting in rows earlier in this class, how did you feel in relation to each other? Remember Deavon's comment that she couldn't see people when they talked? Well, take that comment a step further, how does the arrangement of furniture define how you connect with other students in the room? About how the power is distributed? Chairs aren't arranged by accident or by magic. They are arranged for a purpose. What's the purpose? Who defines that purpose and for what reasons? I want you to think about things you might otherwise take for granted."

Chairs aren't arranged by accident or magic.

Eventually students begin to take their task seriously and engage in thinking about something that they might not have before considered on a conscious level, especially in school — what is the "hidden curriculum" of material school settings?

While the students work, I rotate from group to group, listen to their conversations, take a few notes, and intervene when they get off track.

Group four gets stuck early. Their drawing is one of students seated in small groups.

Emily says: "I'm not getting this. What does how we sit have to do with anything?"

"Let's start with the last question on the handout — yes, I gave you all a handout — 'How do you feel when you work in small groups with other students as opposed to sitting in rows?'" I ask.

"I like it."

I ask Emily why she likes it.

"Because I get to talk with my friends rather than listen to some boring teacher. Don't worry, I'm not talking about you, Tom." Emily says.

"How do you and your friends learn things when you work in small groups?" I ask.

Emily shrugs her shoulders, and Kauri answers instead. "We actually learn from each other, we figure it out."

"Right! So, you guys are the source of each other's learning. How is that different from what often happens when you're seated in rows?"

Kauri puts the eraser end of her pencil to her cheek, looks up to the ceiling for a moment, and then says: "You know, I really never paid much attention when I was sitting in rows. I drew a lot instead."

"Do you pay attention in small group settings?"

"Most of the time," says Kauri, "you really don't have much choice but to pay attention. Plus, I want to hear what someone else says. It's a lot more interesting."

"You guys get it. Just think out loud with each other about these questions. I'll check back in on you in a little bit." I move on to another group.

After the students complete their work, they report their thoughts back to the larger group. Before each group begins sharing, we arrange the chairs in configurations that mirror the particular drawing the group considered. For instance, before group one reports out about the hidden curriculum of chairs arranged in rows, we arrange the chairs in rows. When group two shares their critical reflections of chairs arranged in a large circle, we arrange the chairs into a large circle.

We start with group one, chairs in rows. The group shares that most of their classroom lives have been spent seated in straight rows. Alexxis recalls a time when she was surprised to find a friend who was seated on the far side of the room from her. "I didn't even know she was there for the first couple of weeks of class."

Jason says that he always felt left out. "There wasn't enough room up front for everyone. Only so many students got to sit in the front rows. The rest of us had to fill in the back."

Darren agrees with Jason. "It was like a hierarchy. The same kids go the best seats while the rest of us spaced out in the back."

Deavon added, "I could never talk with anyone, and you know I love to talk."

"Yeah, that was school," added Darren. "The teacher talked and then we were just supposed to listen."

A number of students commented that chairs in rows suggested a classroom where learning begins and ends with the teacher, where power was located up front in a setting that wasn't equal.

"How wasn't it equal?" I ask.

"There was an order," Alexxis says. "Everyone knew who the teacher's favorites were. The kids in the top reading group, the ones who got to monitor recess, they all sat in front. And like Jason said, there was only so much room at the top and that's the way it was."

We move our chairs to form a circle and group two shares its thoughts. I ask Jose to begin. "We like circles because you can see who's talking without having to turn around."

"Yeah," says Zong, "I feel a lot less confined. I can breathe."

Slavic says, "It's like there's room for all of us. We can talk if we want or just listen if we want to, like I always do."

Robert looks directly at me. "And you're not controlling everything. We get to talk with each other."

Herman shares that he's not always comfortable in a circle. "I feel exposed."

"I sometimes do too," says Karley, "but I also feel much more together with everyone else in the class. We can all think out loud together. I feel included."

Perhaps the most interesting and profound reflection that students discuss is the fact that they never before considered classroom arrangements of furniture as anything more than an arbitrary and benign circumstance of learning. The chairs are where they happen to be. Students adjust themselves and their consciousness to a given reality without giving much thought to, as Paulo Freire writes in *Pedagogy of the Oppressed*, critically "considering reality."

The simple act of moving classroom furniture can offer us a point of critical reflection in regard to the first material reality we experience in a school setting, the room in which we sit. We find that we assume that we don't have the power to arrange the material nature of the room to fit our needs. Someone else owns it. Someone else arranges it. Permission is necessary in order to radically change the relationship of desk to desk, student to student, student to teacher. Permission is needed to change the nature of how we learn together in an educational community.

The activity is an initial critical exploration of classroom learning. Simple transformation of furniture will not in and of itself change pedagogy, but it can provide an easy way to think about the places in which we hope to transform ourselves as teachers and students.

I finish the activity by asking my students the "so what?" question. "Given what we did today, what are the larger lessons to be learned? We spent a whole class period looking at classroom furniture designs. Why? What's to be found when we look beneath our desks? Desks and chairs can be arranged in a variety of ways. So what?"

Chance is the first to respond: "Why don't you tell us?"

Deavon says, "I just never thought about any of this before. It makes me think, what else did I miss along the way that has somehow shaped me?"

"You know a lot of us never thought we were very smart and we also thought it was our fault that we weren't doing all that good in school. But maybe it wasn't all our fault, maybe being put in the back row had something to do with it. I don't know." Jason shakes his head as he ponders his words.

Jeremiah springs to life and says, "It's kind of like the worksite [students spend time building low-income housing while at Youth Builders]. We're put in crews and have to figure out things by ourselves. I mean, sometimes the boss isn't around, and something happens that you have to deal with. We work in small groups to figure it out ourselves. I was thinking of that when we were sitting in small groups. We could never build a house if we all just sat and listened to someone tell us how to do it. I figure out how to do it when I do it."

> **"What I want to know is who sets up the chairs? I don't mean here, but out there?"**

"Like I said before," says Darren, "it's about control."

"Tell me more, Darren, how are chairs in rows about control?"

"You learn early on who's in control and who's not when you are just put in rows and told to remember things. You get the feeling that the kids in the front rows deserve to be there and that the kids in back deserve to be in the back," Darren answers.

I direct a question to Jason, "You said earlier that there just wasn't enough room in the front for everyone. How is that similar to what we find in society?"

Jason thinks about my question for a minute before he says, "Now it's like musical chairs out there. Heck, there isn't enough room for all of us in the back row. Forget about the front."

Chance says: "What I want to know is who sets up the chairs? I don't mean here, but out there?"

"What do you mean, Chance?"

"For all my time in school I just tried to find a seat in a room arranged by someone else. I feel like I'm trying to do the same now with my life. I want to know who sets up the chairs out there." Chance points out the window. "How do we get to do something else other than try to find a place in the back?"

"Let's start by trying to understand as much as we can about the structure, the arrangement of things, and then let's see who is making progress turning some of those rows into circles." I know the answer won't satisfy Chance's curiosity, but it's a start.

We can start to uncover a complex system of relationships both in school and "out there" by simply taking stock of where we find ourselves in the world — how we are placed in relation to each other. Once aware, we can try to turn our perspective upside down, to suggest to students like Jason, Darren, Chance, and Deavon that maybe their previous academic and personal failures weren't all their fault, that maybe there are viable strategies that can help students navigate their way through a system that casts them to the rear, a system that teaches them to adjust to a given reality rather than create one. Rather than ending up at the bottom, blaming themselves for their "failure," maybe my students can begin to envision a system, an arrangement, that better suits their collective needs.

And like rearranging classroom furniture, maybe we can think about and change that system one chair at a time. *

RESOURCE

Freire, Paulo. 2000. *Pedagogy of the Oppressed*. Continuum.

Getting Your Classroom Together

BY BOB PETERSON

For years the top of my desk at school looked worse than the floor of my teenage daughter's bedroom, which was quite an accomplishment. But despite my desk's appearance, my entire classroom was well organized. This meant I had more time to plan my teaching and my students had easy access to materials and supplies — all of which laid the basis for successful student-centered projects and, at least for some students, the belief that our classroom was a home away from home.

And given that my social justice beliefs compelled me to regularly teach outside the textbooks and find or create my own curriculum, it was essential to keep materials well organized.

Learning from Others

It took time to figure out how to do it. I learned a lot from more experienced colleagues. During my two semesters of student teaching and six long weeks of substitute teaching, I filled half a notebook with copious scribbles and messy diagrams on what I thought would be good for my ideal classroom. I could hardly wait to start.

However, I got a dose of reality when I finally received my permanent teaching assignment. I walked into a nearly empty room with little more than an old set of dictionaries and a cupboard full of ancient curricular guides and tired posters.

Not deterred, I picked up my notebook and went to introduce myself to other teachers in the upper elementary unit. I wanted to see how they organized their classrooms and what materials they had. I asked them what suggestions they had for me as a new teacher. Most were willing to talk and I gleaned worthwhile advice ranging from generalities ("Don't do any extra cleaning or organizing in your classroom that students can do — they love to help.") to where in the bowels of the school I could find pull-down maps, bookshelves, filing cabinets, and an extra table.

Asking Hard Questions

One suggestion was that I ask myself basic questions when organizing my classroom or thinking about my teaching. "Why am I doing it this way?" "How does this enhance my vision of quality teaching and learning?" "Does this speak to the needs of *all* my students, especially those who are struggling?"

For example, how I organize seating arrangements has a profound impact on classroom life. A "theater-style" seating arrangement assumes a more lecture-based, teacher-centered approach to teaching, while other seating arrangements may promote group work and amplify discussion. These differences in classroom setup are part of the "hidden curriculum" and convey powerful messages to students.

Many elementary teachers arrange their class so that there's a carpet or meeting area where all students can gather in a circle or group for conversation. With older elementary students and larger class sizes that's not always possible.

I varied seating arrangements depending on the nature of the particular group of kids, the number of students in my classroom, and the immediate goals for the class. Flexibility was key because at different times I wanted students to face the front looking at the whiteboard to observe a mini lesson, a video, or presentations and performances by classmates. Often I wanted desks in groups of four or six for cooperative activities and "base groups," which helped with classroom management. At other times I wanted everyone facing each other for class discussions and meetings. Obviously no one seating pattern satisfies all those needs.

Modeling

I regularly modeled how I expected students to modify or change from one seating arrangement to another. For paired sharing I modeled moving chairs so students would sit "eye-to-eye" and "knee-to-knee." While clusters of desks are useful, that meant some students weren't looking directly at the front of the room. I modeled how students were to turn their desks and chairs and look forward. And for classroom meetings, I modeled how to pick up and move their desks to the classroom perimeter and rearrange their chairs in a circle in a safe and quiet manner. Most of my modeling happened at the beginning of the year when I had class discussions about why different arrangements were appropriate for different activities. I also found it necessary to review such procedures from time to time.

The Politics of Bulletin Boards

I often asked myself: What messages were my bulletin boards sending? Whose history or point of view was I presenting?

For instance, instead of Halloween bulletin board I put up a provocative display about Columbus asking, "Who benefited from Columbus' arrival in the Americas?" In February Black History bulletin boards dominated my walls instead of Valentine displays, in March women's history instead of St. Patrick's Day. To be clear, we talked about holidays and exchanged cards on Valentine's Day, but I was aware that my decision on bulletin boards was a political decision.

The same is true for all aspects of the curriculum. When I chose books for my class, I asked: Who and what are represented in the books in the classroom? What books do I read aloud, recommend that my students read, include as part of the reading curriculum? My book choices represent conscious or unconscious political decisions.

I often asked myself: What messages were my bulletin boards sending? Whose history or point of view was being represented?

Wall displays are always contradictory, especially in terms of available space: I tried to strike a balance between displaying student work and putting up challenging questions, posters, maps, and displays. I wanted my students to "see themselves on the walls," both literally — the walls have pictures of students and their work — and figuratively, so the people students see reflect the nationalities of the classroom and the broader world. Given the highly segregated nature of many of our schools and the increase in racist incidents in schools since November 2016, it's very important to have non-stereotypical posters and books about cultural and racial groups not represented in the classroom as part of the environment.

My students helped create bulletin board displays. Their enthusiasm demonstrated that importance of "student voice" being not only spoken in the classroom but also hung on the walls. At the same time, I was aware that what and how such work is chosen might privilege certain groups of students and disadvantage others. (For example, if only the "best" work is always displayed, certain students would rarely have a chance to have their work displayed.)

It's very important to have non-stereotypical posters and books about cultural and racial groups not represented in the classroom as part of the environment.

Two quick ways I got my students "on the walls" were with name poems (see Linda Christensen's "Name Poem: To Say the Name Is to Begin the Story") and a map. During the first days of school students wrote a poem about their names, which after revisions they glued on colorful card stock with a photo that I took — all of which were displayed in the hallway outside the classroom.

And on a bulletin board inside my classroom on a large map of our city, under a large sign "Where We Live" each student placed a labeled stickpin in the map to show where they lived. In subsequent weeks we'd display essays about the students' neighborhoods nearby.

Displaying Educational Posters and Class Notes

The display of educational materials is central to a successful classroom, but space is always a challenge. My classroom had a book corner, a writing center with various types of paper and story starters, a geography area, an art supply drawer, a dictionary and resource center, computers, and a math manipulative cart. I had a specific space for "the poster of the week" and a special display area for the daily agenda, announcements, and the song of the week.

One way to vastly expand the space for displaying word lists, posters, etc. is by stringing a strong cord at a height of about 8 feet between two perpendicular walls in the front corner of the classroom and creating a "poster line" (see diagram on rethinkingschools.org/NTB). Using store-bought hangers (the kind with two movable clamps), one can easily hang 12" x 18" tag board sheets, where I listed words, math-solving strategies, etc.

Accessibility, Responsibility, and Labeling

Because my students were very often involved in projects, they needed access to materials, art supplies, books, rulers, and calculators. I found the easiest way to keep materials accessible and encourage students to be responsible for keeping them orderly and safe — I labeled everything.

I labeled plastic dishpans to categorize different genres and levels of student books; I labeled boxes, drawers, filing cabinets, and bookshelves so that students not only know where things are, but also where they should be returned. A computer, a printer, and some clear contact paper worked wonders when it comes to making neat-looking signs to keep things in order.

Organizing the Paper Load

A key part of classroom organization was managing my students' paperwork — whether it's handouts for daily lessons and activities, the homework, completed student work that needs to be assessed and returned, or school fliers that go home to families.

Eventually I realized I needed two filing systems — one that I had easy daily access to that would expand and vary throughout the school year and another that would become a repository of curriculum, handouts, sample student work, etc. that I would build on year after year. Given that I taught all major subject areas and wrote a lot of my own curriculum, this was essential.

Over time I kept more and more of my lesson plans and handouts on my computer, but I maintained hard copies as well — especially "master" copies of handouts that were essential to student projects and to the social justice content that I wanted to infuse into all curricular areas.

Organizing Student Materials

Of course my being organized as a teacher was only part of the battle. How was I to help my students keep their work organized, especially given that I used many non-textbook materials that I reproduced myself?

I struggled with this question for several years until I borrowed an idea from a high school social studies teacher who gave his students many supplemental materials but was frustrated by their inability to hold on to them.

On the first day of school I gave my 5th graders a three-ring binder, which I called a "people's textbook," and dividers with plastic tabs to organize and maintain non-textbook materials. I asked students to write the divider categories — songs, poems, words, history, news, science, and math — and while doing so I described the wide range of really cool things they would be putting in their binders the entire year. In addition to dividers I gave students formatted sheets for writing down what would go in some sections — such as the song or poetry section where students list the singer and song, or poet and title of poem.

Tracking Student Progress

Part of classroom management is not only the grading and managing of papers and other forms of student work, but keeping all that assessment straight. Various forms of record and grade books exist, but what I have found helpful is a clipboard with a sheet of mailing labels. This allowed me to take notes on each child's work and later I peeled off the label and put it into a three-ring binder of class observations and grades, which had a separate page for each student. Notes ranged from things such as "counting with fingers to solve problem" to "didn't seem to comprehend passage in independent book." These labels accumulated over time. They proved helpful when it came time to write report card comments or during student-led parent teacher conferences. I also used this binder to note any parent contact or student conferences.

I insisted that students keep track of their work and progress as well. Each student had their own hanging folder in a legal-size filing cabinet in front of the room in which they were expected to keep their major projects (which included self-evaluations). The students reviewed these works with their parents during the student-led parent-teacher conferences twice a year and displayed them for the whole school to see at the end-of-year 5th-grade student exhibition. As they left 5th grade for middle school they took their whole portfolio of work home. (See "Motivating Students to Do Quality Work" in Resources.)

Communication

Clear communication with students and parents is an essential part of classroom organization. Some students are visual learners, others are auditory or tactile, most are a combination of all three. In our increasingly multilingual classrooms with students with many different abilities and needs, communicating effectively is essential. Providing handouts about key concepts (to be stored in their "People's Textbook" binders) was a way I helped certain students. Similarly, writing key concepts, vocabulary, steps to a math process on tag board, and then hanging it on the "poster line" made it accessible to all students whenever they needed it.

Given that I wanted parents to know the homework and what was happening in the classroom, my day concluded with me writing down the homework (early in my career on the chalkboard, then overhead projector, then the smart board) for the students to copy on a special weekly homework form that contained items like "show family members flier about all-school parent meeting"; a family member would have to sign each day that they saw the homework listing.

Learning from Doing

Just as I expected my students to learn from their experiences, I worked to do that too. I tried to spend a little time at the end of the day or week, or at the end of a project or major role play, to reflect on how to better teach, organize, and manage my classroom. I had a Word file on my computer desktop — "better ideas for next year" — in which I wrote myself suggestions so that my students the following year would become even more engaged in classroom projects that build their capacity to think critically and problem-solve while nurturing their dispositions toward social justice and civic activism. ✳

RESOURCES

Christensen, Linda. 2017. "Name Poem: To Say the Name Is to Begin the Story." *Reading, Writing, and Rising Up: Teaching About Social Justice and the Power of the Written Word (2nd Edition)*. Rethinking Schools.

Peterson, Bob. 2004. "Motivating Students to Do Quality Work." *Rethinking Our Classrooms: Teaching for Equity and Justice, Volume 2*. Rethinking Schools.

12 Suggestions for New Teachers

BY LARRY MILLER

I was 38 when I started my teaching career. I thought I knew everything I needed to know. I'd been a community and union activist for years and I'd been political all my life. I figured all I had to do was bring my experience and politics to the classroom and I'd be a great teacher. I was wrong. I taught and led schools for 17 years. I've been on the Milwaukee school board for nine years and teach an introductory college education class. I continue to be humbled. When I work with new teachers, I give them the following suggestions:

1. Make respect central to your classroom culture. My students and their parents often say, "You have to give respect to get respect." They're right. Address students as you would want someone to talk to your family members — no yelling, no humiliating. Look for what's good and right in their work or actions and find ways to say something positive. The only way to hold students to your high expectations is to gain their respect and their acknowledgment that your class will lead to real learning that will benefit them.

2. Base your curriculum on social justice. Frame it with a critical edge. I have three questions for assessing my curriculum:

- Does the curriculum encourage a critical examination of the world?

- Is the curriculum challenging and engaging?
- Are students learning the skills they need to be critical thinkers, advance their education, expand their life options, and become active citizens?

3. Keep rules to a minimum and enforce them. Have clear consequences. Don't threaten to take a particular action if you are not willing to carry it out. Talk to young students with respect and high school students as mature young adults.

4. Whenever possible, connect your classroom discussions and curriculum to students' lives, communities, and cultures. Learn as much as you can about your students. For example, I used song lyrics, current events articles, and community speakers to initiate thoughtful and engaging discussions. No matter what subject, including math and science, one can connect social issues and community problems to the curriculum.

5. Learn from other teachers and staff. Talk to teachers who have been in your school for a long time and who appear connected to the students and families and the community. I've always made a point of consulting daily with my colleagues. Learn from the diversity and experience of your colleagues, including the support staff. Their insights can be invaluable.

6. Build students' confidence in their intelligence and creativity. I've often heard my students call kids from the suburbs or those in AP classes "the smart kids." Don't let that go unchallenged. I start the year talking about how "being smart" can take many forms. Students learn in different ways. I find daily examples of students' work and views to talk about as smart and intelligent. Give constant examples of the brilliance of students' communities, past and present.

7. Distinguish between students' home languages and their need to know "standard" English. Work with both. Celebrate home languages in a variety of ways: dialogue, poetry, presentations, etc. Encourage students to code-switch. And ensure that they learn "standard" English. (For a more thorough discussion of home language, see Linda Christensen's book *Reading, Writing, and Rising Up: Teaching About Social Justice and the Power of the Written Word*, which is described on p. 132.)

8. Keep lecturing short. Have students create projects, give presentations, and engage in discussions, debates, role plays, and simulations.

9. Have engaging activities prepared for students when they walk into the classroom. Play a piece of music, put a quote or an editorial cartoon on a document projector to interpret, or put students in "critical thinking groups" with a puzzle, provocative question, or math problem.

10. Connect with students outside of the classroom. Ask family members of students their preferred method of contact — phone, email, texts, or written notes. Call parents during the opening weeks of school to ask about what you need to know to best teach their child. Connect to students and their families in non-school settings. For example, during Black History Month many churches in the Black community have special programs that students perform in. Attend their sporting, music, poetry, and other after-school activities. Be seen in their lives beyond the classroom.

11. Create lessons and assignments that take students beyond the classroom. Organize fieldwork with interviews in communities. Use maps to explore cities and other areas. Use "scavenger hunts" to add fun while encouraging students to be aware of their physical and natural surroundings. Have students use photography and videography whenever possible to document their work. Organize field trips outside of the students' neighborhood or city to visit farms, college lectures, museums, and historic sites that connect to your curriculum.

12. Keep calm. Calmness allows you to make rational decisions. If a student is confrontational or out of control, it never works to react with anger. Let the situation cool down and then try to have a mature conversation with those involved. ✳

How I Survived My First Year

BY BILL BIGELOW

I t was a Friday afternoon and the end of my 6th-period freshman social studies class. As two of my students walked out the door, I overheard one say to the other: "Do you know what this class reminds me of? A local TV commercial."

It was a crushing comment. I knew exactly what she meant. It was my first year as a teacher. And as hard as I was working, the class still felt ragged, amateurish — well intended, but sloppy. Her metaphor, invoking the image of a salesman trying too hard, was perfect.

Many years later, there are still days when my class feels a bit like a local TV ad. But I continue to experiment, continue to study my own classroom practice. And looking back, I think I learned some things that first year that might be useful to pass on.

The first couple of years in the classroom establish what could be called a teacher's "professional trajectory." Most of us come out of college full of theory and hope. But then our lofty aims often bump up against the conservative cultures of our new schools and students who often have been hardened by life and schooling.

How we respond to this clash of idealism vs. cynicism begins to create patterns that help define the teachers we'll become.

Which is not to say that the mistakes we make early on are repeated over and over throughout our careers. I probably did more things wrong than right my first year, and I'd like to think that I've grown since then.

Perhaps the best we can do is to ensure that early in our teaching lives we create mechanisms of self-reflection that allow us to grow and allow us to continually rethink our curricula and classroom approaches. Nurturing these critical mechanisms is vital if we're to maintain our hope in increasingly trying times.

My First Job

Typical of the circumstances of most first-year teachers, principals did not line up to compete for my services. I began on the substitute list, and was lucky to land that spot. I know there are people who enjoy subbing: no papers to correct, no lesson plans to fret over, frequent changes of scenery, and so forth. But I hated it. I didn't know the kids' names; they often began in let's-terrorize-the-sub mode; teachers invariably left awful lesson plans ("Review Chapter 20 and have them study for the test") but resented it if I didn't follow them to the letter; and I rarely had the opportunity to develop a lesson plan of my own, and teach it start to finish.

How we respond to this clash of idealism vs. cynicism begins to create patterns that help define the teachers we'll become.

Finally, in late October I did get a job — at Grant High School in Portland, Oregon, where I had completed my student teaching. It was a school with a diverse student body, about 30 percent African American, with its white students drawn from both working-class and "up on the ridge" neighborhoods. I had two preps: U.S. history and something called "freshman social studies" (and baseball coaching in the spring).

As I was to learn, I'd been hired to teach "overflow" classes, classes that had been formed because Grant's enrollment was higher than expected. Teachers chose the "surplus" students they would donate to these new classes. Then the administration hired a sub to babysit while they sought permission from higher-ups to offer a contract to a regular teacher. In the meantime, the kids had driven two subs to quit. I was hired during the tenure of sub No. 3. My position was officially designated "temporary." In other words, I would automatically lose my job at the end of the year — unless another teacher fell ill, retired, died, quit, or had a baby.

My first meeting with the administrative team of principal, vice principal, and curriculum specialist was perfunctory. I was told that "freshman social studies" meant one semester of career education, one semester of world geography, and no, they weren't sure which came first. Nor did they know which, or even if, textbooks were used. But I could pick up my two-ream allotment of ditto paper from the department chair.

They gave me a key to Room 10 and sent me to review my "work station," as the principal, an ex-Navy man, called it. Room 10 was a runt: a tiny basement classroom crammed with 1950s-style student desks and a loud, hulking heating unit in the rear. But it was mine. It turned out students had been issued textbooks — for U.S. history, something like *God Bless America: We're Number One*, and for world geography, the cleverly titled *World Geography*.

Don't Be a Loner

Before the students came the questions: Should I use these textbooks? How do I grade? What kind of "discipline" policy should I have? How should I arrange the classroom? What do I teach on the first day?

My answers to these and other typical new-teacher questions are less important than the process of answering them. And this is perhaps the most valuable lesson I drew from that first year: Build a community of educators. In September I had organized a study/support group with several teachers, some brand new, others with a few years of experience. We were united by a broad vision of creating lively and thoughtful classrooms where we provoked students to question the roots of social problems and encouraged them to believe that they could make a difference in the world. This group became my haven, offering comfort in times of stress — which was most of the time — and concrete advice to vexing questions.

Of course, I don't mean to suggest that these support groups are only for the inexperienced. I've been in a study/action group, Portland Area Rethinking Schools, for many years, and this group and a subgroup aimed at sharing curriculum on global justice issues continue to offer essential support. They remind me that I'm not alone and they offer practical advice.

We met weekly and usually divided our time between discussion of issues in education — tracking, discipline, teacher union politics, school funding, etc. — and specific classroom problems we encountered. Sometimes we brainstormed ideas for particular units people were developing: for example, Native American history or the U.S. Constitution. It was also to this group that I brought complaints of rowdy classes and recalcitrant students, practical concerns about leading discussions or structuring a major project, and questions of how curricularly adventurous I could be without incurring the wrath of an administrator.

I'm embarrassed to admit it, but I was glad that the group was composed mostly of teachers from other schools. Because of the huge gulf between my classroom ideals and my capacity to live those ideals in my day-to-day practice, I sometimes felt ashamed and was reluctant to share my stumbles and doubts with more experienced colleagues in the building.

There were only eight of us in the group but we taught in four different districts; two were Title I teachers and three worked in alternative programs. The diversity of work situations yanked me out of the isolation of my classroom cubicle and forced me to see a bigger educational picture. Sheryl Hirshon's frequent despair with her reading classes in a rural Oregon community may have been of a different sort from my frequent despair at urban Grant High School. But each of us could learn from how the other analyzed and confronted our difficult situations.

Each of us could learn from how the other analyzed and confronted our difficult situations.

Occasionally our meetings turned into aimless whining sessions. But other times, a simple comment could remind us of our ideals and keep us on the path. I remember in a weak moment confessing that I was going to start relying on the textbook: I was just too tired, scrambling to create my own curriculum from scratch, retyping excerpts from assorted books in the days before we teachers were allowed access to a copy machine, and when personal computers were still a thing of the future.

My friend Peter Thacker, sympathetic yet disapproving, simply asked: "Bill, do you really want to do that?"

OK, it bordered on a guilt trip. But that's all it took for me to remember that in fact I really didn't want to do that. The group was simultaneously collective conscience and inspiration.

The most useful piece of advice in the infancy of my career came from Tom McKenna, my cooperating teacher during my student teaching at Grant High School. It wasn't spoken advice, but he demonstrated it countless times in his classroom demeanor: Show the students that you love and respect them; play with them; joke with them; let them see your humanity. Good lesson plans are essential, yes, but ultimately students respond to the teacher as a human being.

Easier said than done, to be sure. Some days I would start out full of love and humor, but the students' surliness would defeat me by period's end. However, on better days, days when I had designed lessons that channeled rather than suppressed their fitful energy, or when I found some way to coax them to share their real stories — and thus I could share mine — I glimpsed the classroom life that was meant to be. We stopped being boss and workers, guard and inmates.

Moving Beyond the Textbooks

Not all textbooks are wretched, although as I recall mine were pretty awful. But as a beginning teacher I needed to see myself as a producer, not merely a consumer, of curriculum. It's hard work to translate the world into engaging lesson plans, but unless we're content to subordinate our classrooms to the priorities of the corporations that produce textbooks and other canned curricula, that's exactly what we have to do every day.

It's not that textbooks are a vast wasteland of corporate propaganda with no value whatsoever. I've borrowed some good ideas from textbook study guides. But they can easily narrow, distort, and misdirect our efforts.

To offer just one example: In *Lies My Teacher Told Me*, James Loewen's valuable critique of contemporary U.S. history textbooks, he demonstrates that all major texts downplay or totally ignore the history of the struggle against racism in the United States. Especially as a beginning teacher, if I had relied on textbooks to shape the outlines of my U.S. history curriculum, I would have neglected crucial areas of inquiry — and may never have realized it.

In addition to the support group, my planning book was another confidant of sorts. In it I would describe the activities I intended to do each week. Then I would record in some detail what actually happened. This was especially useful the following summer, when I could sit on the porch and leisurely flip through the book looking for patterns in students' responses to various lessons and teaching methods.

When I read back through that planning book today, I'm reminded of how helpless I often felt. From Nov. 28, for example: "Things seem to be getting much rowdier in both my freshman classes. And I'm not sure exactly what to do." I wrote frequently about their "groans." But having the journal to look back on after that first year also allowed me to search out the causes of the rowdiness and groans. I saw that my failure to engage them was more pronounced when I tried to pound them with information. My observations after a lecture on the roots of the Civil War were blunt, and a trifle pathetic: "People were very bored. I guess I should find another way to present it — even though it's interesting to me."

What's obvious to me now was not so obvious at the time: When students experience social dynamics from the inside — with role plays, stories, improvisations — they aren't so rowdy and they aren't so bored. There's a direct relationship between curriculum and "classroom management" that isn't always explicitly acknowledged in teaching methods courses that prospective teachers take.

The following year, I designed a simulation to get at the prewar sectional conflicts, and wrote a role play that showed students firsthand why Lincoln's election led to Southern secession. The role play also prompted students to think critically about the "Lincoln freed the slaves" myth. It was vital that I had some mechanisms to be self-reflective that first year.

Feeling Like a Jilted Lover

The principal made his one and only appearance in my classroom on March 15. Actually, he didn't come in, but knocked on the door and waited in the hallway. When I answered he handed me my official termination notice.

It was expected. I'd known I wouldn't be back because I was a temporary. But still there had been that slight hope. I guess by contract or law, March 15 was the final date to notify teachers if they wouldn't be returning. I had about three months to let my unemployment sink in.

When that June date finally came, I packed my little white Toyota with the files, books, posters, and other knick-knacks I'd accumulated throughout the year. I stood looking at the bare walls, my tiny oak desk, and Hulk the heater. And I left.

My tears didn't start until I was in the safety of my living room.

Tom McKenna had said that at the end of the year he always felt like a jilted lover. "Wait, there was more I wanted to say to you," he would think as the students filed out for the last time. And: "I always cared more about this than you did."

Sitting there on my couch, I knew exactly what he meant. When that first year ended, I was left with the should-have-dones, the sense of missed opportunities, and the finality of it all. The end-of-the-year cry has become one of my work-life rituals: "There was more we had to say to each other."

The school district had made it clear that I was not guaranteed a job the following September. Thanks to this official non-guarantee I was able to collect unemployment that summer — in spite of the state functionary who told me with a sneer: "Unemployment benefits are not vacation pay for teachers, ya know."

But job or no job, benefits or no benefits, I'd made it. I'd finished my hardest year.

I would like to be able to say that the kids pulled me through. I always found that image of "young, idealistic superteacher and students vs. hostile world" appealing. And some years the kids did pull me through. But that first year, the more significant survival strategy was my reliance on a network of colleagues who shared a vision of the kind of classroom life, and the kind of world, we wanted to build.

That first year, we pulled each other through. ✳

RESOURCE

Loewen, James. 2007. *Lies My Teacher Told Me*. Touchstone.

Teaching for Social Justice

There is no way a slim chapter can encompass what it means to teach for justice. Instead, we hope to remind teachers that we are curriculum producers, classroom artists, innovators who seek strategies and content to make injustice and solidarity more visible to students across all subjects and grade levels.

As social justice teachers, our work in the classroom builds students' knowledge and skills, but our work must also seek to make the world a better place. By connecting our teaching to students' lives, and to the broader society, we can work toward a more just and equitable world.

Our opening essay, "Creating Classrooms for Equity and Social Justice," written by *Rethinking Schools* editors, outlines the integrated components that we believe comprise a social justice classroom: grounded in the lives of our students; critical; multicultural, anti-racist, pro-justice; participatory, experiential; hopeful, joyful, kind, visionary; activist; academically rigorous; culturally and linguistically inclusive and empowering.

Here, we include articles by teachers who demonstrate these elements at work in kindergarten through high school science classrooms. Kara Hinderlie Stroman's

"Black Is Beautiful" shows how she teaches kindergarten students to read and write while also celebrating blackness and teaching them about Black people who make a difference in the world. In "Seeing Ourselves with Our Own Eyes," Katy Alexander discusses how she uses poetry to teach her middle school students with disabilities to celebrate their differences by writing praise poems about themselves. Teachers Kim Kanof and Lynsey Burkins show how they embrace the home languages of English language learners while also engaging them in rigorous content.

Over the years, we have created and borrowed teaching tools, which we return to again and again: mixers, interior monologues, read-arounds, role plays. These strategies provoke students to develop their democratic capacities: to question, to challenge, to make real decisions, to collectively solve problems, but also to empathize with others.

Brazilian educator Paulo Freire wrote that teachers should attempt to "live part of their dreams within their educational space." As our editors wrote in "Creating Classrooms for Equity and Social Justice," "Classrooms can be places of hope, where students and teachers gain glimpses of the kind of society we could live in and where students learn the academic and critical skills needed to make it a reality."

Creating Classrooms for Equity and Social Justice

This essay was published in its original form as the introduction to Rethinking Our Classrooms: Teaching for Equity and Justice, Volume I, *and was written by the editors of that book. It was revised by the editors of* The New Teacher Book.

As teachers, we begin from the premise that schools and classrooms should be laboratories for a more just society than the one we now live in. Unfortunately, too many schools are training grounds for boredom, alienation, and pessimism. Too many schools fail to confront the racial, class, and gender inequities woven into our social fabric. Teachers are often simultaneously perpetrators and victims, with little control over planning time, class size, or broader school policies — and much less over the unemployment, hopelessness, and other "savage inequalities" that help shape our children's lives.

But *The New Teacher Book* is not about what we cannot do; it's about what we can do. Brazilian educator Paulo Freire wrote that teachers should attempt to "live part of their dreams within their educational space." Classrooms can be places of hope, where students and teachers gain glimpses of the kind of society we could live in and where students learn the academic and critical skills needed to make it a reality.

No matter what the grade level or content area, we believe that several interlocking components comprise what we call a social justice classroom. Curriculum and classroom practice must be:

Grounded in the lives of our students. All good teaching begins with respect for children, their innate curiosity, passions, and their capacity to learn. Curriculum should be rooted in children's needs and experiences. Whether we're teaching science, mathematics, English, or social studies, ultimately the class has to be about our students' lives as well as about a particular subject. Students should probe the ways their lives connect to the broader society, and are often limited by that society.

Critical. The curriculum should equip students to "talk back" to the world. Students must learn to pose essential critical questions: Who makes decisions and who is left out? Who benefits and who suffers? Why is a given practice fair or unfair? What are its origins? What alternatives can we imagine? What is required to create change? Through critiques of advertising, cartoons, literature, legislative decisions, military interventions, job structures, newspapers, movies, agricultural practices, or school life, students should have opportunities to question social reality. Finally, student work must move outside the classroom walls, so that scholastic learning is linked to real-world problems.

Multicultural, anti-racist, pro-justice. In the publication *Rethinking Columbus*, Rethinking Schools used the discovery myth to demonstrate how children's literature and textbooks tend to value the lives of Great White Men over all others. Traditional materials invite children into Columbus' thoughts and dreams; he gets to speak, claim land, and rename the homelands of Native Americans, who appear to have no rights. Implicit in many traditional accounts of history is the notion that children should disregard the lives of women, working people, and especially people of color — they're led to view history and current events from the standpoint of the dominant groups. By contrast, a social justice curriculum must strive to include the lives of all those in our society, especially the marginalized and dominated. As anti-racist educator Enid Lee points out in an interview in *Rethinking Our Classrooms*, a rigorous multiculturalism should engage children in a critique of the roots of inequality in curriculum, school structure, and the larger society, always asking: How are we involved? What can we do?

Participatory, experiential. Traditional classrooms often leave little room for student involvement and initiative. In a "rethought" classroom, concepts need to be experienced firsthand, not just read about or heard about. Whether through projects, role plays, simulations, mock trials, or experiments, students need to be mentally, and often physically, active. Our classrooms also must provoke students to develop their democratic capacities: to question, to challenge, to make real decisions, to collectively solve problems.

Hopeful, joyful, kind, visionary. The ways we organize classroom life should seek to make children feel significant and cared about — by the teacher and by each other. Unless students feel emotionally and physically safe, they won't share real thoughts and feelings. Discussions will be tinny and dishonest. We need to design activities where students learn to trust and care for each other. Classroom life should, to the greatest extent possible, prefigure the kind of democratic and just society we envision and thus contribute to building that society. Together students and teachers can create a "community of conscience," as educators Asa Hilliard and Gerald Pine call it.

Activist. We want students to come to see themselves as truth-tellers and change-makers. If we ask children to critique the world but then fail to encourage them to act, our classrooms can degenerate into factories for cynicism. Although it's not a teacher's role to direct students to particular organizations, it is a teacher's role to suggest that ideas should be acted upon and to offer students opportunities to do just that. Children can also draw inspiration from historical and contemporary efforts of people who struggled for justice. A critical curriculum should be a rainbow of resistance, reflecting the diversity of people who acted to make a difference, many of whom did so at great sacrifice. Students should be allowed to learn about and feel connected to this legacy of defiance.

Academically rigorous. A social justice classroom equips children not only to change the world, but also to maneuver in the one that exists. Far from devaluing the vital academic skills young people need, a critical and activist curriculum speaks directly to the deeply rooted alienation that currently discourages millions of students from acquiring those skills. A social justice classroom offers more to students than do traditional classrooms and expects more from students. Critical teaching aims to inspire levels of academic performance far greater than those motivated or measured by grades and test scores. When children write for real audiences, read books and articles about issues that really matter, and discuss big ideas with compassion and intensity, "academics" starts to breathe. Yes, we must help students "pass the tests" (even as we help them analyze and critique those tests and the harmful impact of test-driven education). But only by systematically reconstructing classroom life do we have any hope of cracking the cynicism that lies so close to the heart of massive school failure, and of raising academic expectations and performance for all our children.

Culturally and linguistically inclusive and empowering. Critical teaching requires that we admit we don't know it all. Each class presents new challenges to learn from our students and demands that we be good researchers, and good listeners. This is especially true when our racial or social class identity, or our nationality or linguistic heritage is different from those of our students. As African American educator Lisa Delpit writes in her review of the book *White Teacher* in *Rethinking Our Classrooms*, "When teachers are teaching children who are different from themselves, they must call upon parents in a collaborative fashion if they are to learn who their students really are." Teachers need to challenge all forms of privilege, especially white supremacy, in ways that respect and empower the communities and students they serve. And we must embrace students' home languages, helping them preserve their linguistic heritages while also helping them navigate in English-dominant settings.

We're skeptical of the "inspirational speakers" who administrators bring to faculty meetings, who exhort us to become superteachers and classroom magicians. Critical teaching requires vision, support, and resources, not magic. We hope the stories, critiques, and lesson ideas here will offer useful examples that can be adapted in classrooms of all levels and disciplines and in diverse social milieus. Our goal is to provide a clear framework to guide classroom transformation. *

RESOURCES

Au, Wayne, Bigelow, Bill, and Stan Karp. 2007. *Rethinking Our Classrooms: Teaching for Equity and Justice, Volume I.* Rethinking Schools.

Bigelow, Bill, and Bob Peterson. 1998. *Rethinking Columbus: The Next 500 Years.* Rethinking Schools.

Black Is Beautiful

BY KARA HINDERLIE STROMAN

For years, I have struggled to find authentic ways of helping young children — kindergarteners and 1st graders — learn, remember, and appreciate Black history. Come January, the halls of my school are plastered with a variety of Martin Luther King Jr. tributes and artwork that conveniently find their way to being relabeled for February's Black History Month displays — and disappear in time for March's green living tips to save the planet.

But here is what my students need to know: Black is beautiful.

And here is why they need to know it . . .

Currently, in my predominantly white kindergarten class of 27, I see the few Black boys in my class targeted as the ones who did something wrong, as the kids who are called mean, as the kids who are not named as a friend. I see my one Black girl sad on the playground, or looking for a spot at the table with her white peers, unsure how to make space for herself. They are on the periphery of play, usually the "it" in tag, and it reminds me of my own story: In high school a teacher told us that, in our society, the color black symbolizes bad and evil, and white symbolizes good and pure.

I also remember when I was in a human development college class watching a video clip of children choosing a white baby doll instead of a brown one. I remember a little Black girl in the study saying the brown dolls were not as pretty, and the little white girls saying the brown dolls looked dirty. The video and the study itself made me sad for the little

Brown girl I once was, trying to fit in and make friends in school.

One day I came across a stack of books the former librarian volunteer at my elementary school was going to throw out marked "Free books." In it were two copies of *Black Is Beautiful*. It was published in the '70s by Ann McGovern and made up of black-and-white photos of simple black subjects: a black bird, black jelly beans, black puppies, a black butterfly, a young Black girl in dress-up. The words in the book were written like a free verse poem. I loved the simplicity and took both copies to use in my classroom.

Here is what my students need to know: Black is beautiful.

The students listened to me read aloud using a voice of wonderment and adoration — some pages I whispered in reverence. I stopped at the page of the Black girl playing dress-up in her mom's clothes, the only page mentioning black skin being beautiful:

> Black lace, black face.
> Black is beautiful.

"Do you see her wearing her mama's fancy clothes? So beautiful and fun," I said. When I finished, I asked what they noticed in the book.

"I notice the pictures only had black."

"I notice a black bird."

"I noticed beautiful."

"The horse was black!"

"I noticed the candy!"

"Yeah!" the class responded in a chorus of agreement.

I wrote down what they noticed on chart paper. Then I asked, "What can we add to this *Black Is Beautiful* book that the author didn't mention?"

"The tire swing!" Chris said.

"Some people may not see a tire swing as beautiful. How can we convince them it is? I think about how some of you love to push it, and some of you love to ride on the tire swing. Hmm . . . what would some beautiful movement words be that you could say with tire swing?"

"It twirls!"

"It spins around and around!" said Chris, who was now on his knees, having popped up during his share out.

"Oooh! I can't wait to see how you write that!" I popped up too, and smiled.

I moved on, asking for more ideas. I framed their answers in the style and context of the book we read, modeling how to expand their list to sound like a poem. I wrote down their new ideas, and pointed to the ones already mentioned or from the original text: a kitten, a dog, sneakers, a witch.

"I notice the author wrote this like poetry to help us remember how beautiful the things in the book were. What words and descriptions can we add to our ideas to make people see the beauty and goodness of the color black?"

"My dress is soft and cozy," Lori gently patted her black fuzzy skirt, smiling into her own shoulder.

Nadira, who had been gazing away, raised her hand. "Black bird floating in the night sky."

I wrote what they said on the board and asked them to tell a friend three black things they are going to write about in a beautiful way. I know some will only get a picture or a word down while some will fill the page, but I want them all to start by telling someone three things. It gives them a goal and sets the expectation with a starting point.

I sent them off to write their ideas and have "Black is beautiful" written on sentence strips at each writing table for reference. I collected their work, went home, and typed them up.

The next day we reviewed: "Who remembers something that is black and beautiful?"

"Horses!"

"Birds!"

"Sneakers!"

"Rain clouds!"

"Yes!" I said. "Today we are going to look at a different kind of black is beautiful. We know that there are things that are black and beautiful, and people who are Black and beautiful. But it can be a little confusing because is people's skin the color of black paper or a black shirt? No! Black people are all different shades of brown. We just call it black sometimes. Today we are going to write about beautiful Black people and I have a few books to share with you to help give you ideas."

I started off by reading *My People* by Langston Hughes.

"Sunshines, I love this book," I told my students. "The words in this book are so simple and so powerful. This book is actually a short poem that was stretched across the pages so the photographs could illustrate each line of the poem. When I read this poem to you, I want you to study the pictures as you hear the words I say. Look at the faces and features of these Black people and notice their beauty. Notice what Langston compares the beauty to. In one place he compares me to the sun! I always feel so great when I read this poem."

> The night is beautiful,
> So the faces of my people.
>
> The stars are beautiful,
> So the eyes of my people.
>
> Beautiful, also, is the sun.
> Beautiful, also, are the souls
>   of my people.

I told them to listen to ways Langston knows Black- and Brown-skinned people are beautiful. It's a slow book, with only a few words per page, which allows my students to study the sepia-toned photos. Using the same format from the last lesson, we tried to translate the idea of black is beautiful to features of Black and Brown people. After I finished the book, I asked the students to tell me about beautiful Black people. "What did Langston say?"

"Beautiful like the sun."

"The stars are beautiful!"

I am explicit when I talk to the students about the metaphor in this poem. It is hard to understand when you are 5 years old and the world is a literal, concrete place. Some do not make the connections I want them to make, they are not thinking about the Black people of the poem but of their metaphors as the thing of beauty. So I made the connection for them and carried them with me through an example.

"Now you understand why I love this poem. Langston compares beautiful people with the sun and stars. Look at this page." I showed them the page of an elderly man, face raised and smiling at something unseen the reader. "When I look at this page, I see joy and happiness. I see lines around his mouth that say he smiles a lot. His skin looks soft to touch. That is why he looks beautiful to me, and I think that's why they chose this picture to go with the word 'also' in the poem. Sometimes we think of beauty one way and then discover, like in this book, there are other ways that we can see beauty!"

I re-read the poem and asked for "Black is beautiful" examples again. This time there were more accurate answers:

"Eyes are beautiful!"

"Brown skin is beautiful."

"Hands are beautiful."

Brandon, a Black boy who often sits quietly as if in meditation, raised his hand. "Souls are beautiful." He looked at me and we smiled.

We also read *Hair Dance!* by Dinah Johnson, another book with photos of Black and Brown kids playing outside. There is so much visual movement in this book; kids are jumping and hair is swinging. This book is special because the children in the book are from our neighborhood: The author is a parent and the kids were previous students in our school. This interests the children and they study the pictures and recognize some of their playground in the artwork. This time around when kids answered what is beautiful, they moved their heads as if flipping their own imaginary beaded braids. They held their own hair in the air to mimic the pictures they saw while I read the rhythmic words in the book. The resounding agreement was that Black hair is beautiful — and so is jumping! We spent two minutes trying to jump high and fast to get our own hair to dance.

But this time when I sent them to write, they were less confident. Maybe I moved too quickly, or maybe the metaphor was too big of a jump. They stuck pretty close to the examples given in the books: hands, hair, skin. They focused on the metaphor and less on the physical attributes of people as beautiful.

And this was what my students deserve to know: Black is beautiful.

I told the kids why I think it's important to celebrate Black history. I told them my story, of learning about history where no one looked like me or my family. "We have Black History Month as a reminder to teachers that there is not much written about all of the things that Black and Brown people have contributed to our lives. When I was a kid, I only learned about the ways white people changed our lives. There were no books or activities in our school that let us know who those Black people were, or how they affected the way we live. I will share inventors and leaders who paved the way, or made an important discovery through diligence and hard work." They seemed intrigued. Some looked surprised, some totally bored. Buy-in to the unknown is hard, so I gave them an example.

Fresh off the heels of a presidential election with an unexpected outcome in 2016, where girls were coming in wearing pussycat hats and pant suits, I told the class about Shirley Chisholm.

I then told them mostly about inventors or "real firsts," as opposed to firsts for Black people, because they are the most tangible for young learners to understand. It is a clear, concrete contribution to bettering our daily lives: refrigeration, open-heart surgery, stoplights, peanut butter. I want my students to have a basis for appreciating Black people. Later, when they learn about the more complex concepts of slavery, Jim Crow, and civil rights, somewhere in the back of their minds I hope they will remember the beauty of Black and the ways Black people made life better for them. And then maybe, in the front of their eyes, they will see the injustice for what it was and what it still is.

Later, when they learn about the more complex concepts of slavery, Jim Crow, and civil rights, somewhere in the back of their minds I hope they will remember the beauty of Black and the ways Black people made life better for them.

For the next writing exercise, to retain the feeling of reverence, we stayed with the free verse poetry writing style of the first book I introduced by Ann McGovern. The tone of that piece set the mood for the beauty on the page, and allowed them to transition into that poetic mode of writing, thinking, and seeing their ideas in a different light. I had them talk in pairs and instructed them to tell each other who they remember learning about and liked. When I asked them to write, they quickly jotted down their choices: *Stoplights speak to cars in colors, tasty peanut butter on sandwiches for lunch every day, open-heart surgery saving lives.*

When writing with young children, I have to make publishing decisions. In this unit, I wanted the kids to see their ideas from these lessons typed up and put together as a collective piece. If I made them do the extra combining work it could make the unit drag on too long, its message losing potency. So, in this instance, I did it for them.

Once all the parts were typed into one poem, I brought in craft and scrapbook supplies all in black: pipe cleaners, pom-poms, feathers, beads, stickers, textured felt, and dozens of patterned papers; all glittery, soft, and shiny — the jewels of the crafting world. I cropped their poems and let them collage them into beautiful black works of art. I read the poems aloud as I handed them out one at a time, so they could hear each other's work as inspiration.

Resistance

Some years when I do this lesson, I get backlash in the form of parent emails to the principal, disengagement from students, or the fairness argument from both students and parents: "Why just black, why not all colors?" This year it was Andrew, a tall blue-eyed white boy, and a proficient reader and writer.

When he learned about Black inventor Lyda Newman's improved hairbrush, Andrew had whispered "That's not special" to a friend.

When he saw the sentence strips with "Black is beautiful" written on them for a second day, he turned them face down on the tables and exclaimed, "We already did these!"

When Jasmin told her friends something Black was beautiful, he responded, "Black is not beautiful."

Andrew, whose humor sometimes runs in the center of insulting, who often finds delight in others' misfortune, exclusion, or embarrassment, was creating another opportunity for me to change his mind.

When he turned the sentence strips face down exclaiming their completion, I explained this project was going to last the entire month. "Sometimes we remember things better and learn more when we stick with it. It feels like we finished because we did finish one part, but there's more I want to show you and more I want you to try." Andrew said, "OK."

When he said Ms. Newman's invention wasn't special, I noted there is a difference between flashy and noteworthy. "Raise your hand if you have a brush like this one in your house. Raise your hand if you've seen one before. Isn't that cool you're learning about the person who made something we've all seen or used every day? That's why I wanted you to learn about Ms. Newman. She gave us things we use so much they seem boring, but every time someone uses or buys it, she is getting affirmation that what she created was needed, even still today!" I made eye contact with Andrew when I said this, and he nodded in agreement.

When Jasmin came to me upset that Andrew told her Black wasn't beautiful, I took him aside and told him about the power of an ally.

"Why did you say Black isn't beautiful to Jasmin?"

"I was kidding. It is." He tried to get the early exit card by placating me.

"I'm spending a lot of time on black is beautiful because I want you on my team, Andrew. I want you to be the person who stands up and defends black when someone else tries to do what you just did, tries to make a joke about it, and tries to hurt someone's feelings about black. Black isn't just a color of clothes, right?"

"No, it's people and brown skin."

"So when someone jokes about black, it makes us, people with that skin, feel less important. But you have a chance to be a leader. Friends look to you to include them and they follow your lead. If you decide not to treat black as a joke, if you tell a friend why it's not funny to joke like that, you'll be helping the unfairness that is all around us. You will be making this place a better place for more of us. Can you try to do that? Help us feel welcomed and proud of black?"

Some years when I do this lesson, I get backlash in the form of parent emails to the principal, disengagement from students, or the fairness argument from both students and parents: "Why just black, why not all colors?"

Andrew nodded, "OK, yeah! I'm sorry I hurt Jasmin's feelings, Ms. Kara."

"I know, Andrew. Thank you for apologizing. I'm glad you're on my team." Andrew smiled shyly and took a big breath.

Then I took a big breath as he went back to his seat.

Yeah, the work is weighty, little one. Deep breaths help. ✱

Seeing Ourselves with Our Own Eyes

BY KATY ALEXANDER

"Maleeka," he used to say, "you got to see yourself with your own eyes. That's the only way you gonna know who you really are." —The Skin I'm In *by Sharon Flake*

In the lazy heat of summer, looking through next year's class lists, the wisdom from Maleeka's father chewed at the back of my mind. I teach special education to 6th, 7th, and 8th graders, and too often the deficit thinking required by the special education system — in which we document in thorough detail everything our students can't do — makes students see their disabilities and themselves through a negative lens. How could I help my students start to see themselves through their own eyes?

I had stumbled across Trinidad Sanchez Jr.'s "Why Am I So Brown?" when I was in grad school, and it lingered in my heart. I loved the way the poem talked back to dominant culture and white supremacist ideas about skin color. I wanted to teach it to my students, but hadn't been sure about when or how or where to bring it in. I eventually decided to use it at the beginning of the year as a mentor text for students to write poems about their own identities, to create their own "Why am I so . . . ?" poems.

This year, like most years at my school, my students were mostly white, though some were Asian, Latinx, and Black. In a time when "Black Lives Matter" is a phrase we can't take for granted and in a school that is predominantly white, I wanted all my students to start the year with an explicit celebration of brown skin.

The students I work with all have individualized education programs (IEPs), and have academic goals in reading and writing. They have a variety of disabilities, including learning disabilities, autism, ADHD, and communication disorders. My students take most of their classes in grade-level general education classes, but take a literacy class with me to work on their reading and writing goals.

We read Sanchez's poem on the first day of school. "Part of this poem is in Spanish. Do any of us speak Spanish?" I asked. "No? OK, then we will all do our best to read the Spanish lines." We read through the poem together, taking turns to read each stanza:

> A question Chicanitas sometimes ask
> while others wonder: Why is the sky blue
> or the grass so green?
>
> Why am I so Brown?
>
> God made you brown, *mi'ja*
> color *bronce* — color of your *raza*
> connecting you to your *raíces*,
> your story/*historia*
> as you begin moving towards your future.
>
> God made you brown, *mi'ja*
> color *bronce*, beautiful/strong,
> reminding you of the goodness
> *de tu mamá, de tus abuelas*
> *y tus antepasados.*
>
> God made you brown, *mi'ja*
> to wear as a crown for you are royalty —
> a princess, *la raza nueva*,
> the people of the sun.
>
> It is the color of Chicana
>   women —
> leaders/*madres* of Chicano warriors
> *luchando por la paz y la dignidad*
> *de la justicia de la nación, Aztlán!*

God wants you to understand . . . brown
is not a color . . . it is:
a state of being a very human texture
alive and full of song,
   celebrating —
dancing to the new world
which is for everyone . . .

Finally, *mi'ja*
God made you brown
because it is one of HER favorite colors!

Initially, most of my class regarded the poem the way they might regard IKEA assembly instructions, with a mixture of confusion and wariness. I had underestimated the extent to which the Spanish parts of the poem would be daunting and formidable to them. After reading, we watched a video I found on YouTube that 7th- and 8th-grade Latinx students from the Seward Student Network in Chicago had made, with art and imagery to go along with their reading of the poem.

I wanted all my students to start the year with an explicit celebration of brown skin.

I wanted my students to hear the poem read by Spanish speakers, and I wanted them to see the beautiful imagery the students in Chicago selected to go along with the poem, hoping this would illuminate some of the meaning for them.

We also spent time using Google translate to write translations of the Spanish lines. "So if Chicana is a 'woman of Mexican descent' and 'itas' means 'something little,' what would 'Chicanitas' mean?" I asked. Admittedly, our strategy of using Google translate failed us a bit here, as the meaning of the word "Chicana" is much richer and deeper than a "woman of Mexican descent," coming from the work of civil rights activists in the Chicano Movement of the 1960s.

"Little women?" asked Haley.

"Girls! Girls of Mexican descent!" exclaimed Alec.

"What would a boy of Mexican descent be?" asked Elijah.

"Chicano is a man, so that would be Chicanito," I replied.

"That's me, I'm Chicanito," Elijah grinned, rolling the word around in his mouth.

I asked students to share their favorite lines. "Because it is one of

Her favorite colors!" said Mari, grinning a broad brace-filled smile.

"This is wrong," said Ethan. "God is not a woman. It should say Him."

"His god is a woman!" retorted Mari.

The students were intrigued with the subject of the poem. I asked them, "What was working in the poem?"

"That it's in two languages, the English and the Spanish," said Ariana. I was relieved that after spending time working through the Spanish they could see the beauty in the bilingualism.

"That it shows you can be proud of the color you have," said Mari.

"It shows you shouldn't be ashamed of what you look like," said Ethan.

"I like how it's one person asking a question and someone is responding, like dialogue," said Alyssa.

I told them that eventually they would be writing their own poems. But while Sanchez starts his poem with a brief dedication, "for Raquel Guerrero," positioning his words as a response to a question from someone else, I wanted my students to be both the questioner and the responder, to write a dialogue to themselves about themselves — self-affirmation as poetry. They started by brainstorming different things about themselves on the first pages of their workshop journals. "About me" we titled the lists. "All kinds of things," I said. "Here's my list — I'm white, I wear glasses, I'm fat —"

"You're not fat!" said Ethan emphatically. "My mom says that's a bad thing to say! You can't say that about people."

I usually have a conversation with students about my body at some point in the school year. I identify as fat — not overweight, obese, or plus size — and it's important for me that my students see someone using fat in a positive, or at least neutral, way. I think that if fatness can start to be normalized for them, that if they can see fatness as part of the natural range of beautiful difference in humanity,

> I wanted my students to be both the questioner and the responder, to write a dialogue to themselves about themselves — self-affirmation as poetry.

that they may be able to see their own disability someday as part of the wonderful beautiful natural diversity of humanity. I hadn't quite realized that by putting "fat" on my example list, I'd be launching into that conversation now, but I figured that one of the points of the lesson was for us to get to know each other, so we might as well start strong.

"I am fat, and I think it's OK. I don't mind being fat. I feel good about my body. To me, it's just another way of being in the world. Some people are tall and some people are short, and some people have brown hair and some people have black hair or blonde hair, and some people are thin and some people are fat. My mom is fat and my dad is fat and my aunts and uncles are fat, and I come from a fat family, and I am OK with it. Not everyone is OK with it, and some people feel really bad about their bodies. For those people, calling them fat might hurt their feelings and upset them, so your mom is right, Ethan, you have to be careful how you use the word 'fat.' But I'm letting you know right now that I'm OK with the word fat, and you can call me fat, and I don't think it's a bad thing. What are all the things about you, maybe things that some people even think are bad? See how many things you can add to your list."

I walked around, peeking at students' lists. "Funny guy, Italian, brown hair," wrote Alec.

"Male, shy, kinda quiet," wrote Dylan, a student with autism who had hardly spoken in class last year.

We started by making metaphor banks, an idea I got from a workshop with the poet Denice Frohman. She said that when she writes with students, sometimes they start out by listing all sorts of colors, fabrics, food, and so on, so they have something to return to and look through as they're trying to write. We listed fabrics, colors, and weather. We listed kitchen appliances, animals, plants, and musical instruments. "Can we please make lists of car manufacturers?" said Ethan, a student fascinated by cars. We listed all the different kinds of cars we could think of.

We returned to Sanchez's poem and made lists about what we noticed about the style and content of his piece. I took notes for the class while students shared what they noticed.

"It starts with lots of questions," noticed Kayla.

"And questions people wonder about," said Elijah.

"Some parts repeat, like 'God made you . . .'" said Ariana.

"There are metaphors!" said Logan.

"He calls her 'mi'ja,'" said Elijah.

Then I showed them my "Why am I so?" poem, "Why am I so fat?":

A question chubby children sometimes ask
While others are wondering:
Why does the rain fall or

Why does the wind blow?
Why am I so fat?

The Universe made you fat, sweetie
Because it is the shape of your ancestors
Strong people made for hard work
And generation after generation of good cooks and good eaters

The Universe made you fat, sweetie
So your friends would always have a soft shoulder to lean on
Warm arms to hug them
A big heart to love them
And a big tummy to laugh big with them

The Universe made you fat, pumpkin
Because you are
A soft quilt full of down
A wrestler, ready to stand strong
A cumulus cloud, climbing up through the sky
A cello, wide with a deep and resonant sound

Finally, darling, the Universe made you fat
Because the shape of our world is round.

"What do you see that I did that was like what Sanchez did? What did I use from his poem?" I asked.

"You started with questions, too," Kayla said.

"And you said what was good about being fat," said Ariana.

"But you said 'The Universe' instead of 'God,'" said Logan.

"You said, 'sweetie,' sort of like how Sanchez kept calling the girl 'mi'ja,'" noticed Elijah.

"Are you ready to pick a topic for your poem?" I asked them to return to their "About me" lists from the first day of school and to choose something that they wanted to write about. We had noticed that both my poem and Sanchez's poem had described the positive things about that piece of our identity, so we generated lists about all the positive things about our topics.

We had also noticed metaphors used in both poems, and I encouraged students to go back to their metaphor banks to generate ideas. This was challenging for many of them. "I don't know how to do this part," said Alec.

"Well, what's your topic?" I asked.

"Being obsessed with video games," he said.

"OK, so if being obsessed with video games were a type of weather, what would it be?"

"Maybe a tornado?" he replied.

"Yeah, I love that image!" I said.

"I'm done!" exclaimed Ethan. He had written one item on his list about good things about being fast. "You get to places faster."

"What else?" I asked.

"I don't know anything else! That's it! You get places faster!"

"What does it feel like to be fast?" I asked.

"It feels like you get a little breeze on your face when you run."

"Yes, good! Write that down!" I answered.

Some students were ready to begin writing, and other students weren't sure where to start. "Let's look at the first part of Sanchez's poem. If I were going to make it into a 'fill in the blank' for you to fill out, what might that look like?" I asked. "Highlight the parts of the first stanza you would use in your poem," I said. We then created a sentence frame together for the first stanza using what students had highlighted.

After students had a few days in class to work on them, we read our poems to each other. Seth, a boy with a huge heart who had been teased for being perceived to be feminine because of his emotional sensitivity, wrote about his empathy:

Why am I so empathetic?
A question some people ask
While other people are wondering
Why does the rain fall or what is the meaning of life?

Why am I empathetic?

You are empathetic, sweetie
Because you have a heart of a lion,
You want to see what other people see

You are empathetic, sweetie
Because you wish to sacrifice your time and your comfort zone
To help people in need

Finally, sweetheart, you are empathetic because you know that the
  world should
Have been filled with love and support and not with hate and
suffering.

Savannah wrote about her experiences with anxiety:

A question some people may ask,
While others wonder,
Is why am I so anxious?

God made you anxious, precious,
Because you worry for them,
You are always there for them.

God made you anxious, precious,
Because you are like a puppy that just can't wait.

God made you anxious, sweetheart,
Because others in your family have struggled with the same.

God made you anxious, sweetie,
Because you are
A bird ready to fly,
A cheetah ready to run free,

Finally, love, God made you anxious,
Because it strengthens you
every day.

I had been most concerned about my student Dylan with this
writing assignment. Many of the more abstract pieces of reading and
writing were challenging to him. Last year he had struggled to write
metaphors about his name. His poem, about being quiet, blew me
away:

Why I'm so quiet because god made you quiet
you like to listen or be a shadow.
Quiet like silent rocks and plants
Good thing about it is that you can concentrate on your stuff

I like that you like a spy swiftly quietly to a wall or the ceiling
Running to a hiding spot in a swoosh.

Finally, why I'm so quiet because it makes you silent.

Every student read their poem aloud to the class, and while we listened to each other we wrote down appreciations. Before our read-around, I modeled how we would give feedback to each other. "You'll write down a compliment for everyone who reads. You could write down a golden line, or you could say something specific that you loved about the poem, or something the poem made you feel. You could write 'I loved . . .' or 'I felt . . .' And make sure to put who your compliment is to and who it's from." I wrote everyone's name on the board so we would all make sure to spell each other's names correctly. We were still getting to know each other, after all.

After our read-around, I told students to deliver their compliments to each other. They beamed as they read their compliments. "Everyone loved my line about orange like the sun, and orange like the mantle of the earth!" exclaimed Cassandra, smiling and sifting through compliments.

Months later, in December, I was helping a student, Chris, clean out his binder. "Not those," he said, as I was sweeping through for old things to recycle. "Those are all my compliments, I'm keeping those," he said.

So much of the time our school system takes away from students with disabilities, takes from them their "compliments," their strengths, and their value. Part of my job requires me to write long reports and plans that describe in quantifiable detail all the things my students can't do, all the ways in which they don't "measure up," the ways they "don't meet the benchmark," while ignoring the ways their differences are beautiful and wonderful. Instead of seeing themselves through IEPs, evaluations, and test scores, my students have to be able to see themselves "through their own eyes," and to talk back to systems that devalue them. Students with disabilities have to be able to hear the question "Why am I so . . . ?" and answer back boldly with love and truth. Students with disabilities have so much to offer not in spite of their disabilities but because of their disabilities. And if our education system can't recognize it, we have to teach our students to recognize it themselves. *

Presidents and the People They Enslaved

Helping students find the truth

BY BOB PETERSON

During a lesson about George Washington and the American Revolution, I explained to my 5th graders that Washington owned 317 slaves. One student added that Thomas Jefferson also was a slave owner. And then, in part to be funny and in part expressing anger — over vote fraud involving African Americans in the then-recent 2000 election and the U.S. Supreme Court's subsequent delivery of the presidency to George W. Bush — one of my students shouted, "Bush is a slave owner, too!"

"No, Bush doesn't own slaves," I calmly explained. "Slavery was finally ended in this country in 1865."

Short exchanges such as this often pass quickly and we move onto another topic. But this time one student asked: "Well, which presidents were slave owners?"

She had me stumped. "That's a good question," I said. "I don't know." Thus began a combined social studies, math, and language arts project in which I learned along with my students, and which culminated in a fascinating exchange between my students and the publishers of their U.S. history textbook.

After I admitted that I had no clue exactly which presidents owned slaves, I threw the challenge back to the students: "How can we find out?"

"Look in a history book."

"Check the internet."

I realized that I had entered a "teachable moment" when students show genuine interest in exploring a particular topic. Yet I had few materials about presidents and enslaved people, and no immediate idea of how to engage 25 students on the subject.

I also recognized that this was a great opportunity to create my own curriculum, which might help students look critically at texts while encouraging their active participation in doing meaningful research. Such an approach stands in sharp contrast to the "memorize the presidents" instruction that I suffered through growing up, and which too many students probably still endure. I seized the opportunity.

First, I had a student write down the question — "Which presidents were slave owners?" — in our class notebook under the heading "Questions We Have." I then suggested that a few students form an "action research group," which in my classroom means an ad hoc group of interested students researching a topic and then doing something with what they learn. I asked for volunteers willing to work during recess. Several students raised their hands, surprising me because I would have guessed that some of them would have much preferred going outside to staying indoors researching.

Action Research by Students

At recess time, Raul and Edwin were immediately in my face. "When are we going to start the action research on the slave presidents?" they demanded. I told them to look in the back of our school dictionaries for a list of U.S. presidents while I got out some large construction paper. The dictionaries, like our social studies text, had little pictures of each president with some basic information.

"Why don't they just tell whether they have slaves here in this list of presidents?" asked Edwin. "They tell other things about presidents."

"Good question," I said. "Why do you think they don't tell?"

"I don't know, probably because they don't know themselves."

"Maybe so," I responded. "Here's what I'd like you to do. Since slavery was abolished when Lincoln was president, and since he was the 16th president, draw 16 lines equal distance from each other and list all the presidents from Washington to Lincoln, and then a yes-and-no column so we can check off whether they owned slaves."

Filling in those columns turned out to be a challenge.

When my students and I began investigating which presidents owned enslaved people, our attempts focused on traditional history textbooks and student-friendly websites from the White House and the Smithsonian Institution. These efforts turned up virtually nothing. We then pursued two different sources of information: history books written for adults and more in-depth websites.

I brought in two books that were somewhat helpful: James Loewen's *Lies My Teacher Told Me* (Simon and Schuster, 1995) and Kenneth O'Reilly's *Nixon's Piano: Presidents and Racial Politics from Washington to Clinton* (Free Press, 1995). By using the indexes and reading the text out loud, we uncovered facts about some of the presidents. We also did an internet search using the words "presidents" and "slavery." We soon learned we had to be more specific and include the president's name and "slavery" — for example, "President George Washington" and "slavery." Some results were student-friendly, such as the mention of Washington's slaves (and some of their escapes) at mountvernon.org/slavery. There was also a bill of sale for a slave signed by Dolley Madison, the wife of President James Madison. Many websites had a large amount of text and were beyond the reading level of many of my students. So we searched for the word "slave" to see if there was any specific mention of slave ownership.

> "How do we know this is true? Our history books aren't telling the truth. Why should we think this does?"

In their research, students often asked, "How do we know this is true? Our history books aren't telling the truth. Why should we think this does?" I explained the difference between primary and secondary sources and how a primary source — like a bill of sale or original list of slaves — was pretty solid evidence. To help ensure accuracy, the students decided that if we used secondary sources, we needed to find at least two different citations.

Bits and Pieces of Information

Over the next several days the students, with my help, looked at various sources. We checked our school's children's books about presidents, our social studies textbook, a 1975 World Book Encyclopedia, and a CD-ROM encyclopedia. We found nothing about presidents as slave owners. I had a hunch about which presidents owned slaves, based on what I knew in general about the presidents, but I wanted "proof" before we put a check in the "yes" box. And though my students wanted to add a third column — explaining how many slaves each slave-owning president had — that proved impossible. Even when we did find information about which presidents owned slaves, the numbers changed depending on how many slaves had been bought, sold, born, or died.

In our research, most of the information dealt with presidential attitudes and policies toward slavery. It was difficult to find specific information on which presidents owned enslaved people. To help the investigation, I checked out a few books for them from our local university library.

Overall, our best resource was the internet. The best sites required adult help to find and evaluate, and I became so engrossed in the project that I spent a considerable amount of time at home surfing the web. The "student-friendly" websites with information about presidents — such as the White House's gallery of presidents (whitehouse.gov/1600/presidents) — didn't mention that Washington and Jefferson enslaved African Americans. Other popular sites with the same glaring lack of information are the Smithsonian Institution (smithsonianeducation.org/educators/lesson_plans/idealabs/mr_president.html) and the National Museum of American History (americanhistory.si.edu/presidency).

As we did the research, I regularly asked, "Why do you think this doesn't mention that the president owned slaves?" Students' responses varied, including "They're stupid"; "They don't want us kids to know the truth"; "They think we're too young to know"; and "They don't know themselves." (Given more time, we might have explored this matter further, looking at who produces textbooks and why they might not include information about presidents' attitudes about racism and slavery.)

During our research, my students and I found bits and pieces of information about presidents and slavery. But we never found that one magic resource, be it book or website, that had the information readily available. Ultimately, though, we discovered that two presidents who served after Lincoln — Andrew Johnson and Ulysses S. Grant — had been slave owners. While the students taped an extension on their chart, I explained that I was not totally surprised about Johnson because he had been a Southerner. But it was a shock that Grant had owned slaves. "He was the commander of the Union Army in the Civil War," I explained. "When I first learned about the Civil War in elementary school, Grant and Lincoln were portrayed as saviors of the Union and freers of slaves."

When I told the entire class how Grant's slave-owning past had surprised me, Tanya, an African American student, raised her hand and said, "That's nothing. Lincoln was a slave owner, too." I asked for her source of information and she said she had heard that Lincoln didn't like Blacks. I thanked her for raising the point, and told the class that while it was commonly accepted by historians that Lincoln was not a slave owner, his attitudes toward Blacks and slavery were a source of much debate. I noted that just because a president didn't own slaves didn't mean that he supported freedom for slaves or equal treatment of people of different races.

I went into a bit of detail on Lincoln, in part to counter the all-too-common simplification that Lincoln unequivocally opposed slavery and supported freedom for Blacks. I explained that although it's commonly believed that Lincoln freed all enslaved people when he signed the Emancipation Proclamation, the document actually frees slaves only in states and regions under rebellion — it did not free slaves in any of the slaveholding states and regions that remained in the Union. In other words, Lincoln "freed" slaves everywhere he had no authority and withheld freedom everywhere he did. Earlier, in Lincoln's first inaugural address in March of 1861, he promised slaveholders that he would support a constitutional amendment forever protecting slavery in the states where it then existed — if only those states would remain in the Union.

Slave-Owning Presidents

By the time we finished our research, the students had found that 10 of the first 18 presidents were slave owners: George Washington, Thomas Jefferson, James Madison, James Monroe, Andrew Jackson, John Tyler, James K. Polk, Zachary Taylor, Andrew Johnson, and Ulysses S. Grant. Those who didn't: John Adams, John Quincy Adams, Martin Van Buren, William Henry Harrison, Millard Fillmore, Franklin Pierce, James Buchanan, and, despite Tanya's assertion, Abraham Lincoln. The student researchers were excited to present their findings to their classmates, and decided to do so as part of a math class. I made blank charts for each student in the class, and they filled in information provided by the action research team: the names of presidents, the dates of their years in office, the total number of years in office, and whether they had owned slaves. Our chart started with George Washington, who assumed office in 1789, and ended in 1877 when the last president who had owned slaves, Ulysses S. Grant, left office.

We then used the data to discuss this topic of presidents and slave owning within the structure of ongoing math topics in my class: "What do the data tell us?" and "How can we construct new knowledge with the data?" Students, for example, added up the total number of years in which the United States had a slave-owning president in office, and compared that total to the number of years in which there were non-slave-owning presidents in office. We figured out that in 69 percent of the years between 1789 and 1877, the United States had a president who had been a slave owner. One student observed that only slave-owning presidents served more than one term. "Why didn't they let presidents who didn't own slaves serve two terms?" another student pondered.

Using the data, the students made bar graphs and circle graphs to display the information. When they wrote reflections on the math lesson, they connected math to content. One student wrote: "I learned to convert fractions to percent so I know that 10/18 is the same as 55.5 percent. That's how many of the first 18 presidents owned slaves." Another observed, "I learned how to make pie charts and that so many more presidents owned slaves than the presidents who didn't own slaves."

During a subsequent social studies lesson, the three students who had done most of the research explained their frustrations in getting information. "They hardly ever want to mention it [slaves owned by presidents]," explained one student. "We had to search and search."

Specific objectives for this mini-unit, such as reviewing the use of percent, emerged as the lessons themselves unfolded. But its main purpose was to help students to critically examine the actions of early leaders of the United States and to become skeptical of textbooks and gov-

By the time we finished our research, the students had found that 10 of the first 18 presidents were slave owners.

ernment websites as sources that present the entire picture. I figure that if kids start questioning the "official story" early on, they will be more open to alternative viewpoints later. While discovering which presidents were slave owners is not an in-depth analysis, it pokes an important hole in the godlike mystique that surrounds the "Founding Fathers." If students learn how to be critical of the icons of American past, hopefully it will give them permission and tools to be critical of the elites of America today.

Besides uncovering some hard-to-find and uncomfortable historical truths, I also wanted to encourage my students to think about why these facts were so hard to find, and to develop a healthy skepticism of official sources of information. I showed them two quotations about Thomas Jefferson. One was from a 5th-grade history textbook, *United*

States: Adventures in Time and Place (Macmillan/McGraw-Hill, 1998), which read: "Jefferson owned several slaves in his lifetime and lived in a slave-owning colony. Yet he often spoke out against slavery. 'Nothing is more certainly written in the book of fate than that these people are to be free'" (p. 314). The other quotation was from James Loewen (*Lies My Teacher Told Me*):

> Textbooks stress that Jefferson was a humane master, privately tormented by slavery and opposed to its expansion, not the type to destroy families by selling slaves. In truth, by 1820 Jefferson had become an ardent advocate of the expansion of slavery to the western territories. And he never let his ambivalence about slavery affect his private life. Jefferson was an average master who had his slaves whipped and sold into the Deep South as examples to induce other slaves to obey. By 1822, Jefferson owned 267 slaves. During his long life, of hundreds of different slaves he owned, he freed only three and five more at his death — all blood relatives of his. (p. 140)

We talked about the different perspective each quote had toward Jefferson and toward what students should learn. I then explained what an omission was, and suggested that we become "textbook detectives" and investigate what our new social studies text *United States* (Harcourt Brace, 2000) said about Jefferson and slavery. I reviewed how to use an index and divided all page references for Jefferson among small groups of students. The groups read the pages, noted any references to Jefferson owning slaves, and then reported back to the class. Not one group found a single reference. Not surprisingly, the students were angry when they realized how the text omitted such important information. "They should tell the truth!" one student fumed.

No Mention of Racism

I wanted students to see that the textbooks' omissions were not an anomaly, but part of a pattern of ignoring racism in the United States — in the past and in the present. In the next lesson, I started by writing the word "racism" on the board. I asked the kids to look up "racism" in the index of their social studies book. Nothing. "Racial discrimination." Nothing. "Our school should get a different book," one student suggested. "Good idea," I said, "but it's not so easy." I told my students that I had served on a committee that had looked at the major textbooks published for 5th graders and that none of them had dealt with racism or slavery and presidents.

Students had a variety of responses: "Let's throw them out." "Let's use the internet." "Write a letter to the people who did the books." I focused in on the letter-writing suggestion and reminded them that before we did so, we had to be certain that our criticisms were correct. The students then agreed that in small groups they would use the textbook's index and read what was said about all the first 18 presidents, just as we had done previously with Jefferson. None of the groups found any mention of a president owning a slave.

Letters as Critique and Action

In subsequent days, some students wrote letters to the textbook publisher. Michelle, a white girl, was particularly detailed. She wrote: "I am 11 years old and I like to read and write. When I am reading I notice every little word and in your social studies book I realize that the word "racism" is not in your book. You're acting like it is a bad word for those kids who read it." She went on to criticize the book for not mentioning that any presidents had slaves: "I see that you do not mention that some of the presidents had slaves. But some of them did. Like George Washington had 317 slaves. So did Thomas Jefferson. He had 267 slaves." She continued: "If you want to teach children the truth, then you should write the truth." (Michelle's letter and some of the student-made charts were also printed in our school newspaper.)

While discovering which presidents were slave owners is not an in-depth analysis, it pokes an important hole in the godlike mystique that surrounds the "Founding Fathers."

We mailed off the letters, and moved on to new lessons. Weeks passed with no response and eventually the students stopped asking if the publishers had written back. Then one day a fancy-looking envelope appeared in my mailbox addressed to Michelle Williams. She excitedly opened the letter and read it to the class.

Harcourt School Publishers Vice President Donald Lankiewicz had responded to Michelle at length. He wrote that "while the word 'racism' does not appear, the subject of unfair treatment of people because of their race is addressed on page 467." He also argued: "There are many facts about the presidents that are not included in the text simply because we do not have room for them all."

Michelle wrote back to Lankiewicz, thanking him but expressing disappointment.

"In a history book you shouldn't have to wait until page 467 to learn about unfair treatment," she wrote. As to his claim that there wasn't room for all the facts about the presidents, Michelle responded: "Adding more pages is good for the kids because they should know the right things from the wrong. It is not like you are limited to certain amount of pages. . . . All I ask you is that you write the word 'racism' in the book and add some more pages in the book so you can put most of the truth about the presidents."

Michelle never received a reply.

Improving the Lesson

Michelle and the other students left 5th grade soon after the letter exchange. In the flurry of end-of-year activities, I didn't take as much time to process the project as I might have. Nor did I adequately explore with students the fact that most non-slave-owning presidents exhibited pro-slavery attitudes and promoted pro-slavery policies.

But the larger issue, which critical teachers struggle to address, is why textbook publishers and schools in general do such a poor job of helping students make sense of the difficult issues of race. We do students a disservice when we sanitize history and sweep uncomfortable truths under the rug. We leave them less prepared to deal with the difficult issues they will face in their personal, political, and social lives. Granted, these are extremely complicated issues that don't have a single correct response. But it's important to begin with a respect for the truth and for the capacity of people of all ages to expand their understanding of the past and the present, and to open their hearts and minds to an ever-broadening concept of social justice.

I believe my students learned a lot from their research on presidents and slaves — and clearly know more than most Americans about which of the first 18 presidents owned slaves. I'm also hopeful they learned the importance of looking critically at all sources of information. I know one student, Tanya, did. On the last day of school she came up to me amid the congratulatory goodbyes and said, "I still think Lincoln owned slaves."

"You are a smart girl but you are wrong about that one," I responded. "We'll see," she said. "You didn't know Grant had slaves when the school year started! Why should I always believe what my teacher says?" ✳

Author's note: About two years after I completed the research on slave-owning presidents with my students, a wonderful website called Understanding-Prejudice.org was put up by folks at Wesleyan University. This site includes extensive information on presidents who owned slaves (see understanding-prejudice.org/slavery). I learned from this website that three presidents not on my list also owned slaves: Martin Van Buren, William Henry Harrison, and James Buchanan. I am grateful for the additional information on this website, which opens up all sorts of new teaching possibilities.

RESOURCES

For teaching materials related to this article, including the two letters referenced, go to rethinkingschools.org/NTB

This article was written in 2001. In recent years, the word "slave" has generally been replaced with the term "enslaved person," to better recognize an individual's inherent humanity rather than defining someone merely as another's property. I have changed the article's title and in several places used the "enslaved person." I kept the words "slave" and "slave-owner" to remain true to the classroom dialogue and interactions that took place at that time.

Medical Apartheid

Teaching the Tuskegee Syphilis Study

BY GRETCHEN KRAIG-TURNER

When I think of Black Lives Matter, what comes to mind first is police brutality and the resulting lost lives of young men and women in recent times. But as a science teacher, I know that racism in the United States also has roots that extend deep into the history of medical research. Medical apartheid, the systematic oppression and exclusion of African Americans in our healthcare systems, has existed since the time of slavery and continues today in medical offices and research universities. What care people receive, what diseases are studied, and who is included in research groups are still delineated by race.

The term medical apartheid is explained in Harriet Washington's 2007 work, *Medical Apartheid: The Dark History of Medical Experimentation on Black Americans from Colonial Times to the Present*. Washington documents how "diverse forms of racial discrimination have shaped both the relationship between white physicians and Black patients and the attitude of the latter toward modern medicine in general."

Medical apartheid is a reality that many of my students and their families face. I teach in the only predominantly African American high school in Oregon. My students report being talked down to by doctors as a common experience, as is leaving the doctor's office without receiving adequate care. One of my students told us that her uncle's treatment for a heart condition was so substandard, her family sued the hospital for discrimination. Critically examining the history of medical research is a way to bring the experiences of my students and their families into the classroom, and a way to connect our study of bioethics to the often hidden history of African American men and women who fought for their dignity and rights against a medical system that treated them like lab rats.

So I begin my Research and Medicine course, a senior-level course in our Health Sciences and Biotechnology Program, with an exploration of bioethics, a theme that continues throughout all of the units. We focus on the Tuskegee Syphilis Study (TSS), a chapter of scientific and medical history rarely discussed in high school. Particularly as a white educator, I am conscious that leading the school year with a unit on a deeply painful example of Black oppression needs to be done with care. This is the capstone course of the program, and I already know the students when the class starts. Without a level of trust and mutual respect already established, this unit would not be as successful. If I did not know my students well, I would wait until later in the year, after a safe space had been created. Another reason to wait is that the TSS leads to discussions about cell types (particularly types of bacteria) and epidemiology, which are typically covered later in the year.

Day one of the unit starts with me asking a simple question: "In what ways are you in control of your health and in what ways are you not in control?" I list a couple examples: "I'm in control of how often I exercise but I'm not in control of air pollution in my neighborhood." The students do a think-pair-share with the question, scribbling down answers and then sharing with their lab bench partner.

Medical apartheid is a reality that many of my students and their families face.

As we start to answer the question as a whole class, I write their answers on the whiteboard under the headers "In Control" and "Not in Control." Pretty quickly, someone disagrees about the appropriate header.

"One way I'm in control of my health is what food I eat," Robert says. I write "foods" under In Control.

Charene asks, "What if good food isn't available?"

Kia yells out, "Our school lunch is terrible but it's free. Is that a choice? I don't eat that junk!"

After more examples are generated, I ask: "Who does have a choice about what food they eat? Why do some people have different levels of access to doctors? How come some neighborhoods have better air quality? Why can't some people go running safely at night?"

Soon nothing in the In Control column is safe from my kids' scrutiny.

We talk about each item through a social justice lens. For example, going to the doctor regularly is tied to insurance — which is tied to job and education level — and access to transportation. Exercising is linked to living in a safe neighborhood, childcare, money for gyms, air quality, and concern about what police see when a middle-aged white woman is running vs. a Black or Brown youth. The class inevitably concludes that health and healthcare are a complex mix of choice and circumstance, and that those with more social and economic power have a different level of choice.

Sade sums it up: "None of this is a choice for poor people, just for people who can buy whatever they choose, and who has that kind of money isn't always fair."

The Tuskegee Mixer

My students' insights on these intersections in our healthcare system lead into a mixer on the TSS. The TSS exemplifies how race, class, and healthcare have intersected in this country, all themes the students raised during our warm-up.

The "Tuskegee Study of Untreated Syphilis in the Negro Male" (now formally known as the "U.S. Public Health Service Syphilis Study at Tuskegee"), which began in 1932 in rural Alabama, spanned most of the 20th century. African American men with syphilis (the sexually transmitted disease or a different strain of the bacteria known as yaws) were observed, yet received no treatment. They were denied standard treatment — heavy metal treatments at first, and later penicillin — and forbidden to seek medical treatment elsewhere. The architects of the study went as far as barring the men from the World War II draft, where they would have been treated with penicillin. The study continued into the early 1970s, when a whistle-blower, fed up with trying to get the attention of his superiors, took the story to a journalist. After the article appeared, Congress held hearings that suspended the study and led to the passage of the National Research Act, which includes a mandated code of ethics for research on human subjects.

"We're going to look at a time in medical history when informed consent didn't exist," I tell the students as I introduce the mixer. I give each student the role of a study subject, a doctor, a public health official, a widow, or a journalist. There are roles that show the damage inflicted, and also roles that show the resistance and whistle-blowing that ultimately exposed and ended the study. For example, Charles Pollard was a participant who later became an activist:

I am a Macon County farmer, and I started in the Tuskegee Study in the early 1930s. I recall the day in 1932 when some men came by and told me I would receive a free physical examination if I came by the one-room school near my house. So I went on over and they told me I had bad blood. . . . And that's what they've been telling me ever since.

I was at a stockyard in Montgomery, and a newspaper woman started talking to me about the study in Tuskegee. She asked me if I knew Nurse Rivers. That's how I discovered I was one of the men in the study. Once I found out how those doctors at Tuskegee used the African American men of Macon County in their study, I went to see Fred Gray. He was Rosa Parks' and Martin Luther King Jr.'s attorney. He took our case and sued the federal government for using us as guinea pigs without our consent.

Being in this study violated my rights. After I found out about the real purpose of the study, I told reporters, "All I knew was that [the doctors and nurses] just kept saying I had the bad blood — they never mentioned syphilis to me, not even once."

Other roles include Nurse Eunice Rivers and Dr. Eugene Dibble, both African Americans who worked as researchers in the study, supporting the study perhaps as a way to bring both money and prestige to Tuskegee. Roles of the white doctors who designed and orchestrated the study include upsetting quotes. For example, Dr. Thomas Murrell, an advisor to the study's leaders, said:

So the scourge sweeps among them. Those that are treated are only half-cured, and the effort to assimilate into a complex civilization drives their diseased minds until the results are criminal records. Perhaps here, in conjunction with tuberculosis, will be the end of the Negro problem. Disease will accomplish what man cannot.

Once the students read, understand, and are prepared to play the person in their role sheet, I ask everyone to walk around the room, telling people who they are and learning about other participants in the drama.

Their initial curiosity quickly changes to disbelief for some and hardening anger for others. They fill out a question sheet as they meet the other characters, and then spend a few minutes reflecting on questions raised by the mixer, and what surprised, angered, or left them hopeful.

"Why did they do this? What did they learn?"

"Why didn't they give the men penicillin?"

"How long did this last?"

Students start to make the connections between the study and the pre-World War II eugenics movement they studied previously. As David points out, "This is a lot like what the Nazi doctors did in Auschwitz."

Whistle-Blowers

Then we transition into reading the article that brought national attention to the study. In 1966, Peter Buxtun, a U.S. Public Health Service (PHS) venereal disease investigator, tried to alert his superiors about the immorality and lack of scientific ethics of the study, but they would not listen. In 1968, William Carter Jenkins, an African American statistician at PHS, called for an end to the study in a small anti-racist newsletter he founded. Nothing changed. Finally, Buxtun went to the mainstream press, and Associated Press journalist Jean Heller broke the story in the *Washington Evening Star*. She begins:

> Washington, July 25 [1972] — For 40 years the United States Public Health Service has conducted a study in which human beings with syphilis, who were induced to serve as guinea pigs, have gone without medical treatment for the disease and a few have died of its late effects, even though an effective therapy was eventually discovered.
>
> Officials of the health service who initiated the experiment have long since retired. Current officials, who say they have serious doubts about the morality of the study, also say that it is too late to treat the syphilis in any surviving participants.

The students also read the Centers for Disease Control and Prevention's description of syphilis, including the progression of the disease and recommended treatment, and a summary I created of other relevant information.

Then I assign some writing: Using these resources and what you learned from meeting everyone in the mixer, write a first-person testimony that could have been used at the congressional hearings that followed Heller's story. You can be the same person you portrayed in the mixer, or someone else. Explain why you think the study happened, your understanding of the disease itself, and if reparations are appropriate or not. Explain your reasons.

These are quick-writes, not final pieces, but aimed at getting students to understand the human lives behind the medical facts. Lejay writes from the perspective of a widow of one of the men in the study:

> I am Ruth Fields and I became a widow during the Tuskegee Syphilis Study. My husband passed away from the effects of syphilis. . . . In the early 1920s, syphilis was a major health issue and concern. In 1932, a study was conducted of 399 men with syphilis and 201 without. The men were given occasional assessments, and were told they were being treated. In 1936, local physicians were asked to help with the study, but not treat the men, and to follow the men until death. Penicillin became a treatment option for syphilis but the men in the study couldn't receive it. . . .
>
> I endured so much hurt, pain, and loss because of this study, and I just want everyone who was involved to be punished for their actions, because they hurt and killed and destroyed so many lives.

Shirene writes from the point of view of one of the men in the study:

> I am Roy Douglas. Poor, uneducated African American men like myself experienced an outbreak of syphilis. We were sent to hospitals for having "bad blood." Doctors didn't know how the STD worked, the side effects, or the symptoms. To get the information that they needed, they used us as test dummies. More than 400 of us were denied help, medicine, and the proper treatment for years. Some men suffered from mild symptoms like rashes, then spots appeared on the surface of their skin. With time, their nerves, brains, and more shut down. . . . In 1945, penicillin was finally accepted as a treatment for syphilis.
>
> After more than 30 years of researching, the study finally ended in 1972. I personally feel like the study was a small version of a genocide. . . . It was unnecessary and wrong to use poor, Black men as guinea pigs for experiments. Out of the

whole dehumanizing study, the only positive outcome was the cure. There should have been more rules or procedures set up to maintain the health of the sick men. No one deserves to die when there is some type of medicine to cure them. I believe that every person who lent a hand in the study should have gone to prison.

Where Do We Go from Here?

There is so much of the TSS that is hard to swallow. The sheer length — more than 40 years — is astounding for any longitudinal study, let alone one that watched men die from a brutal infection that attacks the nervous system. The fact that researchers went to great lengths to keep the men from finding out that there was a simple cure shows the purpose was not to find treatment. That the study continued throughout and after the Civil Rights Movement is perplexing and contrary to a narrative of racial equity so often spun in history books. But my students' anger is often more personal.

The students are not paranoid. The United States has a history of funding unethical studies on vulnerable populations. We read articles about similar cases in which U.S. doctors and scientists took advantage of vulnerable populations — from sterilizing female prisoners in California to infecting prisoners in Guatemala with syphilis.

It's at this point that I ask students to write up their own code for bioethical human research: If you were in charge of how and what research could be conducted, what limitations would you place? How would you define informed consent? How would you guarantee informed consent? Is anyone off limits? If not, how do you guarantee that they are not being taken advantage of by unscrupulous researchers?

After writing their own codes, I distribute copies of the Nuremberg Code and the Belmont Report. The students then write a reflection on how their codes differ and what might be missing from each of the lists: How is your code similar to the Nuremberg Code and the Belmont Report? How is it different? What did you mention that should be added to those codes?

With their bioethical codes hung in the hallway leading to my classroom and armed with the knowledge that science isn't always ethical, I give students their first major assignment of the year: a research paper on a bioethics topic of their choice.

Before we began this course with a study of the TSS, I read papers about artificially extending life or genetically modified creatures that sounded more like science fiction than real issues affecting my students and their families. But now that we begin with an exploration of bioethics rooted in the history of the TSS, the papers have become more interesting and personal. I still give the students a list of bioethics topics from the CDC website, but through conversations in class and students opening up about their own experiences, the topics have increased in relevance and student engagement. Now students write about why mortality rates of cancers are different for people of different races. They explore how U.S. scientists have engineered studies taking place in Latin America. One young woman wrote a history of gynecology in the United States, from unanesthetized surgeries of women who were enslaved through much more recent forced sterilizations of women of color. Another student wrote about medical experiments by Japanese doctors in Chinese prisoner of war camps during World War II.

Our students are tomorrow's doctors and researchers. We need to give them space to explore how racist practices are a part of science and medicine. As we teach and learn, we can invite students to critically examine the intersections of science, race, gender, culture, language, and socioeconomic status. We must not whitewash our scientific history but rather honor the scientific achievements and contributions of people of color — and empower our students to wrestle with historical and current racial disparities in healthcare and science. ✳

RESOURCES

Materials for the Tuskegee Syphilis Study mixer are available at rethinkingschools.org/NTB

Centers for Disease Control and Prevention. 2016. *Sexually Transmitted Diseases (STDs): Syphilis*. cdc.gov/std/syphilis

Centers for Disease Control and Prevention. 2016. *U.S. Public Health Service Syphilis Study at Tuskegee: The Tuskegee Timeline*. cdc.gov/tuskegee/timeline.htm

Tuskegee University. 2016. About the USPHS Syphilis Study. tuskegee.edu/about-us/centers-of-excellence/bioethics-center/about-the-usphs-syphilis-study

Washington, Harriet. *2006. Medical Apartheid: The Dark History of Medical Experimentation on Black Americans from Colonial Times to the Present*. First Anchor Books.

I hate the textbook I've been given to use.
What can I do?

In order to present students with multiple perspectives on any topic, it is likely that you will need more than one resource. Part of the challenge in becoming a social justice teacher is finding materials to supplement the books you have available in your school. Then there is also the trick of finding the time and opportunities in the weekly schedule to use them. It is not easy, but it is worth the energy you expend.

Take the time to review the textbooks you're given, then determine where you will need to add on to what you've got. Start with your school library. Tap the public library as well for classroom literature.

Monthly book clubs like Scholastic or Cricket often offer quality literature at a great price. They are an inexpensive way to collect multiple copies of books for use in reading instruction. Don't be afraid to ask if there is money in the school budget for your classroom collection.

Songs and poetry are great sources of alternative perspectives too. And you can use data and information from the news to help students explore concepts in math, science, and other curricular areas.

If you still feel you're "stuck" with poor resources, remember that you have the ability to help your students look critically at what they are reading and see the shortcomings for themselves. Help them find ways to "talk back" to the textbook and teach them how to find other perspectives that are not represented in its pages.

—Rita Tenorio

Lots of local institutions — historical societies, science museums, cultural museums, etc. — loan free or inexpensive resources to teachers. Frequently they offer boxes of books or artifacts to supplement a variety of topics and themes.

Many online resources are amazing and lots are free. Some newspapers offer free or discounted subscriptions to classrooms/schools. We get the *San Francisco Chronicle* for free at my school, for example. Sometimes they offer print, sometimes only digital subscriptions are available. Lots of teachers and librarians use and like Newsela, which is leveled and pretty comprehensive.

The Smithsonian publishes a great online magazine called *Tween Tribune* and also has articles in Spanish.

Ask your school librarians or, if you don't have a librarian, someone at the school district admin level. Your district or even state may subscribe or be able to subscribe to databases.

All public schools in the state of California now have access to several high-quality subscription databases covering all subjects and grade levels. Now individual schools and library departments don't have to spend our own small budgets on them. Also, public libraries usually have collections of excellent student databases that students and teachers can access easily with their public library cards.

—Rachel Cloues

If your principal has told you to use the textbook, defying a direct order will generally be considered insubordination and will land you in trouble, or even the unemployment line. However, perhaps there are other people in your school or department who don't like this book. Ask around to find out. Get together with those people. Write up a critique of the book and propose alternative curriculum.

In the short term, go ahead and use the book but use it critically. Invite students to read between the lines: Whose perspectives are missing? Was America "discovered" or "invaded"? See "Students as Textbook Detectives" in *Rethinking Our Classrooms, Volume 1*, or *Rethinking Columbus* for lots of ideas on how to engage students in a critique of their textbooks. (See p. 132 for Rethinking Schools book details.)

In a nutshell: If you feel like you have to use the assigned text, use it, but find other materials as well. Even if you "use" the textbook, any good administrator will expect you to supplement it with lots of other materials.

—Bill Bigelow

Students Bring the World to Our Classrooms

BY KIM KANOF

My period 8 Modern World History class is something to see. Students zip around the room, they dance, they shake hands, they share their cultures. The room comes alive with roaring laughter. Tongues exchange Spanish, Chuukese, Amharic, Swahili, Chinese, Vietnamese, Burmese, Oromo, Farsi, Arabic, and English. Animated hands, bold smiles, and warm body language put everyone at ease. The entire room is a community, including the newcomers who have just arrived in the country. Our class looks like a global convention, with students from Afghanistan, Syria, Ethiopia, Somalia, Rwanda, Vietnam, Mexico, Guatemala, Myanmar, Thailand, Chuuk Micronesia, the Democratic Republic of the Congo, China, and other places around the world. Over the years I've discovered that students learning English need to gain competency in language, but they also need safe spaces where they can grow while learning challenging content that helps them understand history, society, and the role that immigration has played across the world.

Madison High School is a public school in northeast Portland, Oregon, of approximately 1,100 students. Our students speak more than 50 languages. Many are from immigrant and refugee families. Most of my students are new arrivals and have only been speaking English for a few years. Some of my students have experienced severely interrupted formal education and some have had no access to education before entering my classroom. Many of my students and their parents are also learning English and attempting to adapt to life in the United States. They struggle with housing insecurity, and stress and worry over travel bans or obtaining green cards. Some have unidentified learning disabilities, some may be teen parents, some are separated from their families, and many have experienced trauma in their lives. They are all in my sheltered history class designed to support English language learners at levels 1 and 2.

It is easy to get caught up in worrying about students' English acquisition, thinking that students learning English need to be taught vocabulary *before* they can engage in content. I find, however, that when I focus on teaching complex content — while scaffolding language — students' use a wider variety of new words and sentence structures as tools to share their thoughts and ideas. To support them, I provide a variety of entry points. I try to create opportunities for students to bring their lives and stories into the curriculum. To help them comprehend difficult content, I use accessible "texts" like poetry, graphic novels, picture books, photos, leveled news articles, and video. Yes, I teach vocabulary and keep a word wall in my room, but we also play games, create art, and get active with our learning.

Lost Homes Unit

Inspired by photographer Fazal Sheikh's Common Grounds exhibit at the Portland Art Museum, I designed a "lost homes" unit for my Modern World History class. What I love about Sheikh's work is the way he celebrates refugees who have lost their homes and retained their cultural identities. A documentary-based photographer, Sheikh is respected for building relationships over time, recording individuals' stories, and giving displaced peoples voice. Each photo tells a story.

The unit explores the "push" factors that force people to leave home — and the racism, poverty, and culture shock refugees face once they settle in the United States. To teach both content knowledge and language development, I bring in a wide variety of texts, including students' personal stories, the poetry of Warsan Shire, photographs, the documentary *Rain in a Dry Land* that

It is easy to get caught up in worrying about students' English acquisition, thinking that students learning English need to be taught vocabulary *before* they can engage in content.

follows two Somali Bantu families from Kakuma Refugee Camp being placed in the United States, real-world stories from the U.N. Refugee Agency, and news articles. Students also read the graphic novel and animated adaptation of *The Breadwinner*, a story about an 11-year-old who lives under Taliban rule in Afghanistan in 2001. The unit is rich, saturating students in images and stories about displacement, while also teaching them language, reading, and writing skills.

Visuals to Develop Narratives

At the opening of the year, Ade, a Congolese refugee who lived in Kigali prior to moving to the United States, refused to write in English or in her native language. Writing caused her intense stress. If I left her alone, she would sit in the room for 90 minutes and not produce a single word. She, however, enjoyed drawing.

I opened the lost homes unit by asking my students to share a time they moved or lost a home as a way to connect their stories to other stories of migration. We brainstormed objects, people, places, and memories students were forced to leave behind. I distributed art materials and asked my students to draw visual representations of their stories.

As I circulated around the room, I asked Ade to tell me about her drawing. She said, "This is my home in Kigali. There is food. But I do not eat." I wrote down verbatim the words she used to describe her images.

"What kind of food is this?" I asked, pointing to her drawing.

"Bananas, fish, *ugali*."

I wrote these words down on her drawing. I then inquired, "Why are you not eating?" Ade told me her drawing was a memory of her sister's funeral. This was an important story for her to write. She was eager to remember her sister through words.

Another student, Gale, had recently moved to the United States from Thailand. He used Legos to construct a replica of his aunt's house in Thailand. Gale, a 9th grader, had acquired a great deal of verbal English, but he had difficulty writing in English. I asked him to tell me his story. I wrote his words on Post-it notes and stuck them to the doors, windows, and walls of the house he had built.

Creating visual representations helps students build new English vocabulary and gives them confidence as they write and share their narratives with other students. After completing the writing, students post their drawings and sculptures around the room and share their stories orally with one another. I arrange tables in a U shape. Students stand beside their artifacts on a table. They take turns sharing and listening, using their visual representations and the new vocabulary they gained during our conferencing.

Because my goals are to help students develop their thinking and navigate code-switching, not to erase their home languages, I encourage them to speak in Swahili or Spanish or another language depending on their audience. I am only fluent in English, but I know that limiting bilingual students to English can result in missed opportunities for deep, critical engagement.

As they hear other students' lost home stories, students learn about each other as well as new content and vocabulary. Students shared how strange their first time on an airplane was, memories of dancing or playing soccer in Kakuma Refugee Camp, the day they were forced to wear a burqa while traveling through Kabul, Afghanistan, the decision their family had to make to leave Syria, flooded homes in Myanmar, and many more stories about lost homes. Clearly, their personal stories enhanced the content and develop language relevant to later parts of the unit.

After rehearsing their stories orally, using the vocabulary they gain from their visual representations and hearing other students' stories, students write their narratives. My classroom is a mix of students who have newly arrived in the country as well as those who are still developing their English language skills, so the writing depends on their current language level. Some students will conference about their visuals with me to get their writing out, some might write in their home language then translate, others might write the story in English.

Whenever my students share, I use my iPhone to take photos or record their conversations. I also record questions or notes in my teacher journal for further investigation. I write down when a student has demonstrated understanding and areas of confusion. It's helpful to record student thinking and keep these anchors to aid the writing process, but these notes also function as notes for upcoming lessons: What didn't students learn about content or language that I need to work on next?

Building Background Knowledge and Interacting with Text

To expand my students' understanding about other factors that lead to migration, I use a mixer-style role play that my colleague Camila Arze Torres Goitia wrote about immigration push and pull factors — like civil war, environmental disasters, and employment opportunities. A mixer helps students build background knowledge prior to reading a novel, historical text, or watching a documentary. Typically, students receive roles, describing people or events they will meet during their study of the unit (see "Role Plays: Show, Don't Tell" on p. 121).

Before starting the mixer, we update our word wall with the new terms they will encounter in the mixer, such as asylum, refugee, and residency. When learning complex terms, I bring in photos, videos, and translations in many languages, which I find on Google Translate. For example, with the word "asylum," I start with pictures of refugee camps. I ask students, "What do you notice about this picture?" Students commented that people had food, that there was no war, that people had family members with them. To make connections to the complex idea of asylum as a safe place, I bring my yoga mat to class. I show a picture of me on my couch with my dog. Then I tell students, "Draw a picture of your safe space." Once students draw and share, together we write a class definition of the word.

> **I am only fluent in English, but I know that limiting bilingual students to English can result in missed opportunities for deep, critical engagement.**

To make this mixer work with English language learners at levels 1 and 2, I scaffold the mixer discussion. I bold unfamiliar vocabulary as I prepare the roles (see example role below). Next, I shorten the roles to include only the more pertinent information. For example, the role about a refugee from Somalia reads:

I am a 16-year-old **refugee** and I live with my grandmother in Portland, Oregon. Before coming to Portland, I lived in a refugee camp in **Ethiopia** for four years, but my family was originally from **Somalia**. My grandmother cannot **work** and my older brother and younger sister have been missing our father since we have come to the United States. Our family has been working with an **immigration lawyer** for the past couple of years to try and get a **travel/tourist visa** for our father to visit. Because our father is **Somali** and currently **unemployed**, he has not been able to get a travel visa. They say that people who are unemployed are seen as a "high risk" because they may choose to overstay their visa illegally. It seems like our only hope is waiting for my older brother to turn 18, graduate, get a job, and sponsor our father. My siblings and I had planned to visit him this summer but our situation went from little hope to no hope — an **executive order** was signed to **ban** travel for us Somalis. Now my older brother may not even get to sponsor him.

This role is a true story written with the help of a former student at Madison High School. Other roles in this mixer include: DACA recipients, asylum seekers from Iraq and Syria, undocumented youth from Guatemala, diversity visa recipients from Tonga, and H-1B temporary employment visa recipients from India. There are 15 roles in this mixer, with new stories added to represent students in the room or current events of displacement, like the Rohingya from Myanmar, so most students receive different roles. After I distribute the roles, I remind my students that these are true stories and that we need to honor these people by carefully reading and sharing a summary of the most important details. As students read their roles, they highlight important ideas, define unfamiliar terms, and underline what they think is most important for their classmates to know about their role.

Some of my students are hesitant during class discussions because they need time to process in the English language, so I use Flipgrid, a video discussion platform that works on smartphones, iPads, computers, and Chromebooks. Each student records short videos discussing the person whose role they received. This strategy allows them to practice and re-record until they feel ready to share. Instead of walking around and telling each other about their roles, we "mix" by watching the Flipgrid videos students created in class. As we watch students' video clips about people who have been forced out of their countries, students ask each other questions and learn more about the push and pull factors of immigration. Students gather evidence about these factors on a graphic organizer in preparation for a later letter/essay writing assignment.

Gathering Evidence

After the narrative and mixer lessons, students read texts about refugees. Texts in my classroom are more than words, they are photographs, graphic novels, picture books, video, audio, and physical artifacts. And they are also news articles. To help students learn how to move from summaries to analysis in reading, I use a hashtag gallery walk strategy that was designed by my colleagues Maurice Cowley and Tara Jardine.

Many of my students don't know what a hashtag is, so I load a few examples like #blacklivesmatter or #GoMad, our school's social media tag. I explain that hashtags are used to link ideas, describe, or ask questions. Using a photograph of Somali refugees displaced from their homes by floods, I draw a circle around it and we write hashtags to practice making connections. My students wrote things like #wherewilltheylive or #floodsdestroy. Once students have the gist, they create hashtags for other photographs of climate refugees I place around the room.

Our job as teachers is to find ways to link students' experiences to our content and find creative ways to nurture students' language development in the process.

In preparing the unit, I gather articles about climate refugees from a variety of news sources, in a number of languages, and at varying levels of reading using Newsela. Newsela is an instructional platform that provides digital articles with differentiated texts. I seek out articles that described people being forced to flee their homes because of rising sea levels, extreme weather events, drought, and water scarcity.

Before we start reading, I place a quote from the *Guardian* on the center of a large piece of chart paper: "An Environmental Justice Foundation report argues that climate change played a part in the buildup to the Syrian war, with successive droughts causing 1.5 million people to migrate to the country's cities between 2006 and 2011." I circle the quote and model writing hashtag reactions to the text: #climateissuescreateconflict #nowaternohome #droughtsimpactmillions. Then, circling the hashtags and using vocabulary from our unit, I model how I use the hashtags and sentence frames to write a complete thought or reaction. "Climate issues led to conflict in Syria because droughts caused millions to leave home in search of water in the country's cities."

After modeling, students dive into Newsela articles about climate change and climate refugees. Students gather quotes in their notebooks. Then they choose the quote they like the best and create their own hashtag poster. The hashtag posters serve as anchor charts to gather evidence for writing.

I culminate the unit by asking students to write letters to various organizations about ways to help or prevent climate refugees because I want to end on a hopeful note. Later in the year we transition to more formal essay formats, but the letter contains the elements of an essay: an opening with demands or points, several evidence paragraphs, and a call-to-action conclusion. During class, students first brainstorm a list of groups or people they want to write to. Then they gather names of organizations and people out of our readings, films, etc. They discuss what kinds of actions would help prevent the chaos of climate change that creates refugees and ways to help people who experience climate chaos. Many students wrote to the United Nations; others wrote to climate activist Kathy Jetñil-Kijiner, who came to Madison; some wrote to the news media to discuss potential solutions; others wrote government officials about accepting climate refugees.

English language learners lead rich lives and enter our classrooms full of ideas and experiences. Our job as teachers is to find ways to link those experiences to our content and find creative ways to nurture students' language development in the process.

I want my classroom to mirror Fazal Sheikh's photo exhibit, to examine social justice issues in engaging, thought-provoking ways that honor individuals' lives, voices, and cultures. *

Speak Freely

BY LYNSEY BURKINS

I t was a typical morning during writing workshop in my 2nd-grade classroom until Mateo's mother, Luvia, entered the room crying. "Please help Mateo," she pleaded. "He is losing his Spanish. He doesn't know Spanish words, and if he can't speak Spanish, he can't talk to us his family."

She then turned to talk to students in the classroom whom she perceived to speak Spanish and appealed to them individually. In that moment with Mateo's mother and her grief over the loss of his language, my class shared an experience that changed us.

My classroom is situated in a suburban school outside of Columbus, Ohio. All but four of the students in my classroom speak more than one language, and English is not their first. Almost half of these students were born outside of the United States, and some can vividly remember their immigration stories.

Earlier that morning, before school had started, Luvia, her interpreter, and his teachers met to talk about Mateo's progress in school. Teachers shared a lot of information that morning, but it was obvious from what Luvia said in the meeting through the interpreter that her main concern was Mateo's loss of ability to speak his native language. Her concern seemed to be quickly dismissed by the team. Our eyes met mother-to-mother, as she was told, "Well, we can't control that, but we understand how that would be upsetting." I felt her pain.

After the meeting, emotions flooded through my brain. I was angry. As one of two African American teachers at the school, I too had felt the sting that a lack of understanding can bring. When I had tried to speak up during the meeting with Luvia, I was politely quieted by the group. I questioned whether the other teachers, who were all born in the United States and spoke only English, considered the importance of students' home languages and cultures.

Little did I know that it wouldn't be me who stepped in and spoke up for Mateo. It wouldn't be me who would organize and take charge of the effort to help him speak his native language. It wouldn't be me who would reach out to school support staff to join in the effort. It would be his peers.

Within seconds of Luvia's appeal to the students in my class, Maria went to Mateo and said, "I can help you." Then Luis jumped up and said, "Yeah, we can just practice." Soon, a larger circle formed, with multiple voices weighing in.

Classroom Meetings

When Mateo's mother left the room, a stillness took over. The class need-ed to talk and think as a collective unit. Shiv suggested everyone get in a circle to talk about what had happened. Twenty-five 8-year-old bodies sat around a circle ready to have a problem-solving conversation. Some with legs crossed, some on their knees, some lying with their faces poked in.

From the first day of school I introduce and practice the conver-sation circle. The composition and size of the circles varies. Sometimes students are a part of small-group conversation circles; often we conduct circles as a whole class. As a teacher of young children, I am intentional about cultivating a level of talk among children that transforms their ex-perience in the classroom. In the circle, students learn that talking with one another is an important part of their learning process. I want them to understand that engaging in healthy discourse with a diverse group of peers will empower them to solve problems, understand others better, and work as a collective unit to create change in their world.

At the end of the first day of school I prepared students for this daily practice. "Tomorrow you will start a routine that will happen ev-ery morning. You will get into a circle and talk with each other. You will have the chance to share something and also respond to what oth-ers in your circle share. You might share about what you did at home last night, something you are excited about, maybe even something that worries you. It will be like a conversation you have with family or friends. You will need to decide what you want to talk about that day. I won't tell you. This will come from you. Tonight I want you to think about something you might share tomorrow. I'm excited to hear what you all have to say."

The next morning many of the students came ready to share. At first, students started to talk over each other. Some students began covering their ears. One student suggested that they go in order around the circle. The other circle heard this and decided to do the same thing. They continued using that method for a while as they learned how to have a conversation. Some, like Valeria, said pass. She wasn't ready to share she told me. That was OK.

During conversation circles I play the role of note taker, social scientist, and learner. While students share valuable information, I gather information from their conversations to be more responsive to their needs. This knowledge helps me select books, decide how to instruct them, and look closely at their speaking and listening needs. Their conversations help set the course of topics we take up in the classroom. They are the content of our curriculum. Throughout the year I recorded students talking about war in their home country, online bullying, having to move because of their parents' green cards expiring, what it means to be a family, the color of their skin, and many other topics that opened windows to their communities and world.

"We are so lucky, we can just speak freely."

So when Shiv initiated the circle on the day Mateo's mother came to our classroom, students used a familiar practice to make sense of difficult issues.

Mya had the idea that if Mateo spoke both Spanish and English in school he might learn Spanish better. The group agreed with a chorus of "yes" and "great idea."

Then Preeshaa spoke: "Well, why can't we all do that? I know that Neha speaks Hindi like I do. Can we speak both, too?"

Other students chimed in. "I speak Hindi, too! Well, I speak Arabic and so does Eibraham — we can speak with each other."

By the end of the conversation, everyone had a language partner. Each person who spoke a language other than English had someone else to converse with in their native language. As the conversation ended Pranavi said, "We are so lucky, we can just speak freely." She made a "Speak Freely" sign and placed it under the TV as a reminder.

Speaking Freely: Students as Teachers

It wasn't unusual to witness interactions of students blending their languages mid-sentence mid-topic. This was the way we lived. Any opportunity to speak or write was the individual student's choice on how they wanted to communicate. "Speak freely," you would hear a child say whenever a new person entered our class. From the start of the year to the end we ended up with 13 students who either moved into or out of the classroom. It was important to the students that everyone — both children and adults — know our welcoming attitude toward the use of home languages.

Students looked for allies to support their language work. When our bilingual aide entered the room, Luis saw her enter, jumped up, ran to her, and said, "Miss Carla, we are trying to help Mateo with his Spanish. Can you help, too?"

"Sure, Luis. How can I help?"

"Guys come over here." He motioned to Maria, Justina, and Mateo.

"What can we do to help Mateo keep his Spanish? Miss Carla is going to help."

"We can read books and talk," said Justina.

"Miss Carla, we have already been trying to talk more in Spanish during writing time, and we have some books that are in English and Spanish, but we can't read the Spanish. Maybe you could help us?"

From that point on Miss Carla, Mateo, Luis, Justina, and Maria had weekly dates with books that included both Spanish and English text.

Throughout the year the class supported language diversity. The class determined: "Home languages aren't just for home." Students committed themselves to using multiple languages in whatever we were doing throughout the day. It wasn't something that I had to remind them to do because it wasn't something that came from me.

Parents started making remarks about their children coming home saying, "Speak freely," telling their parents how they can speak all of their languages in school.

Students taught me about their languages and demonstrated how they problem-solved language situations. For example, one day Rehema said, "Mrs. Burkins, you said we are getting a new student tomorrow who speaks Arabic. Do you know what dialect he speaks?"

"No, Rehema. I don't."

"Well, I can still help him tomorrow. You know there are different ways to speak Arabic. But it doesn't matter because only some words are different. We will be fine."

Students Advocate for Reclaiming Home Languages

Once students claimed the power of speaking their home languages, they worked as advocates for others who either lost their languages or who didn't have anyone to practice with. Miss Yates arrived for her first day of a high school intern program, which allowed high school students the opportunity to volunteer in a classroom to explore whether teaching was something they would want to pursue. Miss Yates walked in as we gathered on the floor for a story. She had long black hair and light brown skin. Luis glanced at Maria and said, "I think she speaks Spanish!" Without missing a beat, he began to greet her in Spanish. She smiled and said, "Hello, I'm Miss Yates. I'm not able to speak Spanish. I think I used to know Spanish but I lost it." Immediately there was a loud gasp in the room. Preeshaa said, "Oh, no! How did that happen? We have been working hard to keep our home language here. We spoke both all the time."

"Yeah," Luis added. You can practice with us! We can practice Spanish together."

On another occasion, Ava walked up to me after recess. She said, "Mrs. Burkins, I think I know what's wrong with Yuki." Yuki was a student who had recently joined us from Japan. She seemed sad and withdrawn. "She needs a language partner. I saw her at recess with the girls from Mrs. K's class. She looked happy. She was smiling and talking in Japanese. I think that's what she needs."

Speak Freely with Parents

Clearly, many parents whose first language isn't English, experienced the school and home language divide, so our language practice was noticed at home as well. "Mrs. Burkins!" A parent called to me at the end of the day, as she was picking up her child. "Lekesha said that she's been speaking Tamil in class. Is this true?"

"Yes, it is. She's been speaking with Preeshaa and Shiv."

"Yeah, Mom," Lekesha chimed in. "I told you. I'm allowed."

She wasn't the only parent to ask or comment. Parents started making remarks about their children coming home saying, "Speak freely," telling their parents how they can speak all of their languages in school.

During student-led conferences, I noticed a student with her family who seemed to be struggling. I walked over and asked Ami if she was OK. She looked at me with a look of concern. Her father said, "Sorry, Mrs. Burkins we just don't usually talk in English as a family. This is a little different for us."

I asked Ami, "So why are you talking in English?"

Her mother answered. "Well, you are in the room, and you don't speak our language so we will use English."

I turned to Ami and said, "You do what you need to do. This is for you and your family." I gave her a hug. I heard Ami begin to talk in Tamil as I walked away.

Affirming Home Languages Is Social Justice Teaching

Teaching for social justice isn't just a series of projects. Teaching for social justice is also the daily tiny conscious steps we take as teachers to create a structure where children have opportunities to notice injustice, practice questioning their world, learn the art of conversation, and take action in ways that make sense to them. Teaching for social justice is me not being hesitant to take on issues that arise from the day-to-day talk in our classroom. It's me listening more than I talk. It's me responding to students' needs. It's me being culturally responsive.

Speak freely meant these students didn't have to deny a part of themselves the moment they walk through the school doors. They understood that our languages represent who we are. Our languages are our family, culture, and way of life. If we want students to bring their whole selves into our classrooms, why would we have a system that does not welcome and encourage all languages?

"Speak Freely," my students said and I replied, "Yes, speak freely and thank you all for the gift of your home languages and showing me the power in your voices." Speak freely. ✳

How can I teach both content and language to students learning English as an additional language?

As a starting point, we must take time to see students' strengths and to understand their specific language backgrounds. It is important to recognize that each student's language levels and needs will change over the course of a day, month, and year.

Learning a few words and courtesy phrases in students' home languages can be a powerful way to position students as experts and ourselves as language learners. Teachers also must to be learners of our students' cultures. As we listen to students, we can plan projects that build on their background knowledge and weave students' cultures, families, languages, and experiences into the curriculum as Kim Kanof demonstrates in her article (see p. 94).

It is important to encourage students to maintain and develop their first language(s) at school, at home, and in the community. Research indicates that systematically integrating home languages into instruction results in levels of achievement as high as or higher than students in English-only programs. Ideally we would incorporate students' home languages daily, but something as simple as using poetry that has both English and another language — and encouraging students to use their home languages in their writing — can be powerful as well.

By observing and learning from students, we can begin to identify the most effective strategies for teaching complex academic content while developing students' English skills. It can be helpful to use materials that are geared for a specific group of learners (i.e., materials in students' home languages and/or materials in English that are appropriate for students' English reading level). Other strategies include:

- Beginning with visuals — photos, YouTube clips, etc. — to give students images and ideas as a way to connect to prior knowledge before launching the unit or lesson. For example, in a visual gallery walk, students circulate with a partner among collections of images and write thoughts on sticky notes or on the posters themselves.
- Previewing and marking up text with reactions or questions.
- Asking students to share their ideas with a partner before sharing

out with the whole class so that emerging bilingual students can practice formulating their ideas and language to express those ideas before speaking in small group or larger settings.

- Using active methods of learning such as role plays, skits, songs, hands-on science investigations, partner interviews, or other methods that create opportunities for students to develop vocabulary and rehearse language as they engage in new materials and concepts.
- Explaining concepts in students' home languages (invite students, parents, volunteers, or colleagues to help).

From graphic organizers and word sorts to manipulatives and visuals, strategy possibilities are abundant. Our job as teachers of content and language is to hone our abilities to understand where students are and what they might need next.

ADDITIONAL RESOURCES

Art as a Way of Talking for Emergent Bilingual Youth: A Foundation for Literacy in PreK–12 Schools
Edited by Berta Rosa Berriz, Amanda Claudia Wager, and Vivian Maria Poey
Routledge, 2019

Biliteracy from the Start: Literacy Squared in Action
By Kathy Escamilla, Sandra Butvilofsky, and Susan Hopewell
Caslon Publishing, 2013

Educating Emergent Bilinguals: Policies, Programs, and Practices for English Learners
By Ofelia García and Jo Anne Kleifgen
Teachers College Press, 2018

Reading, Writing, and Talk: Inclusive Teaching Strategies for Diverse Learners, K–2
By Mariana Souto-Manning and Jessica Martell
Teachers College Press, 2016

Rethinking Bilingual Education: Welcoming Home Languages in Our Classrooms
Edited by Elizabeth Barbian, Grace Cornell Gonzales, and Pilar Mejía
Rethinking Schools, 2017

Rethinking Schools Special Collection on Bilingual Education
rethinkingschools.org/NTB

Stephen D. Krashen's Website
Information about Krashen's many informative articles and other writings about language learning.
sdkrashen.com

Teaching for Biliteracy: Strengthening Bridges Between Languages
By Karen Beeman and Cheryl Urow
Caslon Publishing, 2012
teachingforbiliteracy.com

The Translanguaging Classroom: Leveraging Student Bilingualism for Learning
By Ofelia García, Susana Ibarra Johnson, and Kate Seltzer
Caslon Publishing, 2016

Types of English as a Second Language and Bilingual Programs

With so much variation across classrooms and schools, it is essential for educators, families, students, and community members to educate themselves about different types of English as a second language (ESL) and bilingual programs and to carefully consider how best to fulfill the needs of their community.

ESL and some bilingual programs, for example, do not have sustained bilingualism as a goal. Districts decide on what programs are offered to families based on a variety of financial, political, and demographic factors. For example, some states and school districts oppose bilingual programs because of their nativist and "English-only" beliefs while others understand the benefits of such programs. In some cases, the lack of a critical mass of students in a single language group or the large number of home languages in one school or district make bilingual programs less feasible.

English as a second language programs emphasize learning and using English in the classroom and on preparing English language learners to function in "mainstream" English language classrooms. English language learners may be placed in Newcomer Programs, an English as a second language class, "sheltered English" classes, or they may participate in a pullout ESL class. ESL teachers may also support classroom teachers in their classrooms. Other languages typically are not used in ESL programs.

In **transitional bilingual** classrooms, students' home language is used as a bridge to English in the younger elementary grades, with the goal of transitioning students to all-English instruction by 2nd or 3rd grade. Such programs have been strongly criticized by proponents of bilingual education for not fostering sustained bilingualism and biliteracy.

Maintenance (sometimes called **"developmental"**) **bilingual** programs aim to develop students' home languages with the goal of bilingualism and biliteracy. Some districts operate maintenance programs through only elementary school, while other districts have such programs through middle and high school. Often maintenance programs start with a high percentage of instruction in the home language and then, by upper elementary, have a balance of English and home language instruction.

Dual-language models generally aim to serve 50 percent native English speakers and 50 percent native speakers of the program's other target language, such as Spanish or Mandarin, although many dual-language programs also serve students with other home languages. In these programs, instruction is in both the target language and English, although the ratios vary with the program. For example, one popular model starts in kindergarten with 90 percent of the instruction in the target language and 10 percent in English, moving toward a 50/50 ratio by upper elementary. Another model maintains a 50/50 balance from kindergarten on.

Immersion programs, in which most or all instruction is in the target language, can involve native speakers of that language, heritage language learners, and/or other students who have a goal of learning the program's language. Other schools teach a heritage language as an academic subject; this is a language class geared toward students with a family connection to the language. Sometimes these students have familiarity with or are already fluent speakers of that language.

Maintenance programs, dual-language programs, immersion programs, and heritage language classes all aim to develop biliteracy and bilingualism, although they go about it in different ways. We believe a community's needs should determine the bilingual program model in a given setting — but we strongly favor programs that help students maintain their languages and have sustained biliteracy as a goal. We also believe that bilingual education should not be a means to track students who speak another language at home, separating them from their peers. And, regardless of the model chosen, the community's and staff's commitment to implementing language inclusion and equity is what ultimately determines a good program.

My students don't bring back their homework. Should I keep assigning it?

First ask yourself some questions: Why are you giving homework? Is there a school policy, or is it up to the teacher? In many places it is a timeworn tradition that students have homework, or it may be that parents demand it or have banned it.

What is the purpose served by homework? Is it a real opportunity for students to review or practice a skill? Is it meant to let families know what is going on in class? Or is it just "busy work"? What happens to the work that students bring back? Who looks at it? How is it used or not used?

These questions are just the beginning.

If you really want your students to take homework seriously, spend time on it and return it. Be sure the content is meaningful and connected to their lives and the classroom.

Homework has to be thought through and planned like any other part of the curriculum. Involve students in the development and use of the information in their homework. Let them know that you and they will need the data they collected, or the words of the person they interviewed, to continue the work in the classroom during the coming days.

Homework can be an opportunity to learn about the lives and perspectives of students and their families. It can be a chance for kids to practice collecting data, to experiment with materials and ideas, to gain expertise in conducting surveys and interviewing others. Asking for the knowledge, ideas, and perspectives of students and their families will give you and your students the rich beginnings of many classroom conversations.

You also have to be sensitive to the circumstances students face outside of school. Is there a place for the student to do work at home? Will there be another person available to help with the work or to see that it's done? What resources does your student have outside of school? Does the family have access to computers or other technology, for example? Don't assume that all your students do or do not have resources. Ask.

If you have students who can't or don't do homework, you can also find ways for them to complete the work at school.

—Rita Tenorio

Promoting Social Imagination Through Interior Monologues

BY BILL BIGELOW AND LINDA CHRISTENSEN

O ne of the most important aims of teaching is to prompt students to empathize with other human beings. This is no easy accomplishment in a society that pits people against each other, offers vastly greater or lesser amounts of privileges based on accidents of birth, and rewards exploitation with wealth and power. Empathy, or "social imagination," as Peter Johnston calls it in *The Reading Teacher*, allows students to connect to "the other" with whom, on the surface, they may appear to have little in common. A social imagination encourages students to construct a more profound "we" than daily life ordinarily permits. A social imagination prompts students to wonder about the social contexts that provoke hurtful behaviors, rather than simply to dismiss individuals as inherently "evil" or "greedy."

Imagining Thoughts of Others

One teaching method we use to promote empathy, and return to unit after unit, is the interior monologue. An interior monologue is simply the imagined thoughts of a character in history, literature, or life at a specific point in time. After watching a film, performing improvisation skits, or reading a novel, short story, or essay, the class brainstorms particular key moments, turning points, or critical passages characters confronted.

Interior monologues tap other people's pain, but they also tap people's hope. After watching *The Killing Floor*, about the World War

I Black migration to Chicago and union organizing in the stockyards, Debbie wrote an interior monologue from the point of view of Frank, a Black worker recently arrived from the South.

I sit and listen to the unfamiliar air of music drifting in through my window. Crickets had made music in the South, but never in a tune like this one. I want Mattie to hear this new music. The sound of white men's feet on the dirt avoiding our Black bodies on the sidewalk. Oh, to share the sounds of coins clinking together as I walk.

The following interior monologue came from a unit on the Jim Crow South. This piece was inspired by a photo of Ezell Blair, a participant in one of the original Greensboro, North Carolina, Lunch Counter Sit-Ins.

I am tired of being a second-class citizen in this country. Tired of secondhand books, and run-down schools. Tired of sitting in the back of the bus. Tired of waiting for whites to be served or stepping off the sidewalk to let them pass. Tired of lowering my eyes. Tired of yes sir and yes ma'am. Tired of lynchings. Tired of low pay. Tired of not being able to get a gosh darn chocolate malt at Woolworth's. I know it doesn't have to be this way. I studied Gandhi. I know what can happen when people come together to make change. And sitting on the stool feels fine. I will sit here all day. They can pour ketchup on me. They can call me names. Nothing they can do can hurt me the way that living in the Jim Crow South has already hurt me. Today. Today. I sit for my freedom.

Students may also choose to write their interior monologues as poetry. In the poem "Fetching Ghosts," student writer Uriah Boyd writes from the point of view of a child whose family house is bulldozed as a result of "urban renewal" programs that displaced people in the Albina district of Portland, Oregon.

Fetching Ghosts
by Uriah Boyd

The place that I call home is humble
and was built by the coarse hands of yesterday.

This place has a spirit —
vibrant though old,
And its creaky floorboards have seen us all
in our most vulnerable state.
Gramma and Grampa dancing barefoot in the living room,
the "shuffle shuffle" of their feet
becoming the musical selection of the evening.
These door frames have held up dreams
Hoisted them upon their broad shoulders
and offered them up to the skies.
That front door has warmly greeted kind souls,
and the back has banished offenders.
I once mopped the floor with Mama's tears,
And the scent of Gramma's sweet potato pie will forever haunt
    this kitchen.
The walnut tree out back has outlived four tire swings.
Even as the ropes slowly wore and unraveled,
the Great Walnut continued to extend skyward.
My great-grandmother fell asleep in her bed
And never woke up.
She hung lavender above every window in her bedroom,
And we wouldn't dare touch them.
In the confines of these walls,
Three of my cousins were born.
And now you tell me that you want to take this place away
For the "greater good."
Whose good?

In our classroom circle, students read their pieces aloud and give positive comments on each other's work (see "The Read-Around," p. 119). Listening to the collection of writings offers students an intimate portrait of the social consequences of events. We feel, rather than observe from a distance. These portraits provide us a way to talk about the film, story, or novel without writing typical discussion questions. We view issues embedded in the text through a more personal lens. The different lives that students imagine and their different interpretations give us opportunities to explore the film or reading more thoroughly.

As is true any time we wonder about other people's lives, our monologues are only guesses, at times marred by stereotype. But the very act of considering "How might this person experience this situation?" develops an important "habit of the mind" and draws us closer together. We write the monologues along with our students and can testify at the startling insights and compassion that can arise. Usually, we — students and teachers — tap into our own well of pain, pride, sorrow, confusion, and joy. Although we may never have experienced war, we know the pain of losing a family member or friend; we have experienced the difficulty of making a tough decision. Likewise, we have felt joy. From these shared emotions we can construct a piece that allows us to attempt a momentary entrance into another person's life.

Collective Text

As students read their pieces aloud in the circle, we ask them to take notes on the "collective text" they create, to write about the common themes that emerge, or questions they're left with. Or we might pose a particular question for them to think about. For example, after we watched the film *Glory*, about the first regiment of African American soldiers who fought in the Civil War, we wrote a dictionary definition of the word "glory" on the board and asked students as they listened to each other's interior monologues to notice: "Where is the 'glory' in the film *Glory*?" Students' own writings and observations became different points of entry to explore the many contradictions in the film and the events it depicts. For example, Eugene wrote, "In our class reading it was commented that there was mostly pain and not much glory. I think that their pain was their glory, the fact that they were willing to be martyrs. They were fighting for a freedom that they knew they would never have, because most of them would die in the war."

> **Interior monologues, by encouraging students to empathize with other people, invite kids to probe for the social causes of human behavior.**

Empathy and sympathy are different. When Ghantel writes her *The Color Purple* interior monologue from the point of view of Mr._____, Celie's uncaring husband, she shows empathy; she tries to imagine how he looks at the world and wonders what experiences made him who he is. But she's not sympathetic; she doesn't approve of his behavior. In fact, she detests him. Interior monologues, by encouraging students to empathize with other people, no matter how despicable, invite kids to probe for the social causes of human behavior. People are not born sexist or racist; and while interior monologues are not analytical panaceas, they can be useful tools in nurturing insight about why people think and act as they do.

Points of Departure for Interior Monologues

In our experience, success with interior monologues depends on:

- Drawing on media or readings that are emotionally powerful.
- Brainstorming character and situation choices so most students can find an entry into the assignment. Asking, for example, "What are five key scenes or moments?"
- Allowing students the freedom to find their own passion — they might want to complete the assignment as a poem, a dialogue poem, or from the point of view of an animal or an object (e.g., Minnie Wright's dead bird, in Susan Glaspell's story "A Jury of Her Peers").
- Giving students the opportunity to read their pieces to the entire class.
- Using the collective text of students' writing to launch a discussion of the bigger picture.

Writing interior monologues won't necessarily have students hugging each other as they sing "We Shall Overcome," but they are a worthwhile piece in our attempt to construct a critical, social justice curriculum. Students need opportunities to think deeply about other people — why they do what they do, why they think what they think. They also need chances to care about each other and the world. Interior monologues are a good place to start. ✳

The Read-Around

A reading and writing strategy

BY LINDA CHRISTENSEN

The read-around is the classroom equivalent of quilt making or barn raising. It is the public space — the *zócalo* or town square — of the classroom. During the read-around, we socialize and create community, but we also teach and learn from each other. This strategy provides both the writing text for our classrooms and the social text where our lives intersect and we deepen our connections and understandings across lines of race, class, language, gender, sexual orientation, and age.

Creating a Safe Space for Sharing

Some students love to share their writing. Reading aloud in class is a conversation, gossip session, a chance to talk with peers in a teacher-approved way. Unfortunately, too many students arrive with bruises from the red pen, so when we begin the year, it's necessary to build their confidence:

1. Seat the students in a circle — or the nearest approximation. This way they can see each other and be seen as they read. Attention is focused on the reader.

2. Distribute as many blank strips of papers as there are students in the class. Ask students to write a compliment to each classmate as they read, focusing on the positive and the specific.

3. Ask students to write each reader's name on the paper. So if Vonda volunteers to read her paper first, everyone in the class writes Vonda's

name on their strip. (This is also a way for students to learn their classmates' names.)

4. Tell students they must respond with a positive comment to each writer. Emphasize that when they listen and "steal" what works in their classmates' writing, they will improve their own. I write a list of ways to respond on the board:

- **Respond to the writer's style of writing.** What do you like about how the piece was written? Do you like the rhyme? The repeating lines? The humor? (Later, these points can change, particularly if I am focusing on a specific skill — verbs, lists, repeating lines, etc.)
- **Respond to the writer's content.** What did the writer say that you liked? Did you like the way Ayanna used a story about her mother to point out how gender roles have changed?
- **Respond by sharing a memory that surfaced for you.** Did you have a similar experience? Did this remind you of something from your life?
- **As the writer reads, write down lines, ideas, words, or phrases that you like.** Remember: You must compliment the writer.

5. As students write each compliment, tell them to sign their slips so the writer knows who praised them.

6. Ask for a few volunteers to share their praise with the writer. This is slow at first, so it helps for the teacher to model it. This is an opportunity to teach the craft of writing.

7. Tell students to look at the writer and give that person the compliment. Typically, students look at the teacher as they talk about what they liked about their classmate's piece. Tell the writer to call on students who have raised their hands. Establish early on that all dialogue in the class does not funnel through the teacher.

8. After everyone has read, ask students to hand out their compliment strips to each other. (This is usually chaotic, but it's another way for students to identify who's who in the class and to connect with each other.) ✳

RESOURCE

Christensen, Linda. 2017. "The Read-Around: Raising Writers." *Reading, Writing, and Rising Up (2nd Edition)*. Rethinking Schools.

Role Plays: Show, Don't Tell

BY BILL BIGELOW

My lecture had put kids to sleep. As I looked out over the classroom, students' faces had that droopy, how-many-minutes-'til-the-bell-rings look. "But how can this be boring?" I silently protested. "We're talking about the Vietnam War." As students filed out of the classroom, I pledged to find a way to ignite their interest. I was just a first-year teacher, but I knew there had to be a better approach.

Over the years, I've concluded that lectures have their place — but only when directly linked to activities that draw students into the intimacy of social dynamics. For me, the teaching strategy that most consistently enlightens and brings students to life is the role play. A good role play invites students to enter the personas of contemporary or historical social groups to learn about issues in their characters' lives from the inside out: Students roam the classroom to build alliances with other groups in the 1934 West Coast Longshore Strike; they meet each other one-on-one to discover similarities and differences in how people throughout the world are responding to climate change; they debate whether the U.S. government should recognize the independence of a united Vietnam at the end of World War II, or who is responsible for the violence against young people coming to the United States from Central America.

I'm talking like the high school social studies teacher that I am, but role plays are valuable in just about every class — science, math,

English — and at just about every grade level. Elementary teachers have written role plays on everything from child labor in the 19th century to the impact of oil pipelines on fictional communities, and have modified many role plays written originally for high school students. Any time there is a division of opinion on an important issue, a role play can help students understand the source of conflict, explore why groups have different positions on an issue, and imagine possible resolutions.

Controversial Question Role Play

One type of role play begins with a controversial contemporary or historical problem: Should the Cherokee and Seminole people be uprooted and moved west of the Mississippi River? Should the U.S. government build the Dalles Dam on the Columbia River? In a role play on the election of 1860, should slavery be banned in the western territories? Are genetically modified crops the best way to feed people today in poor countries? Should high schools adopt "ability group" tracking and standardized testing? In a language arts class, should English be the official language of the United States? In a science class, should glyphosate (the key ingredient in Monsanto's Roundup) be banned?

A role play I wrote with Ursula Wolfe-Rocca and Andrew Darden on the struggle over the Dakota Access Pipeline divides students into five groups: Standing Rock Sioux tribal members, Energy Transfer Partners representatives, Iowa farmers, youth environmental activists, and members of North America's Building Trades Unions. The groups meet with one another in preparation for a presentation to the president on their position on whether the Dakota Access Pipeline should be built. Some differences between groups are stark, others subtle. As in real life, strategic alliances between various groups are possible, and in the course of the role play students usually discover these and work together. The vitality of a role play depends on ensuring that actual social conflicts come to life in the classroom.

In a mock U.S. Constitutional Convention, I include roles for groups that weren't represented at the real convention. So instead of only lawyers, financiers, and plantation owners in attendance, I also invite poor farmers, workers, and enslaved African Americans. Students debate questions from each group's standpoint: whether to abolish slavery and/or the slave trade, whether to allow debt relief to farmers by permitting payment "in kind," and how political leaders should be chosen. This more representative assembly allows students to experience some of the underlying conflicts that were suppressed in the actual Constitutional Convention.

Mixer Role Plays

"Mixer" role plays may include as many as 20 or more roles, and allow students to recognize that there are not just "two sides" to a story — as, for example, with a mixer on the U.S. war with Mexico that includes U.S. abolitionists, New Mexican women, Miwok and Chiricahua Apache Indians, Mexican cadets, Irish Americans who fought for Mexico, U.S. soldiers, and President James K. Polk.

Most mixer roles are short — a paragraph or two — and typically written from the first person. After students read their roles, they highlight key information they want to share, and then get up to meet other historical or fictional "characters." (See "Medical Apartheid" on p. 84.)

Trial Role Plays

Trial role plays begin with an obvious crime — the deaths of countless Taíno Indians during the Columbus administration in the Caribbean, sweatshop abuses in poor countries, the harm to future generations due to climate change. Students represent different defendants and surface ethical issues about sources of injustice in the world. Other subject areas also use the trial format. For example, in Dianne Leahy's language arts class, students hold a trial over who was responsible for the deaths of Romeo and Juliet.

Of course, a role play wouldn't work, or at least wouldn't work as well, if I simply said to students, "You play a poor farmer; you play a plantation owner." They'd have nothing to go on beyond their own preconceptions, often stereotypical, of farmers and plantation owners. So I have to do some research in order to provide students with information on the circumstances in different social groups' lives — circumstances that would contribute to shaping these groups' attitudes on a given issue. Students can do some of this work, but my experience is that they need a base to work from. This is especially true because many of the groups I want to include in a role play have been excluded from traditional textbooks. For example, it's not that easy to find information on the struggles of farmers after the American Revolution or about the Unemployed Councils of the 1930s.

Role Plays and Learning

Amidst the dealmaking, arguing, and oratory, students absorb a tremendous amount of information. But they absorb it in a way that reveals underlying social conflict and solidarity, so they can make sense of that information. In large measure, the process itself is the product. To be effective, the results of a role play needn't repeat history. Some of our best debriefing sessions concentrate on discussing why students made different choices than did the actual social groups they portrayed. Role plays allow students to see that history is not inevitable, that had people understood their interests more clearly, or had they overcome prejudices that kept them from making alliances, events might have turned out differently. I want students to see themselves as social actors, to realize that what they do in the world matters — they are not simply objects to be thrown about by some remote process called History. When they succeed, role plays can help chip away at students' sense of predetermination, their sense of powerlessness.

A final note: A role play aims at nurturing students' appreciation of why people in history and the world today think and behave as they do. But I never want students to sympathize with individuals who behaved in hurtful or exploitative ways, that is, to have some emotional identification or agreement with these people. In my experience, kids are able to make the distinction. This is especially so when in follow-up discussion we critique positions espoused by various groups in a role play, including their own.

In his book *A People's History of the United States*, Howard Zinn critiques conventional nationalistic approaches to history:

> Nations are not communities and never have been. The history of any country, presented as the history of a family, conceals fierce conflicts of interest (sometimes exploding, most often repressed) between conquerors and conquered, masters and slaves, capitalists and workers, dominators and dominated in race and sex. And in such a world of conflict, a world of victims and executioners, it is the job of thinking people, as Albert Camus suggested, not to be on the side of the executioners.

Role plays should bring that world of conflict to life in the classroom and allow students to explore the underlying premises of arguments and to decide: What is just? ✳

RESOURCES

Where some of the role plays mentioned in this article — and a few others — can be found:

"The 1934 West Coast Longshore Role Play," from *The Power in Our Hands: A Curriculum on the History of Work and Workers in the United States* (by Bill Bigelow and Norm Diamond), at the Zinn Education Project. zinnedproject.org

"Rethinking the Teaching of the Vietnam War," at the Zinn Education Project. zinnedproject.org

"The Climate Change Mixer," in *A People's Curriculum for the Earth: Teaching Climate Change and the Environmental Crisis* (Bill Bigelow and Tim Swinehart, editors).

"Elementary Student T-Shirt Workers Go on Strike," by Michael Koopman, *Rethinking Schools*, Winter 2017.

"The Cherokee/Seminole Removal Role Play," at the Zinn Education Project. zinnedproject.org

"Standing with Standing Rock: A Role Play on the Dakota Access Pipeline," at the Zinn Education Project. zinnedproject.org

"*Warriors Don't Cry*: Connecting History, Literature, and Our Lives," by Linda Christensen, at the Zinn Education Project. zinnedproject.org

"*The People v. Columbus, et al.*," at the Zinn Education Project. Elementary adaptation in *Rethinking Columbus* (Bill Bigelow and Bob Peterson, editors). zinnedproject.org

"Testing, Tracking, and Toeing the Line: A Role Play on the Origins of the Modern High School," at the Zinn Education Project. zinnedproject.org

"U.S.-Mexico War: 'We Take Nothing by Conquest, Thank God,'" at the Zinn Education Project. zinnedproject.org

"The Election of 1860 Role Play," at the Zinn Education Project. zinnedproject.org

"Constitution Role Play: Whose 'More Perfect Union'?," at the Zinn Education Project. Elementary adaptation by Bob Peterson ("Rethinking the U.S. Constitutional Convention: A Role Play"), at the Zinn Education Project. zinnedproject.org

"*The People v. Global Sweatshops*," in *Rethinking Globalization* (Bill Bigelow and Bob Peterson, editors).

"Food, Farming, and Justice: A Role Play on La Vía Campesina," in *A People's Curriculum for the Earth* (Bill Bigelow and Tim Swinehart, editors).

"Language and Power Tea Party," in *Teaching for Joy and Justice* by Linda Christensen.

Suggestions for a Successful Role Play

1. Introduce the role play and give students a sense of why the class is participating, and what the general guidelines will be. Break students into groups, roughly equal in size. It's vital that the question(s) each group will address are clear and understood by all.

2. Allow students to connect with the roles they've been assigned. You might encourage students to read their roles aloud in their small groups. I usually ask students to answer questions in writing based on their role: "How do you make your living? Why do you put up with such rotten working conditions?" Or I might ask them to write interior monologues — their inner thoughts — about hopes and fears (see "Promoting Social Imagination Through Interior Monologues," p. 114). Students can read these to each other in the small groups. Have each group make a placard so they can see who's who. You might interview students in front of the class or even bait them devil's advocate fashion: "How do you really feel about that poor farmer in that group over there?" As mentioned earlier, be sure that students' roles are not too prescriptive. I've seen many role plays that tell students exactly who they are and what they think. What's left for the kids? Likewise, some role plays don't give students enough information to participate thoughtfully: "You are a Mexican farmer." That's not much to go on. Also try not to mix up roles by having some economic and some ideological, e.g., steel workers and conservatives; steel workers may be conservatives.

3. It's the students' show, but the teacher's participation is vital. I circulate in the classroom making sure that students understand their roles. I help them think of groups they might want to ally with. I also instigate turmoil: "Do you know what those middle-class people are saying about you immigrants?" It makes for more lively exchanges.

4. Each role should include at least some information that other groups don't have. This requires students to teach and persuade one another. So they need an opportunity to meet. After they have read and considered their roles and positions on issues, I tell students to choose half of their group to be "traveling negotiators." The travelers may meet and "wheel and deal" only with non-travelers, to ensure that the whole class is involved at any given time.

5. It's important that students have an opportunity to present their points of view and hear from other groups. I often structure these gatherings as "community meetings" assembled to discuss the burning issue under consideration. As with the small group negotiation sessions, I encourage students to use the information in their roles in their presentations to teach others. I usually play a role myself, sometimes as a partisan. For example, in the role play on whether "Mother Country" will grant independence to its Asian colony, "Laguna," I play the European colonial governor and chair the assembly. I know some teachers will disagree, but in my experience, it hasn't been a great idea to have students actually run the meetings, as discussion is often heated, and students may jump on each other for seeming to play favorites in whom they recognize. However, at times I'll conduct a meeting with a simplified version of Robert's Rules of Order, which offers students a good deal of say-so in the pacing of discussion. In some role plays, a major aim is to give students practice in making decisions without the presence of an authority figure. For example, a role play on the 1912 Lawrence, Massachusetts, textile strike asks students in a large group format to confront strategic and tactical issues on their own: "With thousands of workers out on strike, how will we make decisions? Should our commissaries feed non-striking workers?" In this role play, students simulate the euphoria and frustration that accompanies grassroots democracy.

6. It's essential to debrief. No activity stands on its own. Before we discuss, I usually ask people to step out of their roles by asking them to write for a few minutes. I might ask them to speculate on what actually happened in history. Sometimes I'll ask them to critique their own positions to give them permission to distance themselves from the points of view they espoused in the role play debates.

From Theme and Evidence Wall into Essay

BY LINDA CHRISTENSEN

One year I decided to make the classroom a shrine, of sorts, to student thinking. I had always posted student work on the walls — poetry, narrative and essay excerpts — as a tribute to student writing. This time I wanted to make the walls a transparent, public display of student ideas throughout a unit. Not a graffiti wall, not an annotation, but something like a classroom dialogue journal, the scroll of our thoughts. This was the birth of the emerging theme and evidence wall, which functions as a unit-long preparation for essays, driven by student passion and ideas, and supported by evidence from one or more texts.

Because the theme wall works as a classroom archive, I begin the wall soon after we start a unit. Here's why: Some of my students struggle with literacy. Partly, some lack vocabulary or reading strategies, others might not have engaged enough with the text to stick with it. Others read as if they are at a movie theater, unconsciously watching a film and eating popcorn. They can recite a summary of the actors and the actions, but not why it matters, not whether it was sexist or racist or problematic in some other ways. They read without a swelling of passion or outrage. I want to teach them to read like social and literary detectives, to read with questions and curiosity. But not only my questions. Not only my curiosity. Theirs. Instead of putting packets together where they answer questions for each chapter, I throw the learning and the work back on them, where it belongs.

That said, let me be clear: I am not hands-off during class. Because we live in a society that wants to distract us from thinking too deeply about the incredible wealth disparity and the deterioration of public schools, unaffordable healthcare, and inadequate public services, I set the stage with initial questions, typically about power and inequality, about who benefits and who is harmed in any situation.

Sometimes I begin the theme wall immediately after the mixer. (See the chapter "Language and Power" in *Teaching for Joy and Justice* for detailed mixer description and materials.) In the language and power unit, for example, I ask students, "What excited or angered you the most? What injustice did you notice? What big ideas seem to be rising up for you?" Harold answered, "I noticed that people were made to feel inferior and that their language was inferior. And that led to a crumbling of their society." On a sentence strip, I write "People were made to feel their language was inferior, which crumbled their society." I hand the strip to Harold.

"Where did you see that inferiority that Harold is talking about in the mixer? Which characters?" I gather a few sticky notes. Daryl follows up with "Joseph Suina. See that was my character. He was sent away to a reservation boarding school, and he learned that his heritage was wrong. His language was wrong." I write "Joseph Suina" on a sticky note and hand it to Harold. "Put that note at the bottom edge of your strip."

I ask, "Who else noticed something about language and power in the mixer?" Denzel raises his hand. "Did you see the movie *Men in Black?* They had a flashlight. And when they flashed the light, people forgot. People we met in the mixer were brainwashed. Their language was taken away by the dominant culture and they were taught that they were wrong." I write this on a sentence strip.

> **I set the stage with initial questions, typically about power and inequality, about who benefits and who is harmed in any situation.**

In the cartoon critique unit, I ask students to notice who has power in the cartoon? Who doesn't? Who gives orders? I also ask them to look at body types and language. (See "Unlearning the Myths that Bind Us" in *Reading, Writing and Rising Up [2nd Edition]*.)

Once students have the idea of the sentence strip and sticky notes, I ask them to gather in small groups and figure out what themes they see emerging and what evidence they have based on their character roles. They post these on a wall in the classroom.

When students return the following day, I ask them to go back to the theme wall and refresh their memories before we start new readings. "What's coming up for you that you want to explore as we learn about language and power? Where's your passion? I'm not going to ask you to write about my topics. You have to find your own, so locate your interest. Yesterday, Denzel talked about how people in power brainwashed the people they colonized into believing their culture or language was inferior, so he might want to keep notes about that topic as he reads today. What thread might you follow?"

Whether they annotate an article with marginal notes, add sticky notes to pages in a novel, or use a more traditional dialogue journal, this active engagement between the student and the text and the classroom prompts students to put their minds in gear while they read. These notes also become the genesis of classroom conversations about the curriculum and ultimately their culminating essay.

The evolution of student thinking is evident as some initial ideas fade away and others bloom with a fringe of sticky notes adhered to the bottom of the theme strip. When students read the novel *If We Must Die* about the Tulsa Race Massacre, the themes "activism through education" and "Berneen's awakening racial identity" have many pieces of evidence stuck to them, but "the role of a newspaper as a catalyst for action" only has two. This was an idea that blossomed early and fizzled out. Also, the students build on each other's evidence within a classroom as well as between classes. Adam from first period might add to the sentence strip Selena put up about power and relationships during third period. More than any other activity, the theme wall claims the classroom as student space.

This strategy also benefits students who have been absent or who struggle to find their way back into class. The wall is a map, helping them return to class discussions they missed, locating evidence for an essay. They still have to do the work, but they can find a more direct pathway back by figuring out specific articles or chapters to read or re-read as they move into the essay.

Bringing in Their Own Lives

Because many of my curricular voyages touch on the daily issues that students struggle with, I also encourage them to bring stories as evidence in their essays. During the language curriculum, Kaanan posted a memory about his teacher reprimanding him for speaking African American

Vernacular English/Ebonics. Alejandro added a sticky note about kids teasing him for his accent in elementary school. And Gina connected the language divide between her grandmother and her as evidence for keeping mother tongue literacy alive. The study of gentrification brought parallel stories of evictions, moves, and displacement. Because I want students to care about their writing and see the relevance of our classroom work in their lives, I explicitly give time to add evidence from their lives as well as evidence from our readings.

Writing the Essay Along the Way

At the end of the unit, the theme wall replaces any prompt I might imagine for students' essays. Instead their curiosity, their reading of the novel or curriculum is literally written on the wall. So when I ask, "What do you want to write an essay about?" They can walk back to the wall and select a topic. For the politics of language, John selected the role of boarding schools in the demise of Indigenous languages. Ryan chose to write about Ebonics, while Cheyenne wrote about the havoc colonization played on communication between generations. Because these themes have been discussed during class, students are ready to write. They have already rehearsed the essay by writing commentary about readings during silent and oral discussions, balancing evidence, sharpening an argument against a classmate's, practicing their own analysis during class talks.

So it is not unusual for a group of students to take down a sentence strip and evidence and circle up their desks and lay out a possible essay. Sometimes students take photos with their phones of topics they might want to write about. And other times, oddly, they ignore the wall and create new essay topics, born on the ashes of the work they have already completed. The theme and evidence wall is one way that students make the curriculum their own — one site where their learning becomes public and collective. ✳

RESOURCE

Christensen, Linda. 2017. "Unlearning the Myths that Bind Us: Critiquing Cartoons and Society." *Reading, Writing, and Rising Up: Teaching About Social Justice and the Power of the Written Word (2nd Edition)*. Rethinking Schools.

Resources from Rethinking Schools

Much of the advice in *The New Teacher Book* centers on the importance of finding and building community as we attempt to become the kind of teachers we want to be. Through the quarterly *Rethinking Schools* magazine and our books, teachers can join together with other educators who are linking values of social and environmental justice with their work in schools.

Founded by classroom teachers and community activists in 1986, Rethinking Schools provides a forum for teachers to share exemplary teaching practices, compare notes on the obstacles to good teaching — and how they are working to overcome those obstacles. Rethinking Schools publications also analyze trends in education and feature inspiring stories about educational activism. For more information on these publications — including tables of contents, sample articles, and information about ordering online — visit our website at rethinkingschools. org. And while you're there, check out everything the website has to offer: articles from past issues of the magazine, excerpts from our books, and special collections on important education topics.

Rethinking Schools — the Magazine
This independent quarterly is written by teachers, parents, and education activists — people who understand the day-to-day realities of today's schools. Every issue is filled with innovative teaching ideas, analyses of

important policy issues, and listings of valuable resources. For information on these and other special issues, see rethinkingschools.org.

Rethinking Ethnic Studies
Edited by Tolteka Cuauhtin, Miguel Zavala, Christine Sleeter, and Wayne Au

There is a growing nationwide movement to bring Ethnic Studies into K–12 classrooms. *Rethinking Ethnic Studies* brings together many of the leading teachers and scholars in this movement to offer examples of ethnic studies frameworks, classroom practices, and organizing at the district and state levels. Built around core themes of indigeneity, colonization, and activism, *Rethinking Ethnic Studies* offers resources for educators in the ongoing struggle for racial justice in schools.

Teaching for Black Lives
Edited by Dyan Watson, Jesse Hagopian, and Wayne Au

Teaching for Black Lives grows directly out of the movement for Black lives. We recognize that anti-Black racism constructs Black people, and Blackness generally, as not counting as human life. Throughout this book, we provide resources and demonstrate how teachers can connect curriculum to young people's lives and root their concerns and daily experiences in what is taught and how classrooms are set up. We also highlight the hope and beauty of student activism and collective action.

Reading, Writing, and Rising Up: Teaching About Social Justice and the Power of the Written Word (2nd Edition)
By Linda Christensen

For almost two decades, teachers have looked to *Reading, Writing, and Rising Up* as a trusted text to integrate social justice teaching in language arts classrooms. This accessible, encouraging book has been called "a profound work of emancipatory pedagogy" and "an inspiring example of tenacious and transformative teaching." Now, Linda Christensen is back with a fully revised, updated version. Offering essays, teaching models, and a remarkable collection of student writing, Christensen builds on her catalog of social justice scholarship with a breathtaking set of tools and wisdom for teachers in the new millennium.

Rethinking Bilingual Education: Welcoming Home Languages in Our Classrooms
Edited by Elizabeth Barbian, Grace Cornell Gonzales, and Pilar Mejía

The articles in *Rethinking Bilingual Education* show the many ways that teachers bring students' home languages into their classroom — from powerful examples of social justice curriculum taught by bilingual teachers to ideas and strategies for how to honor students' languages in schools with no bilingual program. We see bilingual educators work to keep equity at the center and to build solidarity among diverse communities. Teachers and students speak to the tragedy of language loss but also about the inspiring work to revitalize languages on the brink of disappearance and to defend and expand bilingual education programs.

A People's Curriculum for the Earth: Teaching Climate Change and the Environmental Crisis
Edited by Bill Bigelow and Tim Swinehart
Five years in the making, *A People's Curriculum for the Earth* is a collection of articles, role plays, simulations, stories, poems, and graphics to help breathe life into teaching about the environmental crisis. The book features some of the best articles from *Rethinking Schools* magazine alongside classroom-friendly readings on climate change, energy, water, food, and pollution — as well as on people who are working to make things better. *A People's Curriculum for the Earth* has the breadth and depth of *Rethinking Globalization: Teaching for Justice in an Unjust World*, one of the most popular books we've published. At a time when it's becoming increasingly obvious that life on Earth is at risk, here is a resource that helps students see what's wrong and imagine solutions.

Rhythm and Resistance: Teaching Poetry for Social Justice
Edited by Linda Christensen and Dyan Watson
Offering practical lessons about how to teach poetry to build community, understand literature and history, talk back to injustice, and construct stronger literacy skills across content areas and grade levels — from elementary school to graduate school. *Rhythm and Resistance* reclaims poetry as a necessary part of a larger vision of what it means to teach for justice. As Pedro Noguera wrote, "At a time when teachers feel under attack from policymakers searching for ways to raise student achievement and ensure school safety, the authors of *Rhythm and Resistance* show us how easily both objectives can be pursued if we simply open up opportunities for students to write about their lives and share their stories with each other. Teachers who can do that will experience the joy and power of teaching even during these trying times in education."

Rethinking Elementary Education
Edited by Elizabeth Barbian, Linda Christensen, Mark Hansen, Bob Peterson, and Dyan Watson

Collects the finest writing about elementary school life and learning from 25 years of *Rethinking Schools* magazine. The articles in this volume offer practical insights about how to integrate the teaching of content with a social justice lens, seek wisdom from students and their families, and navigate stifling tests and mandates. Teachers will find both inspiration and hope in these pages.

Rethinking Early Childhood Education
Edited by Ann Pelo

Early childhood is when we develop our core dispositions — the habits of thinking that shape how we live. This book shows how educators can nurture empathy, an ecological consciousness, curiosity, collaboration, and activism in young children. This anthology is alive with the conviction that teaching young children involves values and vision.

Rethinking Columbus: The Next 500 Years
Edited by Bill Bigelow and Bob Peterson

Why rethink Christopher Columbus? Because the Columbus myth is a foundation of children's beliefs about society. Columbus is often a child's first lesson about encounters between different cultures and races. The murky legend of a brave adventurer tells children whose version of history to accept, and whose to ignore. It says nothing about the brutality of the European invasion of North America. *Rethinking Columbus* has more than 80 essays, poems, interviews, historical vignettes, and lesson plans packed with useful teaching ideas for kindergarten through college.

Unlearning "Indian" Stereotypes DVD
Narrated by Native American children, the DVD *Unlearning "Indian" Stereotypes* teaches about racial stereotypes and provides an introduction to Native American history through the eyes of children. The DVD includes teaching ideas, lessons, and resources.

Rethinking Mathematics: Teaching Social Justice by the Numbers (2nd Edition)
Edited by Eric Gutstein and Bob Peterson

In this expanded second edition, more than 50 articles show how to weave social justice issues throughout the mathematics curriculum, as well as how to integrate mathematics into other curricular areas. *Rethinking Mathematics* offers teaching ideas, lesson plans, and reflections by practitioners and mathematicians. This is real-world math — math that helps students analyze problems as they gain essential academic skills.

Rethinking Globalization: Teaching for Justice in an Unjust World
Edited by Bill Bigelow and Bob Peterson
This comprehensive 400-page book helps teachers raise critical issues with students in 4th through 12th grades about the increasing globalization of the world's economies and infrastructures, and the many different impacts this trend has on our planet and those who live here. *Rethinking Globalization* offers an extensive collection of readings and source material on critical global issues, plus teaching ideas, lesson plans, and resources for classroom teachers.

Rethinking Multicultural Education: Teaching for Racial and Cultural Justice (2nd Edition)
Edited by Wayne Au
Rethinking Multicultural Education collects the best articles dealing with race and culture in the classroom that have appeared in *Rethinking Schools* magazine over the years. Moving beyond a simplistic focus on heroes and holidays, and foods and festivals, it demonstrates a powerful vision of anti-racist, social justice education.

Teaching for Joy and Justice: Re-Imagining the Language Arts Classroom
By Linda Christensen
In *Teaching for Joy and Justice*, Linda Christensen's sequel to *Reading, Writing, and Rising Up*, she demonstrates how she draws on students' lives and the world to teach poetry, essays, narratives, and critical literacy skills. Part autobiography, part curriculum guide, part critique of today's numbing standardized mandates, this book sings with hope — born of her more than 30 years as a classroom teacher, language arts specialist, and teacher educator.

Open Minds to Equality: A Sourcebook of Learning Activities to Affirm Diversity and Promote Equity (4th Edition)
By Nancy Schniedewind and Ellen Davidson
An educator's sourcebook of activities to help students understand and change inequalities based on race, gender, class, age, language, sexual

orientation, physical/mental ability, and religion. The activities also promote respect for diversity and interpersonal equality among students, fostering a classroom that is participatory, cooperative, and democratic.

A People's History for the Classroom
By Bill Bigelow
This collection of lively teaching articles and lesson plans emphasizes the role of working people, women, people of color, and organized social movements in shaping history. The teaching activities included raise important questions about patterns of wealth and power throughout U.S. history. Through improvisations, role plays, imaginative writing, and critical reading activities, students learn a more accurate and engaging history.

The Line Between Us: Teaching About the Border and Mexican Immigration
By Bill Bigelow
The Line Between Us explores the history of U.S.-Mexican relations and the roots of Mexican immigration, all in the context of the global economy. And it shows how teachers can help students understand the immigrant experience and the drama of border life. Using role plays, stories, poetry, improvisations, simulations, and video, the book demonstrates how to combine lively teaching with critical analysis.

Rethinking Popular Culture and Media (2nd Edition)
Edited by Elizabeth Marshall and Özlem Sensoy
Rethinking Popular Culture and Media begins with the idea that the "popular" in classrooms and in the everyday lives of teachers and students is fundamentally political. This anthology includes outstanding articles by elementary and secondary public school teachers, scholars, and activists who examine how and what popular toys, books, films, music, and other media "teach." These thoughtful essays offer strong critiques and practical teaching strategies for educators at every level.

Rethinking Sexism, Gender, and Sexuality
Edited by Annika Butler-Wall, Kim Cosier, Rachel Harper, Jeff Sapp, Jody Sokolower, and Melissa Bollow Tempel
Rethinking Sexism, Gender, and Sexuality is a collection of inspiring stories about how to integrate feminist and LGBTQ content into curriculum, make it part of a vision for social justice, and create classrooms and schools that nurture all children and their families.

Challenges and Opportunities

The challenges we confront in teaching for social justice are varied. Schools reflect the racial biases and power inequalities of the larger society, as Alejandro Jimenez illustrates in his poem "Mexican Education." Teachers can't erase the larger social influences that impact our classrooms, but we can make them visible and equip students to look at the world with critical lenses.

Sometimes tensions surface when we examine issues like racism, sexism, homophobia, and wealth inequality within our curriculum. Navigating these discussions proves difficult, but not insurmountable, as Jaydra Johnson explores in "Howling at the Ocean: Surviving My First Year Teaching."

Sometimes issues arise with our colleagues, as Anita Stratton and Chrysanthius Lathan point out in their articles. How do we respond to staff members who disrespect racially and linguistically diverse students and colleagues? How do we approach our peers in ways that both advocate for our students and ourselves — and also move the work for justice in schools forward?

The teachers in this chapter use challenges as opportunities; they know they can make a difference by speaking up, by making curricular choices that prepare students with knowledge to help them grow into more empathetic and critically aware human beings. Some choices involve changing classroom dynamics from discipline to inclusion when the impact of injustice in the world threads into the classroom. As Camila Arze Torres Goitia writes in "Restorative Justice in the Classroom":

> I already knew that things that were designated "problem behaviors" were manifestations of deeper issues. . . . When kids are scared, uncomfortable, unseen, or not served by systems, they act out. . . . I needed restorative justice to quell the fear, to bridge the comfort, to make visible those who hid behind masculinity or masks before the fear manifested in an explosion.

Arze's "disciplinary" approach knits restorative justice practices into her curriculum.

Teachers' confidence in the capacity of students and colleagues to change animates this chapter. New teachers can play an important role in exposing inequalities and institutional practices that privilege some and exclude others. Often new teachers have not been inured to the systemic inequality pervasive in many schools, so they can approach institutions with a sense of possibility and determination, as Mykhiel Deych does in their work helping faculty members understand the needs of LGBTQ students. "It's ongoing, this work of showing up for students how they need us to show up."

Mexican Education

Excerpted

BY ALEJANDRO JIMENEZ

My first image of the United States
Came on November 11th 1995
I was waiting in a parking lot
Underneath the lights of a magical place

My uncle said, "here you find anything"
With his help I pronounced my first real words in English
"gu — al — mart . . . walmar . . . walmart!"
My aunt walked out of this place
With a green blanket
She wrapped it around my shivering body
I had illegally crossed the border less than 2hrs before
And now I was warm.

With a big smile on my face —
I thought, I made it.

When my mother registered me for the 3rd grade
In January of '96
My ESL teacher
Had trouble with the multiple syllables in my name
She said — "Alejandro is too long, let's call him alex"

My mother looked at the floor and said, "OK"

It wasn't until a couple years later
When I knew enough English (and assimilation)
That I realized what had happened

Now, most of my family members do not call me by my birth
name.

That same year I met Mrs. Parrot
She would not allow me to go to the bathroom
Until I pronounced my request correctly

Most of the time I would piss myself.

At that time,
I didn't know enough English
To cuss her out
So instead I waited until high school
And I would run by her house and spit on her nice lawn

I also used to poop in her fruit tree orchard.

In 4th grade, an ESL assistant would kick my shins under the table
Every time I would mispronounce any of the words
she was holding on a flash card

Until this day I do not find high heels to be attractive.

In 6th grade,
While in the back of the bus with 3 white kids
Malia Hadley
Whom I had a crush on
Asked me, "alex, is it true that they call Mexicans beaners?"

(I should have known from her smile that she did not actually want
to broaden her knowledge)

I remembered having beans
The night before
That I did not think about
The implications of her question

"Yes," I said

Everybody laughed.

. . .

In 7th grade,
My science teacher compared Mexico to trash
He is the reason why I dislike science.

I also used to run by his house and spit on his lawn.

In 8th grade,
My friends and I jumped each other
And started our own "gang."

We were afraid of what the following school year would hold
After all, that was the furthest any of our parents had gone to
school
I guess punching each other was how we showed support and
guidance

Later, some would drop out
Some would actually join gangs
Some joined the military
And we would not recognize them after their tour
Some would graduate
Very few would go on to college.

In high school,
I was one of 4 brown faces in AP classes
In a school that was 40% mexican

I always felt weird
When my teachers praised me,
"for not being like the rest of them"

What is this rest of that I am not?

I left my guidance counselor jaw-dropped

When I told her I wanted to go to college.

Instead of guiding me through the application process
She asked me to talk to incoming students and their families
About my success story
Of "how you came from nothing to something."

My grandmother's house in Mexico
May not have had running water,
Electricity,
Flushing toilets,
Steak dinners,
Wood floors,
A picket fence,
But
It was
Something.

. . .

I am a green card holder now
I still I have trouble pronouncing some english words
Sometimes my tongue wrestles with itself
It does not know which colonizer's language it prefers.

I ask my intuition for good judgement in navigating this country
but sometimes it feels like I ask for too much.

I am learning how to thrive in a world
Where I am not wanted if my name is alejandro

If my skin is too dark
If my accent is too heavy
If my hands are not rough enough.
If my hands are too rough

When my aunt wrapped me in the warmth of the green blanket,
I thought I had made it.

Mexican education in this country:

They will shorten your name to fit their mouths more easily
Sometimes you will think it is easier too
They will be surprised when you want to be successful
Sometimes you will be surprised too
They will tell you that you are better than the rest
Sometimes you will believe them
They will try to turn you against people that look like you
Sometimes they will win

But now I see that a green Walmart blanket
Cannot protect you from everything and everyone
Set up for you to fail. ✳

Alejandro Jimenez is a formerly undocumented immigrant, educator, TEDx speaker, and Emmy-nominated spoken word artist/poet living in Denver, where he is a restorative justice coordinator in a public high school. Excerpt reprinted with permission of the author.

What I Wish I Had Said

BY ANITA STRATTON

"**G**oodbye everyone," the music teacher sang out as she does every time my class leaves her room.

"Goodbye Mrs. Smith," 22 2nd graders sang back. It was my cue to walk them out. We did the quiet signal for the hallway, and a couple kids gave the music teacher a hug on their way out. Akash walked by her and she called out lovingly, "Bye, Bobblehead!"

Mundane end of the day thoughts ran through my mind: Did I remember to tell Brian his mom will pick him up after school so not to ride the bus? What rotation is it for my after-school duty? What was that one announcement I was going to make? I interrupted myself. *Wait. Did she really just call him Bobblehead?*

Fight or flight. In my shock I froze.

And I said nothing.

Akash arrived from India days ago. He had dark hair and small frame. Our classroom community worked hard to welcome him to our new school. A buddy in the classroom showed him around. We made sure he sat with someone at lunchtime and had a friend to play with at recess. He tried his best to use the English words he knew to communicate. His dark eyes were intensely studying his new surroundings.

Akash consistently nodded his head from side to side when I spoke to him. He smiled often and I hoped he was starting feel comfortable. *Bobblehead?* I thought of the plastic dolls springing their heads back and forth. I felt anger, sadness, and confusion.

Our suburban elementary school in Ohio was experiencing a shift: We had recently become a Title 1 building. The new superintendent was changing the narrative of our diverse population from a challenge to our greatest asset. Although some teachers embraced it, the white teachers' lounge was full of stories of "these" and "those" kids. Avoid the lounge, they always say.

More than half of my class is bilingual: English, Spanish, Hindi, Gujarati, Chinese, Serbian, Arabic. It was the classroom I dreamed of being in as a child where our collective working-class immigrant background was part of our story and not what defined us.

I was in 2nd grade when I moved to Ohio from Japan. Growing up between two languages, I was told I could be a "bridge" between cultures. It felt like a gift and a burden.

Now I was given an opportunity to become this bridge at work. I had the ELL credentials that gave me the "expertise" to express my concerns to a colleague. But I couldn't find the right words to speak to the music teacher.

I took pride in the community my class had created together. Had one of my students said this, my reaction would have been so different. There would have been an immediate private conversation with the student. I would find out what the student said, why it was said, what it means, and ask how words impact others. It may have even turned into a whole-class conversation around how our words hurt people when we don't mean to.

I realized I was more upset about upsetting the teacher than thinking about how I could speak up for my student.

But the comment coming from a colleague made me mute. Why?

What would I say to her?

Was I afraid to say something?

Why?

I decided to confirm the consistent nodding I saw Akash doing as a form of communication. My Google search revealed that head nodding is common in India and most often means "I understand" or "yes." I touched base with the ELL teacher to get an expert opinion. She agreed he was showing respect.

I worried I would upset Mrs. Smith. This teacher traveled. She sings songs in other languages. She teaches students about instruments from around the world. I knew she wasn't trying to be hurtful. I thought if I raised my concerns with her, she would be defensive. I worried she would think I was accusing her of something. I realized I was more upset about upsetting her than thinking about how I could speak up for my student.

Before I came up with a good plan, it was music day again. I picked up my students. They sang their goodbye song. As I walked them out the door, Mrs. Smith turned to Akash and said, "Bye, Bobblehead."

> **If I'm expecting students to have hard conversations with me, I need to do the same with my own peers.**

I was not prepared to hear it again. I had moments to respond. The next class of students were eager to step in to the music room. In the midst of the chaos of transitioning students, I said, "He's nodding yes in his culture."

As the last of my students walked out of classroom, she responded. "Oh. Well, I just called him Bobblehead." Her tone was neutral. Perhaps it was her turn to not know what to say.

This is where the story with this teacher ends.

But it's just the beginning of my own reflection. If I'm expecting students to have hard conversations with me, I need to do the same with my own peers. This won't be the last time I hear a comment that is hurtful. If it were me saying something inappropriate I would want to know.

It was a small step but I said something.

Each time we speak up it gives us the courage to speak again. We need to model for our students how to be allies and work through injustices. Our actions, no matter how small, can have a large impact. I'm thinking about phrases I can tuck away, so I won't be paralyzed in the moment next time. I'm focusing on phrases that share information and support our students.

"His name is Akash" is what I wish I had said. ✳

"How Could You Let This Happen?"

Dealing with 2nd graders and rape culture

BY ZANOVIA CLARK

I was just about to finish my second year teaching 2nd grade. It was the first week of June and school was quickly coming to a close. The sun was out and everyone's energy was extraordinarily high. We were in Seattle after all; when the sun comes around, you rejoice. One morning that week I came to work and noticed I had an email from a parent. This was a parent I had a good relationship with, and she often checked in to see how her daughter was doing. But this email was different. The mother explained that her daughter had been cornered at recess the previous day by some boys who were also 2nd graders. The boys grabbed, groped, and humped her. They told her they were going to have sex with her. Her daughter told them to stop and to leave her alone, but they persisted. As this sweet one told her story of shame, confusion, and hurt to her family later that day, she became so upset that she threw up in the car. Her mother knew this wasn't a miscommunication or misunderstanding. She believed her daughter.

I could feel the anger as I continued to read the mother's message. *Why wasn't someone watching these students? Where were the recess monitors? I just don't understand how students could be doing this and no one saw anything. What are you going to do about it? And how could you let this happen?* I could also feel the hurt and distrust this mother was feeling. Not only in me, but also in our school system for letting her daughter down. I then imagined the fear this 8-year-old student could be experiencing right now as she got ready for school. Fear of her male peers. Fear of the institution that has let her down in more ways than one. Fear that her body and her rights to her body can, and most likely will, be taken without her consent.

As a queer, Black woman, I could understand what this student might be feeling. I have felt that fear before. I have been afraid of males, both peers and strangers. I have felt the anger toward a system that has failed me and continues to fail others.

Why are we punishing, not educating?

I did what many of us are told to do in our teacher preparation programs. I went to the person designated to help guide us through these sticky situations; I knocked on my principal's office door. I told him about the message and asked for his insight and support. I watched him lean back in his chair to the point of a half slouch. He looked up at me with tired, irritated eyes.

"Whose class are the boys in?"

I responded with their teacher's name.

"And whose class is the girl in?"

"Mine," I said, annoyed he didn't listen at the beginning when I gave this information.

He began to speak like he was checking boxes off of a list of things I should have already done myself.

"Well, where were the recess monitors? Did she tell one of them yesterday?"

"I'm not sure; the family didn't say if she told anyone at school. Just the parents so far. And now myself."

His shoulders dropped as he let out a sigh.

"Well, talk with your 2nd-grade colleague and decide how many recesses the boys should miss. Then email the alternative recess teacher and let her know how many days they will be coming."

He went back to whatever work was pulling him away from the conversation. I stood a moment, shocked by his lack of response. I was perplexed that in six minutes, we had "solved" this problem. I reluctantly thanked him for his time and walked out of his office. As I walked down the hallway to my classroom, each step filling my body with anger, I replayed the conversation in my head.

Take away recess? That's it? Recess? Was he even fucking listening to me? And what do you think will happen when they go back to recess, huh? Why are we punishing, not educating? Taking away something they desire and benefit from isn't effectively teaching them to respect the rights that individuals have to their bodies. This does not feel right.

In the end, I did what I was told and collaborated with the other 2nd-grade teachers. Much to my relief, the other teachers were also angered by our administrator's response. We shared the feeling of knowing something was wrong and that we should be doing something about it, but not having enough knowledge or resources to know what should or could be done. We agreed that in the next few days we would all have conversations with our students about personal space and respect for others. We understood that this would not solve the problem or even begin to scratch the surface, but it was better than pretending it never happened.

It is important to note that my district uses the FLASH curriculum. FLASH is a comprehensive sexual health education curriculum created by the King County Public Health Department. It includes puberty, abstinence, birth control methods, consent, and reporting harassment. However, as in many schools around the United States, you do not receive sexual health education professional development, curriculum, or support unless you teach 4th grade or above. Apparently, in our society, if you are not in the midst of puberty, there is no reason for you to learn about sexual health.

As in many schools around the United States, you do not receive sexual health education professional development, curriculum, or support unless you teach 4th grade or above. Apparently, in our society, if you are not in the midst of puberty, there is no reason for you to learn about sexual health.

I chose to discuss personal space with my students during our class meeting the following day. I began with our usual greeting and then dove right in.

"Friends, today I want to talk about something so very important. I want to talk to you about something called personal space. Personal space is this idea that everyone has their own bubble around them." I stretched my arms out in front, behind, and to all sides of me emphasizing the space around me.

I had my students stretch their arms around them and see their personal space.

"Sometimes people or things come into our personal space. How do you think you would feel if someone came into your personal space without asking you?"

"Squished!"

"Annoyed!"

"Mad."

"Yes! Sometimes when people or things come into our personal space without asking, it can make us feel bad. Opposite of that, sometimes people or things come into our personal space because we ask them to or we want them to. It can be good if we want to feel cozy or cared for with a hug. But sometimes bad when it makes us feel uncomfortable, squished, or even unsafe. Everyone is able to decide who or what gets into our personal space. We have the right to say yes or no. And it's important you know that, because sometimes people will get into our personal space without asking and it's OK to say no to that or tell someone to stop. Does this make sense?"

One of my students raised their hand and asked a question.

"But I should tell them in a kind way, right? Use my kind respectful voice?"

"Yes, friend! You are so right. It's during those times we feel uncomfortable or unsafe that our strong, respectful voice is so important. Say something like you mean it and say it proud." I made sure to include the word "strong" because I want my students to know that they need to be strong when advocating for themselves. Conveying to them that their voice is strong from an early age is important because it begins to foster the belief that what they say should matter, even if the person receiving it doesn't listen.

I knew the message I was trying to convey to students would not be understood in one small conversation during the last two weeks of school. Looking back, I'm still unsure about how to best address the complex issues of sexual assault and consent with 8-year-olds. However, I do know what I want them to come away understanding. I want to teach my students to love and accept the bodies of all people, including their own. I want them to understand consent, and that they have the right to say no. I want them to believe that their body is theirs and not at the mercy of others. I also want the boys who have engaged in these aggressive behaviors toward their female peers to be able to heal from whatever traumas and hurt in their lives have led them to believe that they can take ownership of other people's bodies.

As a second-year teacher, I struggled to find the best way to teach my students these things. I wish that there had been time and administrative support for us teachers to meet, talk through these issues, and develop curriculum around them. Working together, we could have leveraged the knowledge of more experienced teachers and brought in outside experts. This problem was not isolated to my classroom, or even to the 2nd grade — it was a schoolwide issue and deserved a schoolwide response. But I didn't know how to advocate for that, and I knew by doing and saying nothing, I would be continuing this cycle of violation, shame, and distrust for these tiny humans. Teaching about personal space during a class meeting was at least a concrete first step that I could take immediately.

I also responded to the family to let them know I heard their concerns and was doing everything I could to help reach a resolution. I told the family that I had gone to the principal to discuss the issue. I also decided to be honest about my principal's response. The family was kind and thanked me. They assured me they would also go to the principal and see if that helped. I explained that in my experience, parents' opinions and views could weigh heavily on the administration, sometimes more than the views of teachers.

A few days went by. The boys completed their consequence and were allowed to return to recess. Our principal had pulled the boys during the course of their consequence to "speak" with them. He told us that he asked the boys if they did what they were accused of and they denied it. He also asked them if they understood what that type of touch meant and they all said no. This led him to believe the situation wasn't as real as everyone was making it seem.

Once the boys were allowed back at recess, the touching resurfaced — just as I had suspected it would. However, the boys now targeted a few more girls. I received more emails and phone calls from families with the same question: How could you let this happen?

I felt I had let these students down. I couldn't protect the ones who needed it most. And I didn't know how to speak to the ones creating these issues. I mustered the strength to talk to my administrator again. And again, I was disappointed. This time, my principal told me, "Younger students don't really understand their actions or what they are doing. They really don't know what sex is, or inappropriate touch." He went on to tell me that "Sometimes parents hold onto things that happen to their children and hold a grudge when their children are fine and not bothered at all." My administrator felt that since the girls weren't distraught at school, or telling us at school directly, they must be fine.

We often dismiss children's ability to understand complex topics. Yet they possess such wonderful ability to understand and process the things we may feel are beyond their reach. Yes, there are things that are developmentally inappropriate to bring up with 2nd graders, but 7- and 8-year-olds can understand and discuss the concept of violating the space, property, or body of others.

I was floored by my administration's response the second time around. I was floored that the leader of my school was telling me that this simply wasn't an issue — that the fear my students were feeling wasn't real. I couldn't understand why we were treating this like a childish dispute over who would go first in Monopoly.

My principal's choices perpetuated rape culture, a culture so deeply ingrained in our society that none of us knows a time when women's bodies weren't at the expense of men.

My heart was telling me how wrong it was to act like nothing had happened. Parents were looking to me for answers, angry that I had let them down. But my head was telling me to use caution. This was my administrator I was talking to. This was my boss. I feared continuing to question my administrator's authority. Would this affect my evaluation? Would he try to push me out? Would he make my life here a living hell? As I reflect back on this time in my career, I wish I had reached out to my union president. I was a new building representative for my school during this time, but still feared the power that principals possess over teachers. I think my union would have supported me and helped me walk through the fire.

Yes, there are things that are developmentally inappropriate to bring up with 2nd graders, but 7- and 8-year-olds can understand and discuss the concept of violating the space, property, or body of others.

I questioned more. If I don't say something, who will? If I don't show my girls they have the right to their own body, who will? And then I realized none of my fears mattered in comparison to the heartache my students were going through and would go through.

The next day I went to my colleague, the teacher of the boys involved, and told her about my second encounter with our principal. I told her that I felt lost and scared, and that I thought I was letting my students down but didn't know what else to do. After a few tears and hugs, we decided to do this together. We wanted to be honest with our principal and try to get him to understand that this was serious.

That day we spent our planning period crafting an email. In that email we told our administrator that his lack of response showed our students that their bodies didn't matter. That we didn't care enough to protect them or educate them, even when they asked us to. We told him we felt strongly that this silence perpetuated rape culture, and that staying silent allowed these societal beliefs to affect our students at younger and younger ages. We know it's hard to understand that these types of behaviors can be happening in 2nd grade, but they are. We asked him to take our parents and students seriously, and to support us in working through these issues.

Unfortunately, the only line from the email that stood out to him was "rape culture." He was defensive and said that we were mislabeling the situation. He asked to speak with each of us privately to discuss the matter further. We were now in trouble.

By the time I was able to schedule my meeting with my administrator, it was the last week of school. I felt defeated. How much problem-solving could we get done in five days? We had already wasted so much time doing nothing. I would be lying if I didn't admit that I was also scared as hell. My principal was calling for a private meeting! Had we gone too far with the email? Was I now not just the loud Black teacher, but also the loud, angry, undermining Black teacher? Could he fire me four days before school was out?

Right before my meeting, a few colleagues stopped by my room to tell me they had heard about what was going on and wanted to let me know they supported what I was doing. They told me to stand strong and fight for my students. I'm grateful for those few people who came into my room. It gave me the strength to stand my ground. Yet I wish some of them had accompanied me to that meeting or encouraged me to reach out to my union. I wish my colleagues had the courage to work with my administrator to change our school's culture.

In the meeting, I told my administrator that I stood by our email. He disagreed with our statement about rape culture because no one was raped and the situation "hadn't been that serious." He said we had done all that we could do and that we were "keeping a close eye" on the students. I repeated that I still felt strongly that we needed to do some educating and he again disagreed. It was in that moment that I realized I wasn't going to get anywhere with him. Not today, not next year, not ever. In that moment I decided to leave that school.

I walked back to my classroom feeling cold and nauseated. I sat at my computer and began filling out the application for a transfer. It made me sick to think of continuing to work for an administrator with so little respect for students' voices and needs. I completed the application to transfer and felt such tension on my heart. I was hesitant to leave the school I had called home for two years. I was hesitant to leave the staff that supported me through my first two years of teaching. I did not want to leave the families who I had grown to know and love as my own. And more than anything, I did not want to leave my students. But I felt that I needed to leave before this situation changed me, before it hurt me beyond repair.

I know that leaving isn't always the answer. For me, at this time in my career, and because of the history with that administrator, it was my answer. With this incident, something in me broke. I lost my momentum, my energy, and my drive. I could not picture myself thriving at that school anymore.

In a perfect world, I would have wanted my principal to do many things differently. I would have wanted him to acknowledge my student and her situation — acknowledge that she was hurting and validated her hurt. I would have wanted him to acknowledge me as a professional and that I came to him with a tough problem. I would have even been fine if he had referred me to the FLASH curriculum or to colleagues who teach that for support. I would have appreciated him problem-solving with me about my conversation with students or making classroom suggestions I might implement. I would even have appreciated my principal simply admitting that he didn't know what to do and showing me respect by listening.

But I also realize that I could have tackled the situation differently as well, by reaching out to my colleagues to brainstorm and plan with me, and by reaching out to my union to stand with me when I feared for my job. I learned the valuable lesson that, when it comes to the essential task of advocating for our students, we cannot do it alone. ✻

Howling at the Ocean
Surviving my first year teaching

BY JAYDRA JOHNSON

n 2016, less than a quarter into my first year of teaching, one of my students was suspended for heiling Hitler at the fall pep assembly. Meanwhile, across the country, Trump's campaign of hate was accelerating while administrators told student athletes they couldn't kneel during the national anthem, and like many other teachers, I regularly found swastikas in smeared pencil on my classroom desks.

This is how I began a careening and collision-filled year of exploring what it meant to be a white, anti-racist educator. In my 20s. In a predominantly white, wealthy school. In the time of Trump.

Through tremendous struggle, I discovered some of what worked and what didn't in the classroom. I discovered that challenging white supremacy guarantees resistance from white people. I also discovered that resistance can be softened. Perhaps most crucially, I discovered my own power to trip and fall and get up and get up and get up.

One incident I think about often occurred in October while I was teaching a unit about Black writers that highlighted resistance and included some study of the Jim Crow South. This unit included poems and literature by Langston Hughes and Maya Angelou, slam poetry and hip-hop by modern artists, and primary source documents from the Jim Crow era. During the debrief of the Jim Crow-era jigsaw activity, a student's comment about "reverse racism" led to a heated class discussion. I gave students a definition for racism that included the notion that racism requires one group to have power over another. I told them, "Black people can't be racist toward white folks because of our nation's legacy of denying full rights to people with darker skin." My class exploded with voices from both my white students and my students of color. We volleyed ideas until the bell rang.

I left class that day energized — it was the most engaged that class had been all year. I felt I had fulfilled my duty as a teacher for social justice and a white ally, encouraging students to question the stories they had been told, to reimagine their own worldview, to get uncomfortable. I had made them think.

But during tutorial period the following day, Sam came in with a couple friends to follow up about our class discussion. White, male, and mad, notebook tucked in the crook of his arm, Sam read to me the definition of racism from the dictionary that he had transcribed from the Internet, then offered, "So you're wrong. Black people can think their race is superior, so they can be racist."

I discovered my own power to trip and fall and get up and get up and get up.

I understood Sam's anger and confusion. These 10th graders hadn't had much opportunity to explore or debate a systems-level definition of racism, and, despite my best efforts, I had ultimately failed to provide that for them. Sam was a white male from a working-class family who felt oppressed and alienated in this school of mostly affluent students. His special education designation pushed him even further to the margins. He couldn't believe that he had any privilege at all. All he knew was that his single father struggled to make ends meet, that he lived in a dog-eat-dog world and was on the wrong end of the fight. I didn't move Sam's mind that day, but as he walked out of my classroom after about 20 minutes of back-and-forth, I did feel like we had a solid conversation, that I had asked some good questions about who has the power to define words, and kept an open mind and heart throughout our dialogue.

The next afternoon, my email pinged me with a message from the principal's secretary. My presence was requested at a meeting the following day about my lesson on racism. I reached down to recover my stomach from its plummet to the floor.

Six weeks into school and I was already in trouble? Would I be put on the naughty teacher list? I was already a first-year probationary teacher, was there such thing as probation probation? Would I be handed a textbook and told to fall in line? How could I defend my own teaching choices when I admittedly felt I had no clue what I was doing?

I immediately ran across the hall to my colleague's classroom. Sarabeth's approach to teaching was similar to mine, and I was full of questions about how to proceed. She advised me wisely and gently, cooling my hot panic and sharing her experience of meetings such as this. Of course, students pushed and wrestled with the content, she said. Our curriculum was challenging the paradigm of white superiority and including some new perspectives. Later that afternoon I reached out to a social studies colleague who was always in trouble for his radical curriculum. He explained that when you're teaching against the grain, this is normal. "Bring a union rep," he said.

I prepared the lesson plan, materials, and rationale that my administrator requested and showed up for the meeting with what poise I could muster, the recommended rep in tow.

"Oh! You didn't have to bring him," my principal remarked in surprise as my rep and I entered his office.

Strike two, I thought. Hoping this wasn't some grave offense on my part, I offered back, "Oh, well, this is my first meeting of this type and I thought it would be best to bring someone, just in case." The principal kindly accepted my plea of ignorance, and moved on to explain why I was there. He had received a message from Sam's dad stating that the definition of racism from my lesson was harmful to their family. He just wanted to get more information to speak in my defense before he called the parent back. I made my case, handed over the materials I collected, and left the meeting feeling grateful for my administrator's support, but still shaken and unsure.

Was I doing the right thing? How could I have messed this up so badly? What was I going to do? Should I pull back on the political in my classroom? It is an English class after all, not social studies. Maybe it would be better for everyone to just read *The Great Gatsby* and answer questions, saving the social justice for when I could do it "right." The hypercritical first-year inner monologue chattered on, but my principal's support and colleagues' empathy galvanized me to keep going.

Students' resistance to that unit and others continued. Late October's lesson featuring rap artists' video and lyrical protests against police brutality fell flat. The choice writing assignment at the end of the Black writers unit was "confusing" or "stupid" and only a handful ultimately made it to my inbox. Our January gender studies unit received a chorus of "Nothing like this happens anymore," and much student writing seemed produced only to placate me.

By the end of first semester, I felt completely inept at teaching for social justice, especially in a school where students report feeling both invisible and hyper-visible, underrepresented and misrepresented at once. I wanted to build a classroom that made my students feel respected, loved, and celebrated while also facilitating a critical analysis of our world. It was hard to see though the daily turmoil how all this was landing with them. My relationships with my students of color felt tepid at best, and I worried constantly that I was doing more harm than good. This felt like a double fail.

Weeks of that year are wiped from my memory due to my anxiety and exhaustion, but I do remember the foggy confusion: How could everything I bring go so wrong and lead to so little student engagement and work?

Perhaps I didn't open my students enough to learning; perhaps they felt I had just been trying to put them in their place or push my own agenda. Throughout the year, my students made themselves heard, one way or another. And it was not just my white students and not just in one class; it felt like every student was in on it. They pushed back by rolling their eyes, refusing to work, and generally spinning the classroom into chaos. I was told to write referrals, manage more, manage less, scaffold more, change topics, change seating charts, call home, ask for help. Nothing seemed to work.

Steadily, my classroom's climate worsened and my efforts to control it seemed to do the opposite. Each class meeting, restorative justice circle, hall pass restriction, phone call home, and visit to the dean was like a burst of wind on a bonfire, the flames of my classroom perhaps visible from space. Parent emails flowed in with questions about my lessons and my competence. Parents asked for meetings. Students complained to administrators. I was labeled as a social justice warrior, an incompetent teacher, and a failure when it comes to engaging students.

And the worst part was that I agreed.

But I kept going to work. I kept trying to make lesson plans that honored the voices of the unheard, asking students to empathize with people's stories, and to share their own. My copies of *Rhythm and Resistance* and *Reading, Writing, and Rising Up* became tattered and tagged. I begged for help from all my teacher allies to help save my sinking ship. SOS.

In January, I actually wished to be hit by a car, injured just seriously enough to take a medical leave. In February, I sobbed on the floor during my prep periods. As the year dragged on, I drowned: in advice, in piles of papers, in emails, and in the certainty that I was the worst teacher who had ever lived. Students dropped my class. I flailed. For a while, I stopped teaching about anything that really mattered to me. For spring break, I drove alone through the firs and fog to the Oregon coast. I hoped to be cleansed by astringent air and whipping grass, to feel right-sized next to waves and horizon and miles of rain-pocked sands. On a cloudy afternoon, I walked to the beach where I howled at the ocean in anger, in grief.

By the time April rolled around, I was empty. I sputtered and stalled out and lurched forward again, fueled purely by the kindness of my small community of teacher friends and heroes. All year I had relied on them for help, and they had given it, joyfully. Reyanna gave me lesson plans, Sarabeth gave me hugs, Linda whole units, and Matt unending enthusiasm. Julia listened with her whole heart, and Emily journaled with me daily. I also leaned on a local group of like-minded teachers, the Critical Educators Collective, and found some sense of solace and efficacy through our activist work and mutual support. Every time I approached my community anew with some failed lesson or bruising critique, I worried I was draining their reserves. Not so. These teachers were gravediggers in reverse, shoveling the dirt off and hoisting me out of the pit. I stood up and breathed. Heave-ho.

By May, I was getting better at knowing how to teach a critical course without steering the ship too forcefully toward my own dream destination. As if by magic, some of the foggy confusion also cleared, and I found myself making fewer "mistakes," perhaps because I started to take a gentler attitude toward myself. I relaxed into my classroom's chaos, spending less time controlling and more time trying to connect with students, bringing their lives into the curriculum. When I did this, authentic learning bubbled up in student poems, narratives, and essays.

I relaxed into my classroom's chaos, spending less time controlling and more time trying to connect with students, bringing their lives into the curriculum.

One unit that really showed me a new path forward was a praise poetry mini-unit that spring. Our model texts included examples of poetry-as-activism. Hiwot Adilow's "Name" talks back to a society that consistently abuses her name, one loaded with cultural and familial significance, with lines like:

I am tired of people asking me to smooth my name out for
    them.
They want me to bury it in the English
so they can understand
. . . .

My name is insulted that you won't speak it.
My name is a jealous god.

Another model I used, Denice Frohman's "Accents," sings the praises of a mother's English, inspiring students with metaphorical language
and a deep reverence for home. Frohman writes:

My mom holds her accent like a shotgun
with two good hands.
Her tongue, all brass knuckle
slipping in between her lips
her hips, all laughter and wind clap . . .
Her accent is a stubborn compass
always pointing her toward home.

These women know how to praise what society diminishes, despis-
es, and ignores. I hoped my students would take on similar topics, perhaps using their own poems to address body image, educational inequities, or poverty. We discussed the content and style of models like these
to get inspired, and I shared my own poem drafts. Then I stepped back.

Instead of dictating the topics I hoped for, I allowed students to
praise what mattered to them, whether it was their favorite video game,
their dog, or, my personal favorite, Cheez-Its. Alex wrote an ode to vil-
lains like "the Joker [who] went from nobody to nightmare in record
time." I could have lamented their reluctance to talk back about "real
issues," but instead I felt a joyous community swelling up as students performed their poems, gave shout-outs, and laughed their butts off. I also
saw how without my nervous dictation, students still got at the issues I
hoped they would, using their pencils to praise their homes, their names,
their role models, and their various cultural identities. Jack sang the
praises of Kendrick Lamar, a critical and political artist-as-activist, in an:

Ode to K Dot
Who is humble
Who teaches the world to love themselves

Who has the funk within him
Who is vibin'
Who is a thunderstorm of words
Who blesses us.

Students also wrote about their Puerto Rican heritage, transgender identities, and broken-yet-lovable alcoholic parents. Most importantly, though, my students found joy, a key ingredient of solid social justice pedagogy. As the school year wound down, I realized that despite the days and weeks of struggle and failure, I had done something real: I had survived the most difficult year of my life. And I was going to come back.

Things didn't improve that year because I quit teaching with a social justice lens. They improved when I realized that being a teacher for social justice didn't mean a forceful fist-in-the-face version of education, demanding that they share my analysis of the world, or a particular definition of racism. They improved when I began, slowly, to figure out what good social justice teaching really looks like: students' stories told and honored, new perspectives taken and validated, poems penned and performed. A little more grace for myself didn't hurt either.

It's impossible to tell how much of the chaos in my classroom was due to my limited skill set, how much to my exhaustion, how much to my social justice curriculum, and how much to a standard rite of passage for new teachers.

But through this long year, I did discover that when I shut students down, or portray one group only as perpetrators, some students will resist. What I needed to do in that moment months earlier was pivot into a place of exploring their notions about racism through compelling content, helping them develop their own ideas and connect their lives to our curriculum. I didn't realize that I had all year to help students uncover the deeply unequal state of our society through poetry, primary source documents, novels, and films, all the while highlighting the contributions of allies who could become role models for my students.

At the time, it felt urgent to squash any hint of oppressive language or ideology in my classroom and in my life, and it was. The 2016 election seemed to embolden those who hurl hate speech, craft xenophobic legislation, and otherwise act out violent and hateful ideologies. But what I didn't yet know was that in the classroom, a full-stop approach was insufficient. I needed a full-start approach instead, a nosedive into the voices of the unheard both past and present.

What I should have also known, of course, is that when I challenge white supremacy, some students and colleagues and parents will push back, and I needed to get used to that. My colleagues of color engage resistance every day, in addition to maintaining resilience in the face of micro and macroaggressions, and it's my responsibility as a white educator to stand against the pushback I receive when I teach for social justice. That said, I also needed to let those at the margins tell their stories and let students question, relate, and conclude on their own. My moralizing wasn't going to do it. Helping them explore questions about racism and hear stories from survivors might.

I am increasingly staying focused on treating myself and my students with a little more love.

I fell far that first year, skidding on my knees into the gulf between my ideals and my abilities. I still have a vision and purpose, to teach toward love and justice, but my expectations and methods are on a constant learning curve.

Some days, I notice the small ways I have grown as a result of trial, error, and seeking help. Some days, I buckle under lessons falling flat, lackluster feedback, and that same old first-year feeling of uncertainty and doubt. But I am increasingly staying focused on treating myself and my students with a little more love. I try to rock them gently from side to side, following the waves, opening up their horizon so they can guide the ship themselves, away. ✳

How Do I Stay in a Profession that Is Trying to Push Me Out?

BY JOHN TERRY

O ne of the first steps I took that kept me in teaching was the decision to step away from many of the canned teaching materials and to rely more heavily on my own knowledge, passions, and experience. I brushed the dust off my books and notebooks from college — from history and political philosophy courses that I had taken — and tried to translate some of what had originally inspired me into something digestible for high school students.

As I reached into these reservoirs of enthusiasm for my work in the classroom, I found myself sharing glimmers of inspiration with a handful of colleagues whose interest in teaching overlapped with mine. Like many educators, I felt that anyone else in the world who was not a teacher could not relate to my daily experience, and it made me crave the camaraderie and compassionate support of other teachers.

Through cultivating these bonds with like-minded colleagues I found new sources of inspiration for my practice. I developed personal relationships and professional networks with other teachers, and in the process my occupation became my vocation. While my hours outside the classroom were still spent related to teaching, they were spent in a way that brought me support and hope. I dug my heels in and tackled the hard work of doing the job right for my students and my school community.

For example, I began meeting with teachers regularly to collaborate on a project to build a model curriculum that integrates human rights principles across disciplines and grade levels. My supervisor at the time recommended that a couple of colleagues of mine and I meet with a group at the state university where a mentor of hers was connecting classroom practitioners to work that supports the mission of the United Nations in promoting and defending human rights. We developed lessons that have been published to the national organization's website, and have been invited to speak at conferences and lead workshops. Through these experiences, I found there is a whole network of educators — at the K–12 level, at the higher ed level, and within the U.N. — who shared my concerns about teaching that promotes human dignity.

Through conversations with other co-workers, I became involved with my local union and attended countywide meetings as part of our Legislative Action Team, where teachers brainstormed ways to fight for policy changes at the state level. I started to connect the dots of political advocacy for the teaching profession from my local school district to our state capital, and came to learn that opportunities existed for me to fight for my own growth as a professional. I showed up to volunteer for phone drives for political candidates in local elections, and turned my new understanding of local policy into productive conversations that could be had in the break room at work, or over the dinner table with family and friends.

I started to connect the dots of political advocacy for the teaching profession from my local school district to our state capital, and came to learn that opportunities existed for me to fight for my own growth as a professional.

I started hanging out with teachers from other nearby districts at happy hours, or at a monthly social book club gathering. When we came together, we talked about some of the larger systemic issues in our classrooms and communities, and I was reminded that there is a larger purpose in what I do. Yes, the obstacles that prevent teachers from being great teachers — or even being teachers at all — are very real, but I learned there are ways to overcome these obstacles, and to breathe meaning and life into our classrooms. I also found there is a lot to be said for being able to blow off some steam with other hardworking people who understand the problems and the joys of teaching. We provide each other with shoulders to lean on, and offer words of comfort to remind each other that we are not insane — rather, it is the conditions in which we work that challenge our faculties to their very limits. Sometimes I leave these conversations depressed or overwhelmed, but more often than not, I leave them feeling supported. They have provided me with a backpack of survival tools:

1. Making a conscious decision to make the goal of creating a better society a central part of my curriculum and teaching strategies.
2. Reaching out to a core group of other teachers in my school and surrounding districts as a regular part of my ongoing professional and personal development.
3. Exploring the possibilities of broader education activism beyond my classroom in my union, state, and local politics.

These strategies have helped me turn my teaching career into something more sustainable and rewarding for me as a practitioner, and something that delivers my best to our kids and our society. *

Dear White Teacher

BY CHRYSANTHIUS LATHAN

Sending kids of color to the classrooms of teachers of color for time-outs on a continual basis is hurting everyone, including the teachers who send them away.

As a Black, female, no-nonsense middle school teacher, white teachers in the building have asked if I wanted to be in on a "difficult" phone call, if I would "talk" to a Black boy who was "acting out" or a Black girl who "needed a mentor." I've gotten used to responding with professional, helpful words, though at times I'd like to choose otherwise: "Baby Boy spends more time in your class than anywhere else. He is looking for praise and mentorship from you. It's phony coming from me. You can call home. His mother doesn't want him acting up, but she wants you to do *your* job too. So, sorry — no, he cannot come to me for time-out."

Don't get me wrong, I appreciate when teachers come to me for advice and understanding regarding students and families of color, but using me solely for repeat time-outs and phone calls does not help anyone involved.

A couple of Januaries ago, I was called into my building administrator's office. I had assumed that I would be asked to do something, write something, or lead something. Instead, I was informed that my child's teacher had written her a referral.

I spent six years teaching at the same school that my children attended, which also happened to be statistically the Blackest school in the city. The school was full of amazing, unique educators who had a good grasp on cultural competence. My child's teacher was a white man who taught on the same floor as I did. I sat with this man through many good and not-so-good staff meetings and trainings. He asked me for writing lessons, which I shared. So how is it that I could share my expertise with him and simultaneously have no idea that my child was having trouble behaving herself in class — until it was crammed into one discipline referral at the end of the fifth month of school? The discipline referral went nowhere, but the confusion remained. I confronted her teacher to clear it up. "Why did you not tell me anything if she'd been doing this since September?"

I was met with a wheelbarrow full of excuses. "I don't want to interrupt your teaching or use you as a crutch," he said.

"Interrupt my *life*? That's my child."

It was my suspicion that his fear of the situation crippled his feet and his dialing fingers, just as fear has defeated many well-meaning white teachers of Black and Brown students. I tell my students, "Don't go running your mouth unless you have multiple reliable sources on which to draw your conclusion." So one day I sent out a special focus group invitation to the students who frequented my classroom time-out leather couch. I grabbed the envelope where I had collected the students' time-out slips (I claimed to have lost them, but was secretly stockpiling them) and began writing invitations.

While most of the class was snuggled into silent reading, I scribbled out 13 invitations. They read:

> **You're invited**
> *A big bucket of Red Vines in exchange for your honest opinions today at lunch*
> *Use this invitation as a hall pass*
> *Don't tell other students — they'll eat up our candy*

Some of these kids were sent by other teachers for a time-out, and some decided to come for their own time-outs; nevertheless, my room was a revolving door with these same students of color, constantly in and out. Some were in my class at least one period a day; others weren't on my class rosters at all. Some were girls, most were boys. All of them were Black or Brown except Josh, a white boy who had attended this school since kindergarten and was now in 8th grade.

What I wanted to know from these kids was: What makes my class so different from their other classes? Why do they behave while they're here but misbehave elsewhere, always get busted, and always get sent to me? I knew that the entire middle school team wanted students to be successful. So what makes Mrs. Lathan's class different? Why were they always circling back to me?

The lunch bell rang and I quickly pushed my class along to get out of the room and get their coats for lunch and recess. I discreetly handed out the invitations to some students. Kids who didn't get one begged to see what they said while I marched the line down to the cafeteria, and drank my soup before I got back upstairs. I set the bucket of licorice in the middle of the hexagonal table, grabbed my flower journal to take notes, and sat. Five minutes later, three kids were escorted in by another teacher, followed by 10 other kids filtering in with their lunches.

I started with my reasoning for asking them to this forum. "Y'all," I said, "I've been teaching for a while, but not long enough. I come to school to learn too. What I learn from you helps me to be a better teacher, for you and for the next year's class. Most of you are in my class at some point in the day, and a few of you aren't. But you guys always come to me for time-out. Look, I counted your time-out slips —"

"Who has the most?" Shawn butted in.

"You," I said, looking over the top of my glasses at him.

The table laughed and grabbed another Red Vine.

"Anyway, I counted your time-out slips. That's why you were invited. And I really need you guys."

"You need us?" Josh asked.

"Yes, Joshie. I need all of you to answer this perplexing question. Right now I'm like the Godzilla meme, with his finger to his brain, thinking, because I can't answer this question: Why y'all always comin' to me for time-out?"

"You really want to know the truth, Mrs. Lathan?" she asked, never looking up. "You're not scared."

"Scared of what? Who? Tell me more, Mai."

"Mrs. Lathan, you know they're scared of us and our parents, too. That's why they don't be calling home. They just send us to you."

Mai's words prompted a firestorm of responses, some funny, some

> **"Mrs. Lathan, you know they're scared of us and our parents, too. That's why they don't be calling home. They just send us to you."**

serious, coming so fast and hard that finally I had to conduct this small lunch group as a class. "One at a time — raise your hand — I can't write that fast."

"It's because he ain't got no control of the classroom, Mrs. Lathan!"

"My mom don't like her because she gave me an F without once calling my mom and telling her I wasn't doing my work."

"Because everybody in here knows Mrs. Lathan does not play."

"You talk to us like our moms and aunts; you expect us to do right, and if we don't, you make us tell our parents what we're not doing."

"They send us here when they get tired of us."

"Only certain kids get sent out for doing the same things white kids do, maybe just a little louder or bolder, so we get caught."

"I think they be watching us as soon as we come in the building."

"You know why, Mrs. Lathan, we ain't gotta tell you why we always get sent to you for time-out. It's because you're Black."

"They don't just send us to you. They send us to the other Black teachers and aides too, Mr. Jones, Ms. Johnson . . ."

"You're not scared of us. We're scared of you, though. Just kidding. I mean, scared in a good way. We're scared to disappoint you. We're scared to go into other classes because we know they're gonna start out talking crazy before we even sit down."

Students spoke of my familiar demeanor and tone, my classroom routines, my allowance of personal space when needed, my low tolerance for work avoidance or refusal, my refusal to kick students out but instead expecting them to work hard, my classroom environment of respect for one another, and so on. All of this sounded like what any good teacher would do.

The "it" factor that lingered was fear. There were two types of fear that the students spoke of: the teachers' fear of them and their fear of the teacher.

As an adult and a professional, there were clearly some issues that I dared not discuss with the group of kids. One is the fact that I'm basically doing another adult's job by doing out-of-class disciplinary work. I work hard, but I have a small lazy bone. I don't want to do portions of other people's jobs, as I'm sure no one else wants to do part of mine.

Another issue is that I am teaching students of color how to navi-

> **"You talk to us like our moms and aunts; you expect us to do right, and if we don't, you make us tell our parents what we're not doing."**

gate a classroom with routines and rules centered in ideals of whiteness, where there is only one "right" way to be a successful student: show in ways recognized by white culture that you respect authority, work to a standard, don't challenge, don't make waves, apologize when you do. I question my own ethics every time I tell a student: "I understand you, your teacher may not. That is a reason to follow their rules." And then I push them right back into that room.

The main issue, though, is the time I spend putting out the fires burning in kids, cooling the burns of the previous classroom mishaps, bandaging them up, and telling them not to play with fire, when I know full well that they aren't playing with fire at all. They are walking into a furnace every time they step into the classroom. That furnace is failure, and it is fueled by fear.

"I Don't Want to Be Called Racist"

Based on conversations with colleagues and my observations, I think that many whites live in fear of their good faith actions being labeled as racist. Rather than facing that fear and seeing what they can learn about themselves from the process, many white teachers seem to believe that a better alternative would be to pair students with teachers who look and sound like them, or like people in their families, in the name of having a positive role model or mentor. There's no doubt that we need more teachers of color in our schools, but we also have to deal with the situation that exists today. Many white teachers are discouraged, believing that they are ill-equipped to meet the needs of students of color simply because they don't have the same experiences as them. In response, they freeze.

They freeze when students like Mai are disengaged and not doing work. She may have issues going on that they can't identify with, and she's probably not going to open up to them anyway because she knows that, too. Does that make it OK to ignore what is clearly work avoidance and instead go to help students who have eager hands in the air? They freeze when students like Isaac storm out and say that they hate the school and every brick in it. Does that justify punting Isaac to Mr. Jones because Mr. Jones goes to church with his family? They freeze when Shauna is watching twerk videos on her phone during science class. Sure, there are rules about phones in school, but do we tell her to put away her personal property and risk a class-melting blowout? They freeze when it's time to call Julius' father because Julius needs a tutor. Julius' father just got out of jail. Does that justify letting Julius fall by the wayside? Or deflecting Julius directly to the principal because his father has a record?

"Phone Conversations with Parents Don't Go Well"

I've had my share of literal and metaphorical hang-ups when it comes to calling parents, but most conversations have been helpful. When I call parents or guardians, I follow these guidelines:

- Address them as Mr., Ms. or Mrs., followed by their name on record. No assumptions. If needed, I ask how to say their name properly — and remember it.
- Refer to their child by their given name.
- Talk to the parents. Highlight the positive, academically and socially.
- When explaining the issue to parents, have concrete evidence without interpretation, and give the parent a chance to respond. For example, "Today when James was with another student, he pulled her chair out, and the student fell," instead of "James hurt another student at his table and caused disruption to my lesson."
- Ask for the parent's help. The student is their child forever, I am their teacher for one year. Look to the parent as an expert.
- Make a deal among parent, student, and yourself as to how all three will help the child be successful in the area of concern.
- Call back in two weeks to update and thank the parent.

"I'm Giving Them Someone Positive to Identify With. What's Wrong with That?"

Although white teachers may feel that they are doing a service to children by sending them to someone identifiable, it's actually a backfire. Each time a child is sent to another adult in the building to manage behavior, the teacher loses a little power, no matter what race the child or teacher is. However, there's a subliminal message that many white teachers are blind to, yet it's a bold, glaring truth to parents and students of color: This teacher does not care. Today, I implore you to care. Care enough about this student to build and fortify your own special relationship with them. Care enough about this student to work at figuring out where communication breaks down between you. Care enough about this student to make them pull their weight and work when it's time to work. Care enough about this student to see if there are academic, health, social, or emotional reasons for their work avoidance. Care enough about this student to call on their parents for help, knowing that a parent is more of an influential teacher than you are. And care enough about your colleagues of color to stop using them to clean up your mess.

Clearly, being uncaring is not the message that any teacher is trying to send. It is inherent that teachers care about the people in their schools. Otherwise, they'd look for jobs that pay more and do less. And just like I don't know of parents who condone misbehavior, I don't know of teachers of any race who intentionally seek to send a message that they don't care.

"I Can't Control that I Am White. How Can I Show My Students of Color that I Care?"

Allowing fear to cripple your ability to develop relationships in your personal life would have devastating emotional effects, so why allow fear to shroud your intelligence as a compassionate educator? The fear of a race of people fuels the furnace of failure for students of color. Just because you are a white teacher and do not experience life through the same lens as your students of color doesn't mean you can't build an environment where realness, rigor, and relationships abound in your classroom.

I think many whites live in fear of their good faith actions being labeled as racist.

If you are a teacher of a student of color, and you have ever asked a co-worker of color to "help," "guide," "mentor," or "just talk to" a student of color that you've had difficulty working with, it's time for you to wake up. Trust me, there's a time in every classroom where a kid needs to go so that either she — or you — can cool off. The revolving door of kids of color, however, needs to stop.

When you send your students to teachers like me, you are inadvertently forcing me to contribute to a racist system, asking me to tell kids how to behave within your four walls and sending them back. That is not fair to them, and it's not fair to me. You need to find that bone in your body that tends to recoil when it comes time to deal with people of color and purposely straighten it back out. You must confront your own discomfort at all costs. Find out why you really don't want to call home, hold the child after school, tell him to sit down, or tell her to finish that essay.

To effectively teach children of color, you need to understand this: I know that you don't look or sound like me, but that doesn't mean that you have no power. My strength in the classroom does not come from my racial identity, and neither does yours. It comes from the way we treat — and what we expect from — kids and families. It is time for you to take back the power in your classroom. By all means, seek out the advice of colleagues of color, but don't send your students to us without first examining the patchwork needing to be done in your teacher practice. ✳

Restorative Justice in the Classroom

BY CAMILA ARZE TORRES GOITIA

Too much of what we do in schools is reactive to student behavior issues, expecting as if we could put Band-Aids on bullet wounds and call it a day. In contrast to most disciplinary methods in schools, successful restorative justice is proactive. The challenge for teachers implementing restorative justice is in going beyond behavioral issues to setting up our classrooms in ways that maximize relationships and learning.

When imagining how I would "handle" behavior in my classroom as a first-year teacher, I spent a lot of time thinking about the ways systems around me addressed this. I had seen the ways students and families get trapped in a criminal justice system that punishes, excludes, and locks up without addressing root causes and without providing support or meeting basic needs. I already knew that actions that were designated "problem behaviors" were all too often manifestations of deeper issues: poverty, drug and alcohol issues, cramped living quarters, and family crises. Too often, students of color are punished when what they need is support. This was clear to me from working with kids in a social work setting. When kids are scared, uncomfortable, unseen, or not served by systems, they act out.

When parents of color pushed back on suspensions and expulsions of students of color in our district, Portland Public Schools initiated restorative justice practices. Parents and community members hoped that by adopting restorative measures, those in positions of authority in schools would change their approach to discipline by shifting the questions they ask about inappropriate behavior. Instead of focusing on blame and punishment, teachers and administrators would ask four key questions when addressing "behavioral" issues: What happened? Who was harmed or affected? What needs to be done to make things right? How can people behave differently in the future?

I teach social studies at Madison High School, one of the most diverse schools in Portland, Oregon. Our administration works to meet the needs of our unique population through various programs and partners. We were one of the first high schools in Portland Public to integrate a full-time restorative justice coordinator on our staff. I had heard of restorative justice when I worked with youth in and out of foster and juvenile detention systems and I was excited to apply it in my classroom. I especially wanted to explore the implications of implementing a restorative approach to schoolwide discipline policy in my own classroom.

I knew the power of relationships in community.

Yet I was also hesitant. The teachers whose classrooms I envied were willing to set aside time for circles, mediations, and other restorative justice practices. I wondered: Where would I find the time? Could I still get through the curriculum? Could I give up 20 minutes once a week? Could I give up 10 minutes once a day? What about the time it takes to move chairs into the circle? What if students just groan?

At the start of the school year, it was easy to push restorative justice to the sidelines. My students were beautiful rainbow-colored unicorns the first week. They quietly awaited instruction, trying to eagerly please and be the favorite. They wrote Post-it notes about how happy they were to have a Latina teacher who wasn't a Spanish teacher.

That lasted about a month. Then my unicorns turned to wild horses bucking and neighing and throwing pencils across the room, fighting in the hallways, crying over stolen boyfriends, and rolling their eyes at me when I asked for attention.

I knew that learning couldn't happen in a room where students felt unsafe or unseen. I knew that I was no disciplinarian who could "solve" these issues through fear or punitive consequences. I knew that I would have to give time to find a way to solve these issues in community. More than that, though, coming from a background in social work, I knew the power of relationships in community. And relationships in my classrooms were a hot mess. By October, I knew something needed to be done.

I needed restorative justice to quell the fear, to bridge the comfort, to make visible those who hid behind masculinity or masks before the fear manifested in an explosion. I needed it to not just recognize but to truly honor students by giving them opportunities to bring their diverse voices into the classroom. This did not mean asking students to talk or write about their deepest darkest secrets or their family life right away. This didn't mean a mediation when they started to skip class (though mediations outside the classroom are imperative to the systemic, tiered restorative justice in schools). It meant doing my part in the classroom to mirror my school's efforts to shift to restorative justice practices. It meant building community by talking about the easy, the fun, and then the silly to make students feel safe. It meant Thank Goodness It's Friday circles where we shared what we were most excited for over the weekend. It meant throwing a ball to a peer, saying their name, and having to do a dance if they forgot their classmate's name. I watched as students who were the most shut in begin to opt in to funny dances even when they knew the names of everyone in the classroom. Ice started to break.

How can we expect our students to be vulnerable, to put their thoughts and ideas out there, to learn if they feel unsafe?

At the beginning of my second year, I decided to commit more time to the practice. I started by building community in fun and easy ways that empowered my students with a safe space that had not always been granted to them either inside or outside of school walls. Restorative justice ultimately helps address both my classroom management and time issues while engaging students in learning; it also parallels a social justice curriculum that honors students' voices and empowers them to act and make changes when they observe injustice.

Restorative Justice First Steps

Our first restorative justice circle was about finding our common values. I opened the circle with a quote in Spanish by Ernesto "Che" Guevara and translated it for students: "The true revolutionary is guided by a great feeling of love." I told them that I liked this quote because it reflected my values of empathy and love. I then handed out a paper plate (a restorative justice staple) to each student and asked them to write a value that was important to them in marker. I gave them an example by showing them my plate where I had written "empathy," "unity," and "love."

I introduced our talking piece, a stone that I found on a beach when I was having a tough week over the summer. I explained that one way we show love in the classroom is by respecting the talking piece. "When we hold it, we have the opportunity to share a piece of ourselves. When we aren't holding it, we have the opportunity to listen wholeheartedly."

Students passed the stone around the circle and shared their values. As students talked, I asked them to place their plates in the middle of the circle like an offering.

As I continue to do this circle at the beginning of each school year, I see a lot of "respect," some "patience," a few "family." This becomes our centerpiece for the rest of the year, so students who find themselves distracted can refocus to the center but also so whenever we have conversations that may be hard, students are reminded of the values they bring to the classroom.

We closed the circle with a primal scream, a student's suggestion, to let out the excess nerves and energy from first-day jitters. This idea has stuck with me; I continue to do it, especially with underclassmen. In subsequent days we opened the circle by sharing our favorite ice cream flavor or scary movie, and then came up with ground rules for the class based on our values.

Building Community

Building a classroom community begins with a sense of home — people knowing our names, giving us nicknames, perhaps being in a place where we hear our favorite songs. Early in the year my students and I came up with nicknames for each other based on the first letter of our names and something we did that we were proud of the previous week. We called each other by the nicknames for weeks using table tents with the nicknames we created during the circle. The nicknames became our classroom inside joke or secret. Students tested me on the last day of school to see if I remembered all the names.

During the second month we compared our lives to our favorite song lyrics. This was one of the shortest circles I'd ever done, but it had a lasting impression on the class as those songs became the soundtrack to our classroom work time. Students began to see more and more of themselves in the classroom and re-engaged when they heard their favorite tune. Friendships were formed when students were shocked to find out that another student loved the same artist.

Midyear, we shared haiku poems dedicated to the students who sat to our left. No groans. I noticed later in the year that one student taped the poem their table partner wrote for them in their binder. A student with a 504 plan for suicide repeated the last line of the haiku written for her like a mantra: "stronger than she knows, stronger than she knows, stronger than she knows."

> **We do this because we desire connection. We do this because it helps us see each other. We do this because it helps us build a foundation to talk about the hard.**

That second year of teaching, I noticed students starting to succeed. Students who were nervous to pair share started to talk through their ideas with their partners. Students who never handed in essays started to submit drafts and ask for feedback. Students who loathed presentations started to joke and bring their personalities to the front of the room. Now when folks at trainings ask me how they can practice restorative justice and teach or stay on top of their curriculum, I respond: How can we expect our students to be vulnerable, to put their thoughts and ideas out there, to learn if they feel unsafe?

Restorative Justice Meets Curriculum

Though these community builders are not limited to the first month in my classroom, we do transition to circles more grounded in curriculum. We still open our circles by sharing something like a dream three-course meal. But then we turn to a circle sharing our narratives about a time we were punished to open up our unit on the criminal justice system in government class. After our World War I simulation paper ball fight in Modern World History, we sit in circle and reflect and empathize — developing a historical imagination and relating it to what we know. In our Stonewall riot role play circle in Gender Studies, we talk about what successful collaboration looks like in circle — taking on the role of activists, sharing those activists' values based on research we had done, and coming up with an action plan for a resistance movement.

After reading a dense text, we pick out our favorite line and toughest line in our circle. The whole room has a chance to contribute and the conversation is enriched. Students whose texts were barely touched are now marked up and underlined, with notes sprinkled in the margins. Folks who I thought for sure would pass share their deep connection to Gloria Anzaldúa's article or the problem with our immigration system. We all develop a deeper understanding through this collaborative discussion format.

Restorative Justice and Classroom Behavior

Because of my students' understanding of and commitment to circles as a part of restorative justice, we are able to talk about the hard issues that arise when we are learning in community. In one of my classes during my third year of teaching, we developed a circle suggestion box. Students submitted ideas for circles they felt we needed or they wanted and specified whether they want to facilitate. As students grew more comfortable with facilitation, restorative justice spread more and more. When students share ideas and stories, even misunderstandings alert me to what I need to add to the curriculum or address in upcoming units.

Students in my leadership class formed a restorative justice club and pushed into underclassmen classes to facilitate circles and lead a restorative justice circle sit-in on sexual harassment in our school. There are currently plans for students to train each other to be peer mediators.

In my classroom we sit in a circle and discuss whether hotdogs are sandwiches or whether water is wet. We choose who we would take with us to the zombie apocalypse (Kanye or Zac Efron?) and who would play us in the movie version of our lives. We tell each other two truths and a lie and share a song lyric that reflects our life. We come up with secret handshakes and play word association games. We share our most prized possession and compete for who had the worst winter break. We do this because we desire connection. We do this because it helps us see each other. We do this because it helps us build a foundation to talk about the hard. We don't do it because it's magic or an unbelievable cure. We do it because it's a process we are loyal to and can stick with through thick and thin. We do this because learning won't happen if we don't. ✳

What are restorative practices and why are they important?

Faced with large class sizes and challenged by "disruptive" behaviors, many teachers, even the most idealistic, fall prey to using a punitive approach to "discipline." Such punitive approaches used schoolwide often lead to unhealthy and unsafe learning environments. An escalating cycle of threats, suspensions, and expulsions spirals into ever more serious problems feeding the school-to-prison pipeline.

An alternative to punitive approaches is called restorative practices or restorative justice. These approaches are rooted in the practices of Indigenous communities around the world. The Indigenous approaches focus on changing one's behavior and reintegration into society rather than isolation and prison. Specific practices, such as sitting in a circle and the use of a "talking stick," also have Indigenous roots.

In recent decades, restorative justice practices have sometimes been used in the criminal justice process as an alternative to mass incarceration. People who have caused harm, their victims, and others from the community participate in "repairing harm" circles. The goal is to agree on a resolution to the conflict, which may include steps so that the offender does not repeat their actions, and restitution from the offender to the victim.

More recently, schools and districts are adapting restorative practices, using them with young children to adults. Restorative practices in schools are a non-prescriptive set of tools for building and maintaining healthy communities through the intentional creation of trusting relationships. They frame conflict — something that will always exist in our classrooms and schools — as an opportunity to develop empathy through discussion, listening, and reparation.

For decades, thoughtful teachers have used such practices to build community and relationships. These restorative approaches include teachers and students developing classroom rules and expectations together, taking time to listen to students who are acting out, and proactive classroom circles that focus on "check-ins," goal setting, curriculum, and community building.

The next "level" of restorative practices is often called restorative justice and attempts to repair harm. Conflicts between individuals are discussed and specific restorative actions are agreed to. This may happen in both whole-class circles and smaller groupings. Students sometimes lead circles. For example, in some high schools a teacher teaches a restorative justice class in which students are trained to lead "repairing harm" circles, where conflicts between offenders and victims can be mediated and resolved.

In the most severe cases, restorative justice "re-entry circles" or "family conference circles" are convened by trained adults who work with individuals, families, and classmates to help a student who has committed harm to reintegrate themselves into the classroom community.

Successful implementation of restorative practices occurs when they are adopted school and districtwide and teachers are provided quality professional development. Unfortunately, in some cases implementation is weak, with responsibilities falling onto a single "program implementer"; this is usually not enough to ensure a qualitative shift in a school's culture of discipline. However, if school leadership, staff, students, and parents can push for a robust and ongoing implementation of restorative practices, educators can create safe and supportive classroom and school environments for all.

—Bob Peterson

RESOURCES

Circle Forward: Building a Restorative School Community
By Carolyn Boyes-Watson and Kay Pranis
Living Justice Press, 2014

The Little Book of Restorative Discipline for Schools: Teaching Responsibility; Creating Caring Climates
By Lorraine Stutzman Amstutz and Judy H. Mullet
Good Books, 2005

"Restorative Justice: What It Is and Is Not"
By the editors of Rethinking Schools
Rethinking Schools, Vol. 29, No. 1 (Fall 2014)
rethinkingschools.org/articles/restorative-justice

Restorative Practices: Fostering Healthy Relationships & Promoting Positive Discipline in Schools: A Guide for Educators
By a Schott Foundation Restorative Practices Working Group
Schott Foundation, 2014
schottfoundation.org/sites/default/files/restorative-practices-guide.pdf

The Restorative Practices Handbook for Teachers, Disciplinarians, and Administrators
By Bob Costello, Joshua Wachtel, and Ted Wachtel
International Institute for Restorative Practices, 2009

Girls Against Dress Codes

BY LYN MIKEL BROWN

"**U**gh, Dress Codes!" The title of one of 15-year-old Izzy Labbe's SPARK Movement blog posts encapsulates what I've heard so many girls say they feel about their middle and high school dress codes.

Izzy wrote her blog after years of frustration, beginning in early middle school when she began to notice girls' bodies become objects of adult interest and surveillance. She honed her critique as part of SPARK Movement, an intergenerational girl-fueled activist project I co-founded in 2010. In her central Maine high school, Izzy and her friend Hannah formed the school's first-ever Feminist Club. On the top of their list was a challenge to the terms of a dress code that penalized girls for wearing shorts and spaghetti-strap tops. After reasoned conversation with administrators failed, club members quietly posted dozens of 8.5" x 11" sheets of white paper with large black print on school bulletin boards: "Instead of publicly shaming girls for wearing shorts on an 80-degree day, you should teach teachers and male students to not overly sexualize a normal body part to the point where they apparently can't function in daily life."

In 2017 another Maine girl, 6th grader Molly Neuner, made national news for challenging her school's dress code. Like so many before her, she joined a coalition of girls across the country using the Twitter hashtag #iammorethanadistraction. Reading her story, two things strike me: This issue is not going away, and most adults don't see the gift the issue offers.

Protests against dress codes get to the very heart of what it means to be an adolescent girl. It's more than a generational claim to personal identity. Dress codes are a stand-in for all the ways girls feel objectified, sexualized, unheard, treated as second-class citizens by adults in authority — all the sexist, racist, classist, homophobic hostilities they experience. When girls push back on dress codes they are demanding to be heard, seen, and respected. This means it's a moment primed for intergenerational engagement and education.

But too often, only two types of adults appear: administrators under fire for defending their schools' policies, and moms complaining about the shaming their daughters have endured or the school days they've missed for dress code violations. Where are the teachers who see the possibility for meaningful conversations about the development of institutional policies, about freedom of speech and choice, about democracy? How about those who see the opportunity to encourage critical thinking about cultural differences or the chance to examine the impact of media and pop culture on gender identity or the influence of rampant marketing and consumerism?

In response to this vacuum of adult engagement, girls are having these conversations without us. Most aren't asking schools to eliminate dress codes altogether. They simply want policies that are relevant to their lives, policies that account for changes in clothing styles, that value identity development, gender expression, and cultural diversity. And they want and expect to be consulted.

> **Dress code policies can become just another example of a hostile school experience for girls of color, for trans girls, for girls living in poverty.**

They also say they want policies that are consistent and fairly applied. One study from the Kirwan Institute for the Study of Race and Ethnicity, for example, indicates teachers are more likely to discipline girls of color for minor offenses like dress code policy violations and are more likely to give them harsher punishments. Dress code policies can become just another example of a hostile school experience for girls of color, for trans girls, for girls living in poverty. Teachers who have not addressed their own unconscious biases (e.g., their tendency to judge a girl's character by how she dresses), who have not confronted their internalized sexism or racism, who struggle with students who challenge the gender binary, cannot apply dress codes fairly. The best way to ensure a policy is applied fairly is diversity and bias prevention training for teachers and administrators.

It also helps to spend some time with students who have struggled with school dress codes and who think critically about bias, prejudice, and injustice. Here are a few things I've learned from listening to what girls say that make for a good dress code policy:

1. "Each dress code rule must have an explanation," Ejin Jeong writes in a 2015 blog post for SPARK Movement. "So much of the discontent with dress codes is that students often don't understand why the rules are in place." As a result, she says, dress codes "often feel arbitrary and unfair." Bex Dudley, who blogs for *Powered by Girl*, tells me her school "tried to enforce 'no brightly colored bras' when the material of the school uniform meant bras were visible. They were literally shaming girls for an 'issue' that they'd created."

2. A good policy applies to everyone; there are no gender-specific rules, no double standards. If girls can't wear tank tops, neither can boys; if girls can't show collarbones, neither can boys. In fact, girls want policies that have nothing to do with gender. "Have a plan for trans students without them having to ask for it!!" Bex exclaims. A transgender-friendly policy means anyone can wear a dress or a suit or earrings or makeup; anyone can wear their hair long or short. Formulated this way, a dress code can do more than prohibit; it can affirm and protect those who are already vulnerable, including transgender students and those who dress outside the gender binary.

3. A good dress code is attuned to cultural and religious differences and allows students to do their hair (Afro, dreadlocks) and wear clothing (hijab, turban, yarmulke) that reflect these differences. And they include rules that protect students from those who appropriate or insult their religion or culture through clothing choices.

4. A good policy is practical. It "gives some room for flexibility and expression," Bex says, "like painted nails and colored hair." And it maximizes student comfort. It accounts for changes in weather, allowing for seasonal clothing — e.g., shorts, sundresses, and tank tops when the temperature rises.

5. Girls say they want policies that do not contribute to sexual objectification by making reference to their body parts or give adults the discretion to use dress code rules to body-shame. Izzy notices that teachers target girls with "curvier figures. . . . [G]irls aren't getting in trouble

for the length of their shorts," she writes. "They're getting in trouble for the shape of their bodies" and "it sounds like we're blaming girls for other people's negative reactions to their bodies. That's misogyny! And it's a problem when it enters classrooms and girls' bodies are treated — by the staff, by boys, and by each other — as dirty, ugly objects that must be covered."

6. A well-crafted policy makes boys accountable for their behavior. Girls want school dress codes that make it very clear they are not responsible for how boys view them and that their clothing choices are not responsible for boys' inability to focus or learn. Such assumptions excuse unwanted attention and harassment. It's a short leap to blaming victims of sexual assault. "Can we throw the phrase 'provocative clothing' out the window, please?" Izzy asks. "Saying that clothing is provocative insinuates that it provokes sexual assault or rape or harassment, which is totally false. Harassers harass and abusers abuse regardless of clothing choices." Instead of policing what girls wear, girls say they want schools to actively teach boys to respect girls and teach everyone to respect transgender students and those who are gender nonconforming.

7. Good dress code policies give boys credit for being more than the sum of their hormones. When girls' bodies are framed as "distractions" to boys, Gabby C. writes in a 2016 blog post for the *FBomb*, "they not only strip girls of their sense of self-respect and free expression, but demean boys as incapable of controlling their basic urges."

8. A good policy clearly prohibits public shaming, which means adults don't make girls kneel in front of classmates to assess skirt length or pull out a measuring tape in public to prove a strap is too narrow. Administrators don't make an example of those who violate the dress code by forcing them to wear baggy T-shirts emblazoned with "dress code violator" like a scarlet letter. Correcting and shaming are not the same thing.

9. A good dress code policy addresses the realities of poverty and social class. Some students wear what they can afford and what's available to them. A short skirt or tight top are not necessarily attempts to ignore school rules. Dress codes can become a way to target and shame students already struggling with the hypervisibility that comes with not wearing the latest styles or the most popular brands, much less clothing that fits well.

10. A good policy does not send those who violate the rules home from school. There is no logic to a policy that takes away a girl's right to education because her skirt is too short. "What's more distracting, my shoulders or the fact that I just missed an entire history lesson?" Ejin asks.

In truth, most everything useful I've learned about girls I've learned from girls. On the surface, this isn't an especially profound statement. But as I look around at the ways adults talk about girls, dismiss what girls know, blame them for the symptoms of societal injustice in all its intersectional forms, create barriers for some and soft landings for others in the guise of concern and protection — I think it's radical to listen to girls and trust them as the experts on their own experience.

However well-intentioned, dress codes are a perfect example of an educational policy that puts compliance before learning; pressures and demands before support; a top-down bureaucratic solution created by adults at the expense of the time and effort it takes to really listen to and learn from students. And if girls are not heard, we should encourage them to advocate for their right to protest if need be. We can't say we want girls to have high self-esteem, to take risks, to lead, and then dismiss or punish them when they take this issue on.

With dress codes, we can see up close and personal what it means for girls to struggle in ways that release imagination and hope for something new. The safe and affirming spaces we offer, the questions we pose, the options we create together with students, are catalysts to critical consciousness, to what Maxine Greene calls "wide-awakeness," and to the possibility that their passionate and forceful reactions to unfairness and hurt will unfold in ways that better their lives going forward.

As Gabby writes for the *FBomb*, "Girls who take issue with these rules aren't blindly rebelling, but truly advocating for their right to be heard as sentient subjects rather than passive objects."

It's time we listened. ✳

RESOURCES

Darling-Hammond, Linda. 2005. "Policy and Change: Getting Beyond Bureaucracy." *Extending Educational Change: International Handbook of Educational Change.* Springer.

Rudd, Thomas. 2014. *Racial Disproportionality in School Discipline: Implicit Bias Is Heavily Implicated.* Kirwan Institute for the Study of Race and Ethnicity.

Inclusivity Is Not a Guessing Game

BY CHELSEA VAUGHT

"Miss, I can't eat this. It's not halal."

Noor's shoulders slumped, clearly disappointed, as she looked down into her treat bag from Ben's 6th birthday party. She walked over, frowning, holding it open to show me the contents. The bag was filled with gummy candy made from gelatin, which is animal-based and generally sourced from pig connective tissue, bone, and/or skin. It was not labeled as halal, which means permissible, and is a way of certifying certain food as being in compliance with Islamic law. Halal gelatin is often either from halal-certified beef or poultry or made from fish or vegetable-based sources.

This wasn't the first time Noor had come to me frustrated with birthday sweets she couldn't eat. Before, the best I could do was tell her I was sorry and make sure she knew I understood her disappointment, but anyone who's ever met a 5-year-old can tell you how poor of a consolation prize that is. This time I was prepared. I'd been saving chocolates and other animal product-free candies from other kids' birthdays to make sure all of my students could fully be part of our class celebrations. Noor was thrilled to be able to exchange her non-halal candy for something she could actually eat. She called her classmates Zeeshan and Amira over, and I traded gummies for chocolates for all three.

After graduating college in the United States, I was hired by a U.K.-based teaching agency to work in a suburb east of London that had a severe teacher shortage. My first placement was as a long-term substitute in the kindergarten classroom where I taught Noor, Zeeshan, Amira, and 25 other 5-year-olds. My school reflected the area's changing demographics: The formerly majority white British suburb was growing, and many of my kids were Muslim and whose families were from Commonwealth countries like India, Pakistan, and Nigeria. I was more aware of their experiences than I previously had been because my boyfriend at the time, who grew up in a British-Pakistani family in the next suburb over, would often talk about his own experiences as a Muslim student in the U.K. He had painful memories of being one of only a few Muslim kids in school, often feeling unintentionally left out or deliberately ostracized. He was never made to feel comfortable embracing his whole identity as a British Muslim. He'd hoped school environments had changed for the better and I wanted to do as much as I could, even if I was playing only a small role, to try to make sure they had. This is part of the reason why I already had an understanding of what the word halal meant and how I could provide an alternative for Noor and others.

Just as providing halal alternatives for students can create a more inclusive environment, so does understanding and making space for Islamic and other religious holidays in school culture and calendars. Being intentional matters. Holidays can be a major part of our students' lives and often exist at the intersection of culture, religion, community, and home. They can help make sure students feel welcome, recognized, and safe inside the school building. Ramadan, the holy month in Islam during which many Muslims fast from sunrise to sunset, might sound overwhelming to unfamiliar teachers and schools acutely aware of the disruption caused by holidays already built into the school calendar. But the month of fasting is not disruptive — like all holidays it can be a great opportunity for learning, celebration of identity, and sharing — and schools can do simple things to be welcoming and accommodating for students who are fasting. When I started teaching in Seattle, I borrowed an idea from another school where I'd taught in London and offered the art room as an alternative to the cafeteria for Muslim students who chose to fast during Ramadan, hosting a coloring and reading club there during lunchtime.

One year, every lunch during Ramadan, 2nd-grader Safa came to my classroom, ready to choose a new how-to-draw video from a favorite YouTube channel or to draw from her imagination. Occasionally she brought her friend Wardah. Fasting is not required in most traditions for most elementary-aged kids, but Safa liked being part of something her parents and older siblings were also doing. I cherished the opportunity to learn more about my student's life, hearing how her family was planning to celebrate Eid al-Fitr (the celebration to mark the end of Ramadan) and her plans to visit extended family halfway around the world later that summer. Safa liked feeling supported at school in her faith, and I knew from her mom's emails that the support was appreciated by her family as well.

Through all lessons and subjects, our students' lives and the politics surrounding their identities are always present. As essential as it is to create inclusive spaces for students to simply be, we should also aim to create opportunities to incorporate their culture and religion into projects and lessons. This doesn't mean that we should make assumptions about how students will choose to identify, but rather that we should be deliberate and direct in letting students know they are safe to include whatever aspects of their identity they choose into their projects.

Last year, I had to confront whether I was doing enough to create an inclusive environment in my art room as the 3rd graders began a printmaking project based on their cultural identities and heritage. Students were asked to design two motifs that represented their culture. I chose images of the Midwest and Indiana for my examples, and our whole-class discussion produced ideas related to food, clothing, and flags. Culture is a complicated subject, and open-ended and autobiographical projects typically need a little extra scaffolding, so I wasn't alarmed when most of the class hesitated after the demonstration and discussion. I expected it to be a challenging but rewarding project. I met one-on-one with kids and discussed their

We should be deliberate and direct in letting students know they are safe to include whatever aspects of their identity they choose into their projects.

ideas in small groups, and eventually most picked up pencils and began sketching. Then I noticed Ibrahim quietly staring down at his sheet, his eyebrows looking unmistakably frustrated.

Our students are of course not immune to the Islamophobia, xenophobia, and racism we hear every day in media, in our communities, and from the current administration and those supportive of its views. Ibrahim's ideas for his motifs seemed to bump up against this. He wanted to explore his identity as a Somali American Muslim, but was hesitant to begin his sketch.

Not all of my students felt this hesitation (for example, one of Ibrahim's classmates raced to include Pakistan's flag as one of his motifs — the other being a not-quite-explained dinosaur) but Ibrahim felt differently. He was unsure if he could include the stylized Arabic script for Allah as part of his project and asked me for permission. "I can do that?" he said, seemingly surprised that I said he could. I don't think he said more than "Well, you know" when I asked why not, but I wanted to reassure him he could use it if he wanted to. Without being certain of the source of his hesitation it's easy to assign my own biases and political anxieties, but I wanted him to know his self-expression was always safe in my room.

Any teacher with Muslim students can start by creating opportunities to listen to students, parents, and families as they speak and share their needs.

Ibrahim chose a Somali flag as his other motif. He took his time on his planning and on the final print, meticulously coloring in the Styrofoam printing plate and carefully printing a repeating pattern of his two motifs on a long strip of paper. He was proud of his final project and his classmates enjoyed learning about these two important parts of his identity from him when they talked about their projects as part of small-group "verbal exit tickets."

Making classrooms and schools safe for all students is an exercise in lifelong learning and listening. I have often relied on the help and advice of Muslim friends and now my husband (who grew up in a Muslim family and country), as well as online research. It's a privilege to have these close resources, but any teacher with Muslim students can start by creating opportunities to listen to students, parents, and families as they speak and share their needs. We can use or create curriculum and projects that allow students to learn about and incorporate their culture and religious practices if they want to. We can be deliberate in including, making space for, and recognizing our students in all aspects of their identities. Making schools inclusive doesn't have to be a guessing game. *

"I Believe You"

Responsive teacher talk and our children's lives

BY MICHELLE STRATER GUNDERSON

To all of my students: I believe you.

Every Monday morning Lilly would walk into our 1st-grade classroom with downcast eyes and a heavy heart. She would wait for everyone to settle in and then quietly beckon me over to her seat and say, "My head hurts."

It became a routine. I would stroke her head and say, "I know you miss your dad. Let's try participating in school and see if it helps you feel better." This seems like a reasonable response from a seasoned veteran teacher in her 31st year of teaching. My message to Lilly was I understand children, I understand your life, and I know what is best for you.

I had Lilly in mind when Olympic gymnastics physician Larry Nassar was sentenced to 175 years for multiple sex crimes perpetrated on some of our nation's most vulnerable young people. While watching the news and listening to some of their testimony during the sentencing hearing, I kept saying to myself over and over again, "I believe you."

Thinking of Lilly and her Monday morning headaches, I realized that I was discounting Lilly's experience and not fully listening to her. It was then that I recognized that I needed to change my response when children report to me — headaches, scraped knees, someone hurting their feelings — by saying "I believe you" before responding to the incident. Although Lilly was not reporting serious assault or abuse, as in the case of the gymnasts, I have come to believe that fostering a culture of belief in children and their words is a step toward giving them the tools to advocate for themselves in all aspects of their lives.

I teach an inclusion classroom, a blend of both general and special education, in a neighborhood school in Chicago. There are five adults who work together serving 27 children, nine of whom have special needs. The adult roles in our classroom include myself as the general education teacher, a special education teacher, two classroom assistants assigned to individual children, and a student teacher. There are many moving parts in our classroom and luckily the adults take time to talk and plan together. For the most part, all of us are on the same page when it comes to teaching children. We are justice-minded and strive to keep developmentally appropriate practice in our classroom.

Fostering a culture of belief in children and their words is a step toward giving them the tools to advocate for themselves in all aspects of their lives.

The week of the Dr. Nassar news reports, I approached our team with the idea of deciding to respond with the "I believe you" sentence stem to children reporting incidents or concerns to us. We talked about the need to validate children's experiences and feelings. We debated whether or not to say, "I hear you." But in the end we concluded that telling a child you believe them gets to the truth we hoped to impart. My student teacher, Emily Lanz, said, "You can always tell someone you hear them, but believing someone is a whole different story. It is the investment in the truth of the child's life."

After several days of practicing "I believe you" as our response to children, we took time in our team meeting for reflections. Todd Reynolds, the special education certified aide in our room, is queer. He often tells us how hard it was to grow up in Springfield, Missouri, and that he was often misunderstood by his teachers and peers. During our discussion he said, "I can't imagine how much different my life would have been if someone had said 'I believe you' instead of 'You'll grow out of it.'"

Rolling Out "I Believe You" in Our Classroom

We spent the next three weeks putting this practice into our teaching routines. As a team we would note the occasions when we used "I believe you" with children, and we would discuss its effectiveness. All of us experienced a shift in our classroom climate and our relationships with the children. Emily said, "Our room just feels gentler now."

At one point during this three-week trial period, a child came to me and said, "David hit me." I responded, "I believe you; let's go talk to him to see what he has to say." If the incident reported by a child involves someone else, we always give the other child a chance to respond. "I believe you" doesn't mean that we think the child is telling the whole truth, but it is the truth from their perspective. The next step is helping the child see the other person's truth.

Here are some more examples of our work that give a picture of this shift in practice.

One student said, "Mr. Reynolds, my brother gets all of the attention at home." Mr. Reynolds responded, "I believe you. Let's find ways to celebrate you at school."

"Mrs. Gunderson, I just love Debby," Jonah said to me on Valentine's Day. "My heart is bursting." My reply included coaching: "I believe you. Debby is wonderful. Let's talk about what it means to love someone in 1st grade, and what it looks like."

And because we teach 1st grade, some of the reports include the typical squabbles of 6-year-olds. As we were walking out the door on Friday, a little one came up to me and said, "Jeff pretended to fart on me." "I believe you," I said. "Let's go talk to Jeff about how to treat friends."

One of the dilemmas I confront as a teacher of young children is how to respond to a child's report when I think they are not telling the truth or exaggerating. I was listening to two children happily playing in the block center when the blocks came crashing down. Zora ran to me and said, "Tommie always knocks down my buildings." I said to her, "I believe you about being upset about your building. Let's talk about what the word 'always' means."

One of the complications we experienced was dealing with tattling, a normal part of teaching 1st grade. Children at this age become reporters of every transgression, and it is important that educators help children learn to independently work on their own problems. In our classroom we define "tattles" as saying something just to get someone in trouble and "tells" as reporting something a child needs adult help with or something an adult should know. It is an imperfect system, and takes a long time for children to process the difference between the two.

When reflecting on our new process, Todd said, "Some of these examples are 'tattles' and others are 'tells,' but by saying, 'I believe you' you let the child know that no matter the outcome, their concerns were not dismissed when they came forward. I think it is not about a new way to handle conflict resolution — we will still use the opportunity to help the child distinguish between a 'tattle' and a 'tell' and each will be dealt with appropriately — but 'I believe you' sends a strong message to children that the adults in their lives are present and take their safety and concerns seriously."

Making Our Practice Public with Our Students

After three weeks of practicing and analyzing our "I believe you" focus, we were ready to talk to the students about it. Our kids love it when we gather them on the rug to have a serious life talk. They quietly sat down in our gathering space and looked at me with the seriousness that always settles over our special talks.

I told the children how much we care that they experience school as a safe and caring place. Then all of the teachers explained that we have been very intentional in using "I believe you" when they come to talk to us. We gave the children our examples and our explanation about our decision. I talked about an incident that happened the day before when Elsie told me that someone had taken her place at the lunch table and that it hurt her feelings. Elsie remembered that I had said, "I believe you. Let's go see how that happened" while taking her by the hand to talk to the group of girls.

We then read the book *Mae Among the Stars* by Roda Ahmed. This is an illustrated biography of Mae Jemison, the first African American female astronaut. Of special interest to my students, Dr. Jemison was a student at Morgan Park High School on Chicago's South Side. In this picture book, Mae explains to her parents her dream of becoming an astronaut. They take her to the library and buy her a telescope. She is determined to "see Earth from out there." But on Career Day, when Mae told her teacher that she wanted to be an astronaut, her teacher said, "Mae, are you sure you don't want to be a nurse? Nursing would be a good profession for someone like you." The subtext of this encounter being that as a Black female, this would be the obvious profession open to her.

After we read the book I asked our students to write what they were thinking about how the teacher treated Mae.

One student wrote, "What I was thinking is that it was mean to treat Mae like that. She should chase her dream, not the teacher's."

Another child said, "If I was going to have a new teacher, I would want to be told 'I can.'"

"I was thinking the teacher did not treat Mae how a teacher should.

Like she didn't care deeply about Mae."

Our students are very young, yet they understand the subtlety and subtext of adult and child interactions. We noticed that the children's writings were not as rich and developed as the whole-group classroom discussion we had. For example, John said during the discussion, "In the story, the teacher put Mae in a box," which is a very colorful description of the story event. In his writing, however, he said, "I was mad." This is to be expected. Many times 1st-grade students can verbally explain complex thoughts, yet their writing does not capture it all. This is one of the reasons we allow children to talk issues through, draw, and write in our classroom. Multiple responses are important in order to engage children on different levels. All of their responses reaffirmed to our team that we were on the right track. After reading through the children's work, our student teacher said, "Imagine if our students insisted on being spoken to fairly throughout their lives."

Students are now recognizing "I believe you" moments on their own. The other day we read *Amazing Grace* by Mary Hoffman in order to develop a character study, totally aside from explicit teaching of "I believe you." In this book, Grace is told by her classmates that she cannot be Peter Pan in the play because she is Black and a girl. Grace eventually takes on the persona of Peter Pan and astounds her classmates at the audition. At the end of the reading, Elsie said, "That was an 'I believe you' story.'" We all agreed.

This is how we embarked on our journey together with our students, letting them know that our words and actions are intentional, and that we care deeply about them. After our Mae Jemison lesson our team discussed our hopes for our students. We concluded that our hope is that we are building a pathway to empowerment for them.

Many of the people I have spoken to about this have told me instances where an adult saying "I believe you" would have changed their lives. Imagine the difference across race, across class, across gender if we would say "I believe you" to one another instead of "really?" or "well, actually . . ." It is no small thing we do when we structure our classrooms around respect and empowerment — our words can make all the difference in the world. ✳

On Behalf of Their Name

Using they/them pronouns because they need us to

BY MYKHIEL DEYCH

"When someone with the authority of a teacher describes the world and you are not in it, there is a moment of psychic disequilibrium, as if you looked into a mirror and saw nothing." —Adrienne Rich

Adrienne Rich's quote illuminated the projection screen welcoming teachers as they entered the library for a 90-minute training on Gender & Sexuality Acceptance led by the Queer Straight Alliance (QSA) — a student organization that I am the staff advisor for. Our large, urban school holds about 100 staff members. Few looked forward to this training. The rest, sitting with their arms crossed, present only because admin mandated their attendance.

The QSA kids pushed for this training all year. The principal was on board in theory, but elusive about scheduling it. At last, late February here we were. In my final year of probationary teaching — I stood mere weeks away from receiving my permanent contract. Job security slinked at the brink of my reach. And I feared ruining it all.

I felt panic at the thought of losing my job for being a transgender and queer teacher leading the transgender and queer students. This progressive, liberal community and its wealthy, demanding parents held power and sway that made my nerves pulse irregularly. I woke some nights in a sweat from dreams of tantrum-throwing parents and their hate-inspired monologues directed at me: "What even are you!? Despicable! Unfit to be around kids — how dare you. Stay away from my kid!"

When you are a member of a marginalized group — especially one that's been villainized and degraded — safety is not an automatic privilege, even when you're white. Although my whiteness does provide shelter that trans and queer teachers of color are not afforded.

The students and I met to plan the staff training for several weeks before the Monday night meeting. Kids were both gung-ho and non-committal. The students really wanted to yell at the staff, misgender, and ridicule them. These students hurt and wanted to lash out to ease some of their pain. Many of them felt strongly, but few of them wanted to stay after school for two hours and say anything into the sea of mostly hetero-sexual entirely cisgender teachers. They were great balls of fury and they wanted to pitch fire in every direction at once. Few had the courage necessary to face the staff in a meeting. These teachers were supposed to be theirs. Students say, "*My* teacher." This simple possessive pronoun makes the pain of not being seen by said teacher feel like a self-inflicted wound.

Some teachers ridiculed students in front of the class, scoffing at the idea or trouble of using they/them pronouns. One teacher flat-out said, "Well, what is the kid biologically — that's what they are to me." The incredulousness of this statement essentially translates to: "What's that kid's genitalia — students are equivalent to their genitalia." No teacher needs to be thinking about children's genitalia.

During the weeks of planning for this training, I floundered in a borderland where I wanted/needed to be with the kids — really have their backs and support their lived experiences, listen to them, validate them. But also being an adult and a colleague, I worried that yelling at staff wouldn't change anything. And we really needed staffwide change. Kids skipped classes, kids hurt — each other and themselves, kids avoided their education because adults couldn't just get their names right. Everything begins with a name. We exist because we know each other by name. Students change their names because this gives them the power to exist. To refuse to call a student by their painstakingly chosen name — whether it matches the gradebook or not — denies a student's right to be wholly present. This erasure snatches away identity just barely emerging.

> **Students say, "*My* teacher." This simple possessive pronoun makes the pain of not being seen by said teacher feel like a self-inflicted wound.**

I kept asking the QSA the questions: "What outcome do you want? What is your purpose in this training? Do you want to educate the teachers? Share your stories so they're known?" Aliya said, "We want to be seen. We want them to try." Sal added, "How is it so hard to use my right pronoun?"

While politicians and professionals and teachers argue about the morality of gender variance, real children are disappearing in the classroom — figuratively and literally. Two trans students dropped out, another on the verge, QSA members barely hung on, and Grant lost a transgender student to suicide the summer that followed this training. And this in a very progressive district at a high school with gender neutral bathrooms.

I let them hash out their ideas for a couple meetings without much of my own input. I would nod and say yes. I'd empathize and I meant it all, but inside I was kind of freaking out. Will this implode? Is staff just going to scoff and roll their eyes? Will they even listen or just be on their phones the whole time? What if students don't show? What if my colleagues blame and hate me for all this? What if I get fired? Am I really going to come out to my whole staff in this training?

Yes, I am.

> **While politicians and professionals and teachers argue about the morality of gender variance, real children are disappearing in the classroom — figuratively and literally.**

As soon as the staff settles into their table group seats we start off with a video of Olive, the vice president of the QSA. Olive nods at me with tightened lips, and I hit play: "My name is Olive Reed and I use they/them pronouns." The video follows Olive moving through their day and discussing their experiences with school being safer than home but that they are called a faggot nearly every day. Olive says, "Everything in our society is binary, it's not just gender. But when you don't fit into that binary, take a step back and you're like, but what about me? And it's just — it feels like — there's not a place for me in this society." Teachers are watching, rapt with attention. Olive believes that "no one should have to hide who they are because of fear. No one should have to be afraid of being able to be who they are." When I first saw this video, I knew I couldn't support the students in this training and not come out to my colleagues. I owed them the overcoming of my own fear, I owed them my vulnerability. Olive's video ends with a quiet call to action: "People are accepting enough that you can come out, that you can openly be who you are, but people are not accepting enough for everyone to be safe. Yeah, we've made a hell of a lot of progress, but no, we're not anywhere near resolving anything."

At the video's end I instruct staff to write down striking thoughts, questions, etc., before sharing out at their tables. Many of the responses reveal appreciation for Olive's bravery and vulnerability. To not overcook Olive's anxiety about being the center of attention we move on to our intros. Three (of several) students and I give our names and pronouns.

"My name is D'Angel I use he/him pronouns."

"My name is Olive, I use they/them pronouns."

"My name is Asuna, I use she/her pronouns."

My heart pounding against my vocal chords, I finish us off: "My name is Mykhiel Deych, I use they/them pronouns." Shuffle, shuffle. Swallow.

A thrumming of invisible energy ripples through the four of us and out over the crowd. Air shimmering like the waving heat over an open grill in the hot of summer. D'Angel says with a smile, "Now please go around at your tables and say your names and pronouns." Some eyes roll and lips snarl, yet most of the staff conform to the simple task. A QSA member is seated at nearly every group table to help with intros. I mean, it is simple, isn't it? Just state your name and pronoun. Not far from the common instruction to state your name and birthdate or name and subject you teach. The norm of introductions at the start of a meeting feels familiar. Why the resistance to pronouns then?

The prefix "pro" means on behalf of. In English, we have gendered pronouns, so to use a pronoun in place of a person's name imbues onto the person a slew of gendered meaning that acts to define and/or limit the identity of that person. Students struggle to come into their identities no matter what. Becoming a *self* challenges everyone. One's gender *should be* a given, right? The easy part, the part of identity you've had since you were a kid, right?

Along with a handout, the next video, *Sex & Gender Identity: An Intro*, briefly defines and explains key terms: **Sex** is the biological classification of being female or male or intersex and is assigned at birth. **Gender Identity** is one's deeply held sense about gender and is not the same as sex. **Gender Expression** is the external manifestations of gender expressed through a variety of ways, including but not limited to clothes, hair, name, pronoun, voice, behavior, etc. **Transgender** is an umbrella term for people whose gender identity and gender expression differs from their sex. **Cisgender** is a term for people whose sex at birth matches their gender identity and gender expression. **Genderqueer** is a term for people who do not identify as part of the female/male binary and may experience themselves as both or neither. **Genderfluid** is a term for a gender identity that varies over time. And lastly, the verb that brought us into the room: **Misgender**. To misgender someone is to identify a person with a gender that they aren't. For example, when you call me a lady or ma'am you have misgendered me.

Teachers start sharing out about any newfound understandings or questions on the video. One teacher shares a painful incident. Mr. Xon says, "I don't know about these things but what I know is that I let a student go to the bathroom and they take a very long time and when they return I ask them where they've been and the student says, 'I had to go to the gender neutral bathroom.' OK, but I don't know if that's really what's happened or not." He stays standing for a moment palms open, facing up. He is trying to understand.

The room hushes; I take a slow breath, and another. But before I say anything, Asuna steps forward to respond, "The only gender neutral bathroom is far from your classroom, and there is almost always a line for it. This is really hard for us. We need you to believe us." This raw bravery and unapologetic vulnerability inspires me and I shiver. Are teachers who most need to hear this absorbing anything? All the students' hard work — is this going to change anything?

> **"Messing up isn't the problem — we know it's hard to get used to. We actually just want you to try."**

To provide a few tangible tools we put up a slide that has problematic phrasing replaced with simple solutions. Sally reads off "Instead of calling the class to attention with 'Ladies and Gentlemen,' try 'Scholars' or 'Mathematicians.' Instead of dividing by 'boys and girls,' use 'favorite foods' or 'wearing blue,' etc. Avoid blanket statements like 'all boys this' or 'all girls that.'" Discussion abounds.

A teacher shares out apologetically, "I don't use the they/them pronouns because I just know I'll mess it up." Griffin replies, "Messing up isn't the problem — we know it's hard to get used to. We actually just want you to try." They don't say it with a smile, but it comes out calm. An audible and affirmative "hmm" sounds out at a few of the tables. After sitting for a long time we shake things up.

Kaitlin instructs into the mic: "Please stand up and if you are a dog person stand over here and if you are a cat person please stand over there. She points to the far ends of the room and a gap in the middle widens as teachers move to where they belong. A few students and teachers vacillate between the two sides and end up in the middle with furrowed brows and heads tipped to one side. One teacher raises her hand and says, "Well, I don't like either." Another says, "I used to like dogs but now I'm more about cats. Where should I go?" And another asks with a deep shrug, "But I like both. Where do I belong?"

Thank you, allies, I need your help — students need you.

Where do I belong? The question hangs in the air as several teachers release audible gasps as they catch on to the metaphor they've just played out. "Wait, I get it, students maybe feel like this about their gender. Or sexuality too, right?" Ms. Smith says and taps a finger to her lips. Some eyebrows furrow. Some grins appear. Nods slowly bob through the clumps of solidly "dog people" and solidly "cat people." If only gender was a simple choice.

Teachers chat it out as they return to their seats to try role plays where they practice four important interactions: asking for someone's pronouns, using they/them pronouns in a conversation, correcting someone misgendering someone else, and correcting themselves misgendering someone. I circulate around the tables. At least one student sits amongst each of the table groups. The role plays open a flurry of activity at each table. The air full of electricity, my breathing feels steady until suddenly, one table gets superheated. I rush over to intervene and arrive in time to hear Kaitlin nearly shout, "It is grammatically correct, we already use they/them pronouns when referring to one person when we don't know a person's gender." I lock eyes with Kaitlin and she grins, "I got this M. Deych. Thanks, though." She is proud of herself. Proud to debate a teacher we already knew going into this training would be a wall to take down brick by brick.

When we come back together as a whole group, another teacher asks, "Are we really expected to keep track of when it is and isn't OK to use a student's preferred name or pronoun?" After so much of the training going well, the hostility in this question stuns me speechless. *My head races. You know how we have all that training about getting to know students, building relationships!? Well, this is that!* To my appreciative surprise, another teacher responds, "Well, we're not talking about a huge percentage of your class here. This comes down to a few students on your whole roster probably." Thank you, allies, I need your help — students need you.

The training finishes with a panel that responds to teachers' anonymous questions and answers written on scraps of paper that were at each table throughout the whole training. Three students, a parent of a transgender student, and I sit on the panel. Unfortunately, the final question deflates a lot of the gains we'd made: "I just can't use they/them pronouns, it's wrong, and I just can't. What do I do?" I probably don't hide the irritation when I say, "No one is expecting the grammar to change. It isn't wrong. You use it grammatically, *not* 'they *is* home sick' but 'they *are* home sick.' And if it helps to know, the reason many of us — the reason I — use they/them pronouns is because it reflects the multiplicity that I experience in my gender. So it is actually very right." Griffin relays their story of battling depression and ends with their head held high, "We actually just need you to try."

It's ongoing, the work of showing up for students how they need us to show up.

The students left feeling hurt by this last statement/question. It haunted them. And though issues persist with certain teachers, overall progress accumulates. Multiple teachers thanked me for supporting the students in that training. One said she felt defensive at first but then it really was good to hear about the students' experiences. Another came to me to hash out and discuss the issue with "ladies and gentlemen." It's ongoing, this work of showing up for students how they need us to show up. With 41 percent of transgender people attempting suicide (compared to 1.6 percent of the general population), we have to because they actually *need* us to. ✳

Measuring
What Matters

Grades serve as a kind of currency for schooling. From A-plusses to big red F's, from "Advanced Proficient" to "Below Basic," from "highly effective" to "needs improvement" — and all the many variations in between — grades and test results are how schools reward and punish, sort and label.

Today this is no longer limited to students. Educators, schools, even whole districts and states are frequently ranked, sorted, and labeled with shorthand letter or number ratings. These labels reduce the evaluation of learning and performance to clickable rankings, good for superficial hasty judgments, but bad for kids, teachers, and schools.

It doesn't have to be that way. In this chapter we look at what assessments can be when they're designed to improve teaching and learning and to support transparency and collaboration, instead of producing dubious data for external monitoring.

We look first at the long and harmful history of standardized testing and the damaging impact it continues to have on schools and classrooms. But we move quickly to constructive responses and alternatives. In "Testing Assumptions," activists from the Providence Student Union describe creative campaigns to educate both the public and policymakers about why assessment policies need to become less punitive and more supportive. In "My Dirty Little Secret: I Don't Grade Student Papers," a master teacher discusses how to put motivation and communication at the center of grading practices. "Authentic Assessment for Learning" offers specific examples of assessment tools that serve students well while engaging educators in rich conversation and collaboration — the best kind of professional development.

Finally, we look at better ways to evaluate teachers and schools. In Montgomery County, Maryland, a model system for sustaining a districtwide culture of professional learning emerged from collective bargaining ("Taking Teacher Quality Seriously"). "Beyond Test Scores" describes an innovative effort to develop "a more holistic picture of school quality" underway in a cohort of Massachusetts school districts. As project director James Noonan explains, "Importantly, the information collected using this school quality framework will not be used to rank schools. Rather, the information will be used to more precisely communicate the work of schools and to allow district and school leaders to better allocate energy and resources toward improvement."

Collaborative, holistic, student-centered, teacher-made. These are key elements of assessment in democratic schools where even the tests are aligned with social justice.

Time to Get Off the Testing Train

BY STAN KARP

Tests have always been part of schooling. Almost everyone who has gone to school can remember some version of spelling tests, pop quizzes, take-home essays, and final exams. Assessments that provide feedback about student learning, including different kinds of tests, can be powerful tools for students, teachers, even whole schools and districts. Assessments can also provide important information for parents about their children's progress.

But something fundamental has gone wrong with testing in schools. In recent decades, a sprawling, suffocating — and highly profitable — apparatus of standardized testing has replaced teacher-designed assessments with a "data-driven" mania that is the engine of test-and-punish reform. Data from deeply flawed multiple-choice tests, commercially designed and often scored by machines, is used by policymakers far removed from classrooms to make decisions about whether students get promoted or graduate, whether teachers keep their jobs, even whether schools are closed.

Like weeds in a garden, the spread of testing is strangling the curriculum, narrowing the range of what is taught, and impoverishing school experience. Children who need music, art, play, and poetry are instead getting worksheets and test prep. Students who need to critically explore gender, climate, and race issues are being taught to dissect multiple-choice questions. Active learning that helps students find meaning and purpose in their education is being replaced by standardized, scripted curriculum, often tethered to computer screens and produced by the same companies providing the tests.

Test-driven schooling is also undermining professional development. Instead of collaboratively developing engaging curriculum, building bridges to families, and undoing racism, teachers are spending valuable time parsing student growth scores and building data walls.

To be sure, data can be a useful tool. It can inform discussions about learning progress and make patterns of discrimination and inequality visible. Some districts, seeking balance, strive to be "child-driven, data informed."

But when the bipartisan No Child Left Behind (NCLB) law was passed in 2001, test scores became the most powerful force shaping federal and state education policy. Gaps in scores among student subgroups were used to label schools as failures without providing the resources or strategies needed to address the gaps. State and national policymakers used the inequalities reflected in the test results to create a narrative of failure that undermined support for public education and drove educational policy away from equity concerns and toward punishment and privatization. Poor communities of color especially were targeted by waves of school closings, the spread of privatized, unaccountable charter schools, and systematic disinvestment in public education.

It is not an accident that modern standardized testing has roots in theories of white supremacy and eugenics. During World War I, standardized "intelligence" tests were used to sort and segregate racial and immigrant groups. This led to expanded use of such tests in schools and colleges. The results have been disguising race and class privilege as "merit" ever since.

The limitations of using "quantitative metrics" like test scores to measure learning are well known. They were summed up by social scientist Donald Campbell in a famous maxim known as "Campbell's Law":

> The more any quantitative social indicator is used for social decision-making, the more subject it will be to corruption pressures and the more apt it will be to distort and corrupt the social processes it is intended to monitor.

The cheating scandals, drill-and-kill pedagogy, testing company blunders, and destructive policy choices of the past several decades have provided ample evidence of the counterproductive impact of test-driven reform.

The development of a new generation of Common Core tests doubled down on these practices. Millions of public and private dollars that might have been used to reduce class size, fight racial segregation, or build better school facilities were instead poured into creating harder standardized tests. The results were so disastrous they sparked a national revolt. A test "opt-out" movement mobilized millions of parents and students. Researchers debunked and teachers rebelled against efforts to extend test-based assessment to teacher evaluation. Polls have repeatedly shown that parents think there is too much testing and too much emphasis on the results. A summary of the *Phi Delta Kappan* annual poll of attitudes on public education noted, "Parents say standardized tests don't measure what's important to them, and they put such tests at the bottom of a list of indicators of school quality."

The limits of what standardized testing can tell us are also well documented. The National Assessment of Educational Progress (NAEP), often called "the nation's report card," is the only long-term measure of student test score outcomes. The relative consistency of the NAEP math and English language arts tests over several decades has produced comparative scores that show mostly predictable results. Overall, the Math and ELA scores of public school students have risen modestly and gaps between racial and socioeconomic groups have persisted.

Like weeds in a garden, the spread of testing is strangling the curriculum, narrowing the range of what is taught, and impoverishing school experience.

But it's also worth noting the differences between the way NAEP is used and the way individual state and commercially produced exams have been misused. NAEP uses statistical sampling to identify representative student subgroups (e.g., gender, race and ethnicity, school location). NAEP tests are administered to different sets of 4th- and 8th-grade students every other year and at least once every four years to a sample of 12th graders. By contrast, NCLB required states to test every student every year in every grade from 3 through 8 and once in high school. This led to dramatic increases in the amount and frequency of testing.

Moreover, mandated federal tests are often just the beginning. In many elementary and middle schools, students — sometimes as young as 4 and 5 years old — are regularly tested on a biweekly or monthly basis on computers and then subjected to computerized drills "at their level" as part of federally and state-mandated interventions. There are pre-tests, interim tests, post-tests, and practice tests. It's the difference between giving a patient a blood test and draining the patient's blood.

Federal law also prevents NAEP from identifying the results with specific schools, students, or educators. NAEP's anonymous sampling provides comparative results about student performance and trends without labeling or ranking individual students or schools. By contrast, the NCLB-induced testing juggernaut aims to tattoo a score every year on every student's forehead and every school's data wall as a basis for making high-stakes decisions about school practice and policy.

Assessments for democratic schooling should be designed to improve teaching and learning, not primarily to produce data for external monitoring.

Like all tests, NAEP has limitations and arbitrary features. For example, in the 1980s the proficiency levels for NAEP were set artificially high, well above "average performance" for particular grade levels. As a result, even in states with the highest NAEP scores (typically Massachusetts and New Jersey), the majority of students still usually fail to score at "proficient" levels. Instead, they are categorized as "Basic" or "Below Basic" based on arbitrary and unrealistic scoring standards no real schools have ever met. As one recent analysis of NAEP scoring levels put it, "The vast majority of students in the vast majority of nations would not clear the NAEP bar for proficiency in reading, mathematics, or science. And the same is true of the 'career and college-readiness' benchmarks in mathematics and English language arts that are used by the major Common Core-aligned assessments."[1]

Still, the many flaws of standardized testing do not mean we should ignore the real inequalities reflected in the results or the need for schools and educators to be accountable to the communities and students they serve. Transparent assessment practices have a central role to play in making sure schools work for all children. But democratic schooling for social justice needs more authentic types of assessment.

Assessments for democratic schooling should be designed to improve teaching and learning, not primarily to produce data for external monitoring. They should include real tasks for real audiences and be thoroughly integrated with the curriculum. To be authentic and useful, results should come from multiple sources and be used to inform collaborative discussion among educators, parents, and students. Assessment outcomes should also be used to generate new learning strategies and new curriculum goals, not labels and punishments. Although they may include various types of tests, they should not be defined by any single format, particularly standardized multiple-choice tests. (For specific examples of better assessment models in schools, see "Authentic Assessment for Learning," p. 213.)

The assessments our schools and communities need will not be found on the testing train. Educators seeking a future of hope and justice for our children will need to get off, and in the words of the legendary organizer Myles Horton, "make the road by walking." ✳

ENDNOTE

[1] Harvey, James. February 2018. "The Problem with 'Proficient.'" *Educational Leadership* 75(5): 64–69.

ADDITIONAL RESOURCES

Pencils Down: Rethinking High-Stakes Testing and Accountability in Public Schools
Edited by Wayne Au and Melissa Bollow-Tempel
Through articles that provide thoughtful and emotional critiques from the front lines of education, *Pencils Down* deconstructs the damage that standardized tests wreak on our education system and the human beings that populate it. Better yet, it offers visionary forms of assessment that are not only more authentic, but also more democratic, fair, and accurate.
rethinkingschools.org/books/title/pencils-down

Rethinking Schools
Articles in the quarterly magazine and on the website critique standardized testing and offer suggestions for authentic forms of assessment.
rethinkingschools.org

WHAT'S WRONG WITH STANDARDIZED TESTS?

Multiple-choice & short-answer tests are poor measures of student achievement,

particularly of the ability to understand and use complex material.

High-stakes tests cause curriculum to be narrowed to just what is on the test.

Teachers feel pressed to boost scores, even to cheat, and educational quality often suffers.

Test scores are not reliable.

An individual's score may vary significantly from day to day due to testing conditions or the test-taker's mental or emotional state.

There ARE BETTER WAYS to evaluate achievement and ability:

Good teacher observation, documentation of student work, and performance-based assessment are most useful.

Tests do not reflect current knowledge about learning.

There has been enormous progress in this area. Tests are mostly based on outdated assumptions.

Test-makers can't remove all bias.

Cultural assumptions built into tests often remain.

Standardized tests are not objective.

Decisions on what to include, how questions are worded, which answers are "correct," and the uses of results are all made by subjective human beings.

Standardized tests are NOT fair & helpful evaluation tools.

They reward quick answers & do not measure deep or creative thinking in any field.

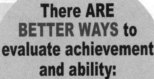

Find out more at www.fairtest.org

Authentic Assessment for Learning

Alternatives to high-stakes, standardized tests are being successfully implemented across the country. Although these more authentic assessments vary in focus and scope, they are generally designed to meet some common principles:

- Support improved learning. The assessment is designed to provide feedback that helps students demonstrate what they know and identify areas for growth.
- Help teachers improve instruction. Good assessment provides an array of information that teachers can use to improve their teaching practices and promote student learning.
- Integrate seamlessly with the curriculum and instruction. Assessment works best when it flows naturally from, and is part of, authentic student work — e.g., a math project that becomes part of a student portfolio.
- Be classroom based. Most information for authentic assessment is drawn from classroom work done by students over a period of time.
- Use a variety of measures. Good assessment draws data from both students' learning and schoolwide measures, such as attendance and graduation rates.
- Good assessment practices provide flexibility and don't constrict or dominate the curriculum.

- Be free of cultural, racial, class, or language bias.
- Don't steal time from teaching and learning. Test prep, test taking, and data input and analysis should occupy only a small portion of the school day and year.
- Involve educators, parents, and the broader community. Raising academic performance requires more than assessing individual student achievement. It requires schoolwide efforts to improve curriculum, school climate, teacher support, and parent/community collaboration.

Models of Authentic Assessment

Portfolio-based assessment and learning records. During the school year, teachers and students gather work samples that show student progress and achievement in various subjects. Students are encouraged to reflect on the work that has been selected, what they have learned, and their own learning processes and goals, all of which contribute to the overall goal of improving student learning. In some approaches, the teacher periodically examines the portfolio and evaluates the work based on a scoring guide. Sometimes students or their peers also score their work. The teacher ultimately records a score or evaluation on what is sometimes called a "learning record," attaching evidence such as a poem or essay a student has written.

Performance assessments. These assessments are based on students "performing" certain tasks, such as writing an essay, conducting a science experiment, or doing an oral presentation that is digitally recorded. Performance assessments can "drive the curriculum" in a holistic and useful way. For example, they can encourage more hands-on science experiments where students learn the scientific process and how to reflect on and analyze data, rather than merely answer questions at the end of a textbook chapter. Having teachers collaboratively score/evaluate performance assessments can promote deep professional development. Many districts have found this to be the case, particularly with writing assessments.

Exhibitions. Midyear or end-of-year exhibitions of student work across various grade levels and subject areas can provide strong motivation for students to produce high-quality work. Teachers and students can plan assignments designed to produce purposeful work and projects that will be shared with real audiences, including parents, students, and other members of the community. This reinforces a schoolwide culture of positive assessment for learning. In order to graduate in some high schools, students have to complete "capstone" projects and present their work to a committee of adults — somewhat similar to the oral exams common for postgraduate degrees.

Student-led parent-teacher conferences. Teachers help students prepare presentations about their work, reflect on their progress, and describe their learning goals and accomplishments to their parents or guardians. Giving students the opportunity to prepare and lead conferences increases student engagement in learning and motivates students to produce quality projects. It also helps parents concretely see the projects and learning that are going on in the classroom.

Schoolwide assessments. Because student success is intimately related to the culture of learning in an entire school, assessments that address schoolwide issues can be powerful. With a "School Quality Review Team" assessment, teams of trained educators and community members visit schools, usually for up to a week. The teams observe classrooms, follow students, examine the curriculum, and interview parents and teachers. Based on their observations, they write up a formal report, with specific recommendations for improvement. To be most effective, the recommendations need to be shared with and acted upon by both teachers and parents — which often requires additional time and resources. (For more on whole school evaluation, see "Beyond Test Scores," p. 242.) ✳

ADDITIONAL RESOURCES

Defending the Early Years
An organization of early childhood educators and advocates who rally educators to take action on policies that impact the education of young children, especially around testing and standards.
deyproject.org

FairTest: The National Center for Fair and Open Testing
FairTest works to end testing practices that undermine fair, valid, and educationally beneficial evaluations of students, teachers, and schools. Provides excellent materials in English and Spanish on alternative forms of assessment and problems with standardized testing.
fairtest.org

Learning Policy Institute

Conducts research and advocacy on a range of policy and equity issues, including assessment.

learningpolicyinstitute.org

New York Performance Standards Consortium

A network of schools using high-quality assessment alternatives to standardized testing.

performanceassessment.org

14 Days SBAC Took Away

BY MOÉ YONAMINE

"Do I have to do this?"

Miguel pleaded with me. He hadn't even logged in and sat at the computer, deflated. I nodded. I couldn't get myself to feign a smile. Twenty-one 6th graders were sitting in the room — some with Spider-Man or a Ninja Turtle emblazoned on their shirt, a few who sported baseball caps with flat brims they carefully kept the original gold sticker on, girls who still wore colorful ball ponytail holders and beads in their braids and pigtails, and the girls who made sure to keep their lip gloss nearby. Twenty-one students — 11- and 12-year-olds. It was May and that meant SBAC time. The Smarter Balanced Assessment Consortium. The Test.

The neon lights in the computer lab glowed rudely on our faces. Blinds closed — too bright for this Oregonian crowd; Aaliyah immediately lowered them as we walked in, even on that beautiful spring morning. Some barely pushed the "on" button on the computer to the chorusing of that single tone humming, telling me, the teacher, that they were late in following the test's directions. Why won't they get it going?! I struggled within myself, both wanting to shut down the whole testing — maybe there will be a miraculous overload of the computer system from so many of us (upstairs and downstairs) testing at once — and at the same time, wanting them to please finish on time or even early because we just couldn't waste any more class time.

Having come from teaching in a local high school where social studies teachers were never assigned to proctor a standardized test, I felt clumsy in piecing together how we would get back to our unit on climate justice. It's just four days I told myself — two days of practice testing and two days of taking the test. Right? I started counting: Well, actually four additional days where the other 6th-grade teacher also has to do SBAC with the same kids for math and science. OK, eight scheduled days of kids who will no doubt be brain dead. But who's counting?

There was no way my child was going to take that test — an inaccurate and unfair test that assesses a child's intelligence by how they perform on computerized questions while ignoring inequities in background knowledge, in hardships from neighborhood poverty, and in the distribution of educational resources.

Aaliyah whistled from across the room, twiddling her hair, staring blankly at the login screen. "Shut up, Aaliyah!" said Malcolm. Aaliyah rolled her eyes and looked at me.

"My mom already opted me out. She told me she did," she said with her arms crossed.

"I don't see you on the opt-out list, but I'll call Mr. Reynolds down and maybe he has more information."

"Mm-hmmm," she said, as she rolled her eyes while looking away — that slow-motion eye-rolling that lets her get away with it while still being able to claim she wasn't doing anything.

"Ms. Yonamine, didn't you opt Kaiya out?" asked Fata, sitting up straighter as if eagerly waiting for some validation. Kaiya, my daughter, was a grade older in the same school. I had opted her out of SBAC immediately. There was no way my child was going to take that test — an inaccurate and unfair test that assesses a child's intelligence by how they perform on computerized questions while ignoring inequities in background knowledge, in hardships from neighborhood poverty, and in the distribution of educational resources. Fata looked at me blankly waiting for an answer. I looked at the open door of the computer lab, back at Fata, and said nothing. "Aren't there like 20 people who got out of it?" Fata prodded.

"She can't tell you," said Kalani, who was sitting next to him and looked up from behind his glasses.

I wanted to tell them that this test is not about who's smart and who's not. This test is not about if you will be successful in college. I wanted to say to them, "Don't take it, honey. This test is not a measure of who you are or how smart you are. You are brilliant," as I had told Kaiya for weeks leading up to this moment. Although I considered the test wrong, as a third-year teacher, I felt trapped between my disgust for the test and the expectations to adhere to the school's protocols. As we repeatedly analyzed data comparing the growth of our students' test scores (or lack thereof) at our "high-poverty" school, I felt the weight on my shoulders to show that my students can rise from their low test scores. Meanwhile, many of my teacher colleagues at affluent schools on the other side of the city expressed excitement in closing out their year with meaningful projects full of joy and social justice.

I read the first set of instructions to walk everyone through the log-in process and to proceed with their first series of vocabulary and reading comprehension questions. Malcolm sat by squatting on top of the chair. We made eye contact and he said, "What? This is comfortable."

"OK," I said, putting my finger to my lips to remind him to be quiet and pointing to the computer, pushing him to get started.

Jimena sat there crossing her arms. She was actually from the other 6th-grade cohort but she had been absent during her class' SBAC time in the computer lab. She was on the screen with the first question. "I hate this," she said.

"Try your best, Jimena. Get started," I said in a low voice standing behind her. She turned back to the computer, chose an answer too quick to have read the question. Knowing I was still standing there, she proceeded to pick up speed, clicking through random answers.

The rest of the students were trying hard to read. Every time she finished a question, Leigha drew a smiley face on her white, copy paper that had been handed out for scratch — a way to encourage herself to keep going. Ashley took notes on the content of every question asked, reading the passage again and again before selecting the answer. Malcolm was now facing me, straddling his chair backwards and smiling.

"What's wrong?" I asked him.

"This is so boring. I don't even know what it's saying."

"Do you want to take a break?"

"Yeah. I wanna take a break from the whole thing," he said, loudly directing his voice to the center of the room to the laughter of his friends.

Even though the main office was literally two feet from the doorway and we faced the window to the secretary, I was not allowed to step out. I called Matt, the secretary, who was standing at his raised computer. I watched him pick up the phone without taking his eyes off of the computer screen through the window. "Can you ask Mr. Reynolds to come down please?" I said softly, trying not to stir students' anxious curiosity.

Matt immediately sighed, "OK. But it'll be a while. Everyone needs him," he said in a flat voice and hung up, cutting our conversation short.

Minutes went by and now Malcolm sat on the floor, this time with the chair on top of his head. I tried to keep my laughter from exploding and fought to keep my strict teacher look. "Put it down please, Malcolm." His smile turned into a straight face with a pouty lip as he pulled the chair down to the ground slowly again, all to his friends' laughter.

I noticed Miguel reading his book, with the first question still on the screen.

"What's going on?"

"I can't do it," he said, not even looking up from the book.

"Why?"

"Because I'm stupid. I told you I can't do this," this time looking at me with pain in his eyes. My nose tingled from the sadness that flooded over me: Miguel had been fighting all year to overcome his own internalized idea that he was not smart enough because he was one of the few pulled out over and over until he passed the English Language Proficiency Assessment (ELPA) test. In class, he struggled to write just one paragraph and he constantly kept his eyes on his peers to compare himself to their pace of writing. "You are smart, you are smart, you are smart," I whispered firmly. But the weight of this test was winning over anything I said.

Mr. Reynolds quietly stepped in with a walkie-talkie in hand, already looking worried.

"Malcolm needs a break and Aaliyah says her mom opted her out." He beckoned for Malcolm to come with him as Malcolm skipped diagonally across the room to leave. Mr. Reynolds looked at Aaliyah. "I'll go check," he said, seeming too busy to even take a breath.

Aaliyah mumbled, "I am not doing this," still resisting eye contact with me and looking out the window.

"Then read your book, Aaliyah," I tried to calm her. She grabbed the book next to her and slapped it open loudly to a random page, signaling to everyone that she was not happy.

Fifteen minutes in and the silence began to break into sighs and chairs creaking as more kids swayed their bodies with comforting rhythm. I looked at the Fred Meyer bag of gum and granola bars provided by the administration to help students weather the test. But the kids needed them already. I walked around and quietly put orange Trident next to each student's keyboard. Gasps of excitement could be heard, and smiles of "thank you" politely captured at the beat of the gum coming down. "Is there food?" whispered Fata. I nodded. "Is it chocolates?" he asked. I quietly held up the chocolate chip granola bar I pulled out from the bag. He put up two fingers — two granola bars he wanted. I shook my head. He pouted. By the time I finished distributing the snacks, some of the kids had only a wrapper left.

Kalani, though, had opened nothing — unusual for the sweet, funny, and loving boy that he was — full of affection in his body language even if he was a kid of few words. He was on the third question. I walked over to stand behind him. We were discouraged from having any conversations as teachers but I stood there to tell him I was right there. Something was wrong. He didn't turn around and smile like he always did. Nothing. He wiped a tear from under his glasses as he still faced the computer. "Hey, what's up," I whispered. He wiped the other eye, and then again. "Do you want to not do this right now?" I asked. He nodded, keeping his hand under one eye to stop the tears from falling. "OK. It's OK. You don't have to," I said, putting my hand on his shoulder. Kalani had been through so much outside of his school, and this was not what he needed. This was never what he needed. Nor anyone. I hated that I was forced to do something that brought so much harm, something that I would not allow for my own child.

I hated that I was forced to do something that brought so much harm, something that I would not allow for my own child.

Fourteen days this testing went on. Four from my complete two hours that these 6th graders had with me in our double-blocked humanities, and then four from the other 6th-grade teacher's, who did her complete two hours for math and science with SBAC — leaving me to receive brain-dead kids who were quiet and wanted to do nothing except to run around and scream outside. Many of our kids didn't finish within the scheduled time. Eight were pulled out for three more days, and then five more were pulled for three days even after that. Fourteen days I couldn't carry out my teaching because we couldn't leave out the remaining kids. Fourteen days I lost during those May weeks.

On the second SBAC day, I told Miguel to try again — his mom had not turned in an opt-out form. Minutes in, he began repeatedly banging his head with the inside of his wrist. "I can't do this," he said. He didn't get back on the computer that day and had to spend it in the other 6th-grade classroom while we carried on the test. He would be pulled out of our class later for three more days until he finished.

Jimena eventually blew out, her comments of outrage were no longer just in the quick clicking of her hands. "This is bullshit," she shouted from across the room as the testing coordinator walked in to check on our progress. She beckoned Jimena out to the hallway. Jimena angrily shoved another chair out of her way as she got up. She had to take a time-out and start again the next week. She was absent for the week that followed.

Fourteen days SBAC took away. We ended our year without returning to building community for our climate justice unit. We ended the year with a rushed celebration of each other. We could have been so much more. Fourteen days SBAC took away. Fourteen days I enforced SBAC testing to be the priority of our classroom learning — or rather, our classroom "unlearning." Fourteen days SBAC took away. ✱

Testing Assumptions

BY CAULDIERRE McKAY, AARON REGUNBERG, AND TIM SHEA

Passersby in downtown Providence jumped, startled, as a ghoulish-looking crowd of young people turned the corner of Kennedy Plaza. Green skin sparkled, sunken eyes stared, and torn, "blood"-spattered clothes dragged as they shuffled down Westminster Street. The dreadful-looking young men and women gathered at the entrance to the Rhode Island Department of Education (RIDE), where, instead of battering down the door in search of brains, these zombies showed they had plenty already. One demonstrator stepped forward, megaphone in hand. "We are here to protest the use of high-stakes standardized testing, and the zombifying effects it is having on our state's young people," he proclaimed. "To base our whole education, our whole future, on a single test score is to take away our life — to make us undead. That's why we're here today, in front of the RIDE, as the zombies this policy will turn so many of us into. We're here to say: No Education, No Life!"

Our organization, the Providence Student Union (PSU), has been organizing against high-stakes standardized testing in Rhode Island since 2012, when RIDE began implementing a new testing-based graduation requirement. Students had to score high enough on the New England Common Assessment Program (NECAP) to receive a high school diploma, regardless of grade point average or other evidence of scholarly success. PSU members, although recognizing creativity was not an important skill for the test, nonetheless felt it might serve us in opposing the new graduation policy.

The youth-led PSU organizes around our mission: "to build the collective power of students across Providence to ensure youth have a real say in the decisions affecting their education." Students have consistently agreed with supporters of high-stakes testing that it is time to raise expectations and standards in our schools. But we were outraged at the narrow-mindedness of those who believed that simply slapping a high-stakes standardized test onto the end of our 12 years in crumbling, underfunded schools was going to magically solve the poor educational outcomes for low-income districts like Providence. For us, it is an issue of equity — this policy disproportionately puts low-income students, students of color, students learning English, and students with disabilities at high risk of being denied a diploma.

In essence, high-stakes testing punishes individuals — youth! — for systemic failures. In doing so, it makes an implicit argument that educational challenges are not the result of larger economic or political problems, but rather the fault of these kids who are too dumb to pass their tests, and of their teachers who are too lazy to teach them properly. In fact, students and their teachers are currently the only people being held "accountable" for our education system's failures. Not RIDE, which is in charge of setting education policy; not our school district, which has failed to create the engaging learning communities we need; and certainly not our state's elected officials, who have consistently underfunded our schools and social services while cutting taxes for Rhode Island's wealthiest citizens multiple times in the last decade. Arguably, the latter group is most responsible for the fact that 42,000 Rhode Island children, or about one in five of the state's kids, live in poverty. Yet the logic of high-stakes testing implies that the ones to blame and to be punished for the failures of the system are the very people who are doing their best to teach and learn in difficult circumstances.

Even worse, this policy has vastly increased our schools' obsessive focus on raising test scores, with disastrous results. RIDE has framed this as a good thing. "We're finally giving students the extra supports they need to pass the tests," the department has repeatedly claimed. But what this actually means is that friends of ours are getting pulled out of their classes to do "NECAP boot camp."

Students Become the Walking Dead

Two PSU members had been talking all year about how much they loved their computer class and how useful it was. One day they came to our meeting with frowns — they had been taken out of that class and put into a test-prep class with all the other students who had scored "below proficient." Other PSU members began arriving with more horror stories: time spent during history and gym classes on math remediation, interesting class projects replaced by test-prep computer modules, and on and on. Students most in need of engaging instruction and creative learning were being squeezed into narrower, less individualized, less active classes focused on test prep and basic math skills. In short, the scope and depth of our entire education were being sacrificed for the sake of correctly answering five to eight additional questions on the standardized math exams to get students across the pass line.

Rhode Island students are familiar with this story. But the average person — and especially the average elected official — in our state had no understanding of these concerns when we began our campaign in the winter of 2013. High-stakes testing is a complicated issue and, if people had heard of Rhode Island's new policy at all, it was likely through the distorted cliché that "testing will raise standards, and we all agree we need higher standards." Our organization knew we needed to correct this misperception by getting the matter on the public's radar and changing the frame through which people saw the issue.

In essence, high-stakes testing punishes individuals — youth! — for systemic failures.

But how? We had already organized a "normal" rally at the Rhode Island State House (the usual kind of protest with a crowd and speeches) and spoken at a number of state board of education meetings, but we needed to get more creative if we really wanted to vault the issue into the public eye. Then we had our brainstorm.

We were having a conversation about what high-stakes testing does to students when PSU member Cauldierre McKay mentioned that it basically turns students into test-taking, unthinking zombies. A collective light went on. We all agreed the zombie image was a perfect symbol for our message about how this policy undermines real student success, and it was a metaphor we knew the public would be able to grasp quickly and easily. In addition, we knew zombies were hot — *The Walking Dead* had 16.1 million viewers and for a while was the most-watched drama series in cable history — and we figured that dressing up like zombies would be fun and attract students. So why not organize a zombie march against

RIDE to demonstrate to the world exactly what we felt we were being turned into?

Countless amounts of talcum powder, red food coloring, corn syrup, eye shadow, and ripped shirts later, the protest was a big success. Students had a great time and we attracted a lot of local news coverage. After all, what reporter would want to miss the scoop "Zombies Converge on Downtown Providence?" In the following weeks, pundits turned their attention to the broader issue, and new organizational allies stepped forward.

However, our zombie action also brought increased pushback. RIDE officials began a talk show blitz and testing supporters published op-eds hawking the absolutism that anyone who was against high-stakes testing was against high standards. A number of commentators tried to discredit our activism, saying we should stop wasting our time with gimmicks and instead focus on studying. After all, if we weren't so lazy and just did our work, we should be able to pass the test.

Once again, we needed to reframe the conversation. PSU member Kelvis Hernandez was particularly upset by one adult commentator who showed his ignorance by claiming that students should be able to pass the test easily. "If they think it's so easy, why don't they take the test and see for themselves?" Kelvis demanded. A new idea was born: We decided to debunk the "high standards" messaging by pointing out what this test actually measures, what it misses, and how "easy" the test is.

"Take the Test" Event

After the success of the zombie action, we knew we could get attention using untraditional tactics. The plan for the "Take the Test" event was simple: get as many successful adults as possible to take the NECAP. Of course, we encountered some complications. First, it is illegal to have an actual copy of the NECAP, so we created a mock exam using the questions RIDE releases every year. We did our best to approximate the same ratio terms of content, format, and "depth of knowledge" questions as the real test.

Second, we found that our biggest detractors were least willing to risk failure by taking the test. Every member of the Rhode Island Board of Regents who had voted for the testing policy declined to participate in the event, as did the director of the state's Teach for America and the spokesperson for Rhode Island Democrats for Education Reform. When asked, then-Commissioner of Education Deborah Gist responded that, since she has a doctorate and has taken many tests, she did not feel the need to prove herself to anyone. (It is worth pointing out that PhD candidates are primarily evaluated with performance-based assessments; they are required to be able to think and do, rather than fill in bubbles.) Fortunately, there were lots of other people who did have the courage to put themselves in students' shoes. After several weeks of outreach to all the elected officials and successful professionals we could think of, we had a respectable group of test-takers.

We assembled a very brainy, well-dressed crowd in the basement of Providence's historic Knight Memorial Library. Our accomplished group of about 50 volunteers included state representatives, state senators, city council members, senior aides to the mayor of Providence, accomplished attorneys, directors of major nonprofits, Ivy League professors, a former Democratic nominee for governor, an NBC news anchor, and a scientist or two.

A buzz of anxious conversation filled the room until a group of youth stood up to collect the adults' attention. The students quieted the crowd, read instructions, and distributed test booklets and answer sheets. At last, PSU member Monique Taylor announced: "You have one hour to complete the first section. You may begin now." Pencils up, heads down, they started filling in bubbles.

Of the 50 successful, talented professionals who participated, 30 — a full 60 percent — did not score high enough on the mock exam to graduate under Rhode Island's high-stakes testing graduation requirement!

As you might imagine, this event quickly became a media sensation. The next day, newspapers were filled with pictures of the confused and frustrated adult test-takers struggling over their mock exams. When we called a press conference to announce the results of the graded tests a week later, every outlet in the state showed up to hear the outcome. They wanted to know: how many passed?

The results? Of the 50 successful, talented professionals who participated, 30 — a full 60 percent — did not score high enough on the mock exam to graduate under Rhode Island's high-stakes testing graduation requirement! The fable of the necessity of standardized tests to produce a "career-ready" populace had been vanquished. As it turns out, test questions don't measure the constellation of skills, knowledge, and attitudes it takes to succeed in the world.

We had made it difficult for RIDE and its allies to argue students needed to pass the test to be successful in life, when so many clearly successful people had just failed it. It became easier to break through the shallow "they don't want high standards" frame, and to point out the arbitrariness of holding a high school diploma hostage to a single standardized assessment. And it taught our 50 volunteer test-takers valuable lessons, too, creating many new, important allies. Many of these elected officials subsequently were key to persuading the state's general assembly to pass a resolution condemning the testing graduation requirement.

Students kept up the pressure. We held a major public forum on alternatives to high-stakes testing, led a sit-in at RIDE, met with Rhode Island's governor, and more. Through it all, we in the PSU have been inspired by the acts of testing resistance around the country, from Seattle to Portland to Chicago to New York and everywhere in between. These actions gave us the courage to raise our expectations, and we now feel part of an emerging national movement. ✳

Postscript

In June 2014, the Rhode Island General Assembly passed legislation placing a three-year moratorium on the use of standardized testing as a graduation requirement. During the debate on the floor prior to voting, many legislators explained that it was students' activism that changed their thinking on the issue.

In 2016, the General Assembly adopted new graduation requirements eliminating the state testing requirement (although districts can still adopt local testing rules).

Members of the PSU — who have been working toward this for years — were excited. But there's no time to rest; we still have lots more work to do to ensure all students in Rhode Island receive the education they deserve.

ADDITIONAL RESOURCE

More Than a Score: Ending High-Stakes Testing in Rhode Island
The Providence Student Union's history of student-led campaign against high-stakes testing.
pvdstudentunion.org/more-than-a-test-score

My Dirty Little Secret: I Don't Grade Student Papers

Helping students find their passion helps them learn how to write well

BY LINDA CHRISTENSEN

I have a secret: I haven't graded a student paper in the last three decades. Now, don't get me wrong. That doesn't mean I toss them in the fire, "accidentally" lose them, turn them over to student teachers, stamp them with a six-trait writing analysis and plug in numbers, or push them through some kind of computerized grade machine. I discovered early on that if I wanted to produce writers I needed to let go of grades.

Creating Meaningful "Work"

Our grading should match our pedagogy. In my classroom I attempt to prefigure aspects of the kind of society I want my students to live in: a society where the work is meaningful and intrinsically rewarding, where people grapple with big ideas they care about in an environment where they can talk, read, write, and think without worrying about failure or ridicule.

Students need to feel that their work is important, relevant, and meaningful. If not, why should they spend time working on it? I was reminded of this when I demonstrated a narrative lesson in a classroom at Madison High School in Portland, Oregon. Madison's students come from diverse cultural, racial, linguistic, and economic backgrounds. Students had just read *Breaking Through*, a short memoir by Francisco Jiménez about growing up in a migrant family and trying to fit in as a teenager. The students and I examined a point in the memoir where Jiménez describes going to graduation wearing a white T-shirt because his family couldn't afford to buy him the required white shirt. We also read Gary Soto's "The Jacket," as well as a number of stories written by my former students. (See "Can't Buy Me Love: Teaching About Clothes, Class, and Consumption" in *Teaching for Joy and Justice*.) We talked about buying clothes to fit in, desiring clothes we can't afford, receiving clothes that we don't want from people we love. The topic fits my criteria. It's about big ideas: poverty and acceptance. Students struggle with finding a place to belong, but they also want to avoid being a target for other students' ridicule by wearing the "wrong" clothes or shoes. Many are desperate to fit in — even when "fitting in" means joining a group that rejects the standard teen scene.

As we started the writing, I told the students, "Find your passion. Write your way into a story that you want to tell." Damon didn't write about clothes. He wrote about getting a gift he didn't want from his foster parents. He wrote about living in foster homes, about learning how to lie about gifts he didn't want; he also wrote a list of questions about his next home and his next school — he was headed into his 12th home the week after I gave the assignment. He wondered if his new "family" would like him. He wondered if he would make friends at his new school. Fitting in meant a lot more to Damon than wearing the right clothes.

Because the assignment was open enough for Damon to write about what was important to him, he did. Because I want Damon to keep writing, I didn't put a grade on it. Instead we had a conversation at the end of the period where I talked to him about what I loved about the piece, and I told him the truth: Many adults and students need to read his piece. I gave him a few suggestions for revision.

He's experimenting with taking his story and making it into a narrative essay, tied together with vignettes about the skills he's learned in foster homes. He sent me the next draft via email from the library near his new "home." Damon's not writing for a grade. He doesn't even attend Madison anymore. He's writing because this is a topic he cares about. He's writing because someone is listening to him, and he hopes that through his writing, more people will understand what it's like to live in a foster home.

Grades as Wages

In too many classrooms, grades are the "wages" students earn for their labor. Teachers assign work, students create products, and grades exchange hands. There are problems with this scenario. Students who enter class with literacy skills are rewarded with higher grades. They already know how to write the paper; they just need to figure out what the teacher wants in it. Essentially, they take what the teacher talks about in class and reproduce it in a paper. Students who lack these basic skills or whose skills are underdeveloped are at a disadvantage. Unless there has been an explicit teaching of how to write essays and narratives, they may not know how to produce the products the teacher expects. As a result, they receive lower grades.

In too many classrooms, grades are the "wages" students earn for their labor.

Instead of rewarding or punishing students with grades, I believe that we need to "live out our ideals," as Myles Horton exhorted us, by creating situations where students, like Damon, learn to care about the work they produce. Of course, this means creating meaningful and important work that students want to do and creating communities where good work can happen. It also means explicitly teaching students how to write essays, articles, stories, poems, and memoirs and finding real audiences to read that work.

Revision: It's Never "Done"

Numbers on a rubric or grades for content and mechanics on the top of the papers don't teach students how to write, nor do they push them to their next drafts. These methods assume that students are "done" or that they will care enough to go back and attempt to fix their drafts in order to raise their grades. Numbers and grades "assess" or judge the paper, rather than provide feedback about how to improve it. Too many of my students learned to negotiate the difficulties of writing by turning in hurried drafts pulled together without much thought. They received their C's or D's, and they were "done" with their writing. The grades let them escape learning how to write. Without feedback or instruction on how to revise a draft, students do not improve their writing. The first draft is what they know about writing at the moment of writing. The revision, after instruction, helps them become better writers and better thinkers.

When Keith Caldwell from the National Writing Project visited the Oregon Writing Project, he used a great analogy. He said, "As soon as you put a grade on a piece of writing it's done. Don't grade it and you signal that it can still be revised, still worked on." He compared writing to baking pastries. Grades, according to Caldwell, are the frosting. They signal that the donut or the sugar cookie is heading for the showcase. It's done.

Because I want my students to view their writing as a process, I refuse to let them be "done." If students turn in drafts that represent their best work at that point in time, they receive full credit for the writing, say 100 points, for getting the first draft completed. If students don't have drafts, they receive no credit. If they turn in rushed drafts that clearly aren't their best efforts, I return them and ask them to redo the paper until it is a substantial draft.

After students write their first drafts, I give additional instruction based on the kinds of errors in content or style that I noticed in the class. Frequently, these whole class feedback lessons include how to analyze evidence, transitions, and sentence craft lessons. Some students need more individual attention to deal with grammar and punctuation errors. But everyone revises. (See "Responding to Student Work: Teaching the Writer, Not the Writing" in *Reading, Writing, and Rising Up, [2nd Edition]*.) Students regularly write and rewrite papers they care about. I remember Anne Lennon, a senior, lamenting in her end-of-the-quarter portfolio: "Seven drafts on this essay and I'm still not done!"

> **Because I want my students to view their writing as a process, I refuse to let them be "done."**

Too often, writing — and thinking — in school becomes scripted (hence the five-paragraph essay) because scripts are easier to teach and easier to grade. Unfortunately, they fail to engage students in real writing. Real writing is messy. And students often don't "get" how to write narratives or essays the first time we teach them. They need lots of practice without judgments; they need to be told what they are doing right, so they can repeat it; they need to examine how to move to the next draft.

But What About Report Cards?

Because I work in public schools that still churn out report cards, I must give students grades at the end of each quarter and semester. And I do — based on the total points earned for each grading period. The difference is that I don't put grades on individual papers. (And I don't give quizzes or tests, nor do I assign or accept extra credit work.) They receive all of the credit possible or they redo the papers. For example, a first draft of an essay is typically 150 points; a revision is 300 points. But they only receive the points — all of the points — if they write a paper that meets the criteria. (See "Essay Criteria," p. 235.)

I'm sure there are folks who will shake their heads at the lack of rigor or standards in my system, but I believe my system is rigorous and I hold students to meaningful standards. They don't pass my class if they can't write an essay or narrative — even if they complete all of the class work. I will work with them until they can write, but I will not accept work that doesn't meet the exit criteria.

Student Reaction

Nicole's reaction to my grading philosophy cemented my belief that I was doing the right thing. Nicole enrolled in one of my classes every year beginning with her sophomore year. The first year, Nicole was frozen by her fear of making a mistake. She attended daily, she responded to other students' papers, but she resisted writing — and this was in Writing for Publication, where writing was essential. In the opening days of her junior year, when a rather smug student made a negative remark about a classmate's paper during a read-around, I didn't have to say a word. Nicole jumped in and talked about the importance of finding what works in a paper. She set the tone for the year — and she finally wrote.

In a midyear class evaluation of my senior course, Contemporary Literature and Society, Nicole raised her hand. "I like that you don't grade our papers. I went through Sabin Elementary School and Beaumont Middle School with Mira. Every time the teacher would hand back our papers, Mira's would have an A and mine would have a C. It made me feel like I wasn't as smart as Mira. Now when I look over at Mira's paper, I see that we both have comments from you written all over them. It's a conversation, not a competition."

Mira, the valedictorian, also liked comments instead of grades. "What tells me more about my writing? A grade or the comments and questions you write in the margins?" In fact, Mira looked for colleges that wrote narrative evaluations of their students rather than grading them. (Now, she teaches writing at the college level and writes magnificent poetry.)

As social justice teachers, we need to align our grading policies with our ideals. We need to recognize that grades are one more way we privilege those who arrive knowing how to write papers or lab reports, conjugate verbs correctly, speak with confidence in front of an audience without fearing ridicule for their accent. If the work in our classrooms is meaningful, our students recognize the reward of learning and growing as writers and thinkers instead of working — or not working — for a grade. ✳

ADDITIONAL RESOURCE

Teaching for Joy and Justice: Re-Imagining the Language Arts Classroom
By Linda Christensen
In *Teaching for Joy and Justice*, Linda Christensen demonstrates how she draws on students' lives and the world to teach poetry, essays, narratives, and critical literacy skills. Part autobiography, part curriculum guide, part critique of today's numbing standardized mandates, this book sings with hope — born of her more than 30 years as a classroom teacher, language arts specialist, and teacher educator.
rethinkingschools.org/books/title/teaching-for-joy-and-justice

ESSAY CRITERIA

Assignment: Write a persuasive essay that clearly states your opinion on a contemporary issue. Support your opinion using personal experience, anecdotes, statistics, evidence from everyday life, novels, magazines, TV, movies, etc. In this essay, also focus on tightening your sentences and using active verbs. Attach this sheet to your essay.

1. Thesis Statement: stated or implied. Write it in the space below.

2. Introduction: What kind of introduction did you use?
   ____ Question   ____ Quotation
   ____ Anecdote   ____ Wake-up call

3. Evidence: Prove your point. Check which of the following types of evidence you used below. On your essay, mark each type of evidence with a different color:
   ____ Personal Experience: Evidence from your daily life
   ____ Anecdotes: Stories you've heard that illustrate your point
   ____ Statistics/Facts
   ____ Examples from novels, magazines, TV, movies
   ____ Other _____

4. Conclusion: What kind of conclusion did you use?
   ____ Summary   ____ Circle back to the beginning
   ____ Possible solution   ____ Restate and emphasize thesis
   ____ Further questions to think about

5. Tight Writing:
   ____ Active verbs   ____ Lean language
   ____ Metaphoric language   ____ Sentence variety

6. Grammar, Punctuation, Spelling Checked and Corrected

On the back of this page, describe what you need to do to revise this essay:

Taking Teacher Quality Seriously

A collaborative approach to teacher evaluation

BY STAN KARP

I f narrow, test-based evaluation of teachers is unfair, unreliable, and has negative effects on kids, classrooms, and curricula, what's a better approach?

By demonizing teachers and unions, the corporate reform movement has actually undermined collaborative efforts to improve teacher quality and evaluation. But in reality there is a lot of common ground among educators, parents, and administrators on the need for:

- Better support and evaluation before new teachers get tenure (or leave the profession, as nearly 50 percent do within five years).
- Fair and timely procedures for resolving tenure hearings when they are initiated.
- A credible intervention process to remediate and if necessary remove ineffective teachers, tenured or non-tenured.

Good models for each of these ideas exist, many with strong teacher union support. But overreaching by corporate reformers has detached the issue of teacher quality from the conditions that produce it. Class sizes are growing and professional development budgets are shrinking. Federal and state plans have poured millions of dollars into data systems and tests designed to replace collaborative professional culture and experienced instructional leadership with a kind of "psychometric astrology."

These "data-driven" formulas lack both statistical credibility and a basic understanding of the human motivations and relationships that make good schooling possible.

But better alternatives do exist. One promising model is the Montgomery County (Maryland) Public Schools' Department of Professional Growth Systems (PGS), which has taken a collaborative approach to improving teacher quality for more than a decade. Several defining features make the Montgomery model very different from the test-based "value-added" or "student growth" approaches. The Montgomery County PGS:

- Was negotiated through collective bargaining rather than imposed by state or federal mandate.
- Is based on a clear, common vision of high-quality teaching practice.
- Includes test scores as one of many indicators of student progress and teacher performance without rigidly weighted formulas.
- Includes a strong PAR (peer assistance and review) component for all novice and underperforming teachers, including those with tenure.
- Takes a broad, *qualitative* approach to promoting system-wide teacher quality and continuous professional growth.

Developing and sustaining good teachers, rather than "getting rid of bad ones" has always been the main goal of the Montgomery system. But real consequences for persistently poor performance are part of the process. The *New York Times* reported that since its inception in 2000, the program has provided "extra support if they are performing poorly" while "getting rid of those who do not improve."[1] In its first decade, the PAR processes led to some 500 teachers being removed from the classroom in a countywide system of about 160,000 students with approximately 11,000 teachers and 200 schools. Over the same period, nearly 5,000 teachers successfully completed the PAR process.[2]

But PAR is only part of a professional growth system designed to improve teacher capacity throughout the system, not just identify and remove ineffective teachers. It's a qualitative approach growing out of a shared vision of high-quality professional practice. The PGS begins with "six clear standards for teacher performance, based on the National Board for Professional Teaching Standards" and includes "performance criteria for how the standards are to be met and descriptive examples of observable teaching behaviors."

The six standards are:[3]

- Standard 1: Teachers are committed to students and their learning.
- Standard 2: Teachers know the subjects they teach and how to teach those subjects to students.
- Standard 3: Teachers are responsible for establishing and managing student learning in a positive learning environment.
- Standard 4: Teachers continually assess student progress, analyze the results, and adapt instruction to improve student achievement.
- Standard 5: Teachers are committed to continuous improvement and professional development.
- Standard 6: Teachers exhibit a high degree of professionalism.

A system of supports and professional development activities, including detailed protocols for assessing progress toward these goals, is outlined in various handbooks, evaluation rubrics, and contractual agreements. The system also provides resources necessary to turn these ambitions into real commitments, though sustaining these investments is an ongoing challenge.

For example, the PAR system relies on about two dozen "consulting teachers" who are recruited from master teachers with five years of experience in Montgomery County Public Schools (MCPS). The consulting teachers (CT) make a commitment to work for three years as CTs and then return for at least two years to a school in a teaching or other non-administrative position. CTs receive special training to work intensively with an average of 16–18 "clients" who include new teachers and experienced teachers referred to PAR by their principals. The supports provided by CTs include:[4]

- Informal and formal observations.
- Written and verbal standards-based feedback.
- Equitable Classroom Practice ("Look-Fors").
- Coaching sessions.
- Lesson planning.

- Model lessons.
- Co-teaching modeling.
- Peer observations.
- Classroom management.
- Time management.
- Alignment of school supports.

CTs document their work, but do not do formal evaluations. Their reports go to the PAR panel made up of eight teachers appointed by the Montgomery County Education Association (MCEA) and eight principals appointed by the administrators' association. The panel reviews the documentation and makes a recommendation for nonrenewal/dismissal, an additional year of PAR, or "release" to the "regular" PGS evaluation process that covers all staff. If either the client or the principal disagrees with the panel's recommendation, he/she can initiate an appeals process that allows all parties to present additional info and speak to the panel, which ultimately reaffirms or alters its original decision. A tenured teacher dismissed through PAR does retain tenure rights and can appeal a dismissal decision. But in practice, the PAR process generally documents fully the basis for such decisions and formal challenges to PAR decisions are rare.

Although the system is spelled out in detail, what really makes it possible is the level of cooperation that grew out of years of developing a collaborative approach to issues of teacher quality. The commitment to collaboration between the MCEA and the district is summarized in unusual contract language:

> We define collaboration as a process in which partners work together in a meaningful way and within a time frame that provides a real opportunity to shape results. The purpose of the process is to work together respectfully to resolve problems, address common issues, and identify opportunities for improvement. To be successful, the collaborative process must be taken seriously and be valued by both parties. The process must be given the time, personal involvement and commitment, hard work, and dedication that are required to be successful. The partners will identify and define issues of common concern, propose and evaluate solutions, and agree on recommendations.[5]

Beyond PAR, the larger PGS system is based on a belief that "good teaching is nurtured in a school and in a school system culture that values constant feedback, analysis, and refinement of the quality of teaching." Formal performance evaluations are part of "a multiyear process of professional growth, continual reflection on goals and progress meeting those goals, and collegial interaction." The aim is to support "a collaborative learning culture among teachers in each school, integrating individual growth plans into school plans, and utilizing student achievement and other data about student results."[6]

Besides teachers, there are separately articulated PGS standards and evaluation protocols for administrators, non-classroom professionals, and support staff. Ideally, this contributes to a schoolwide sense of accountability and collective purpose that helps sustain healthy school communities.

Montgomery County is not the only district that has implemented collaborative peer approaches based on collective bargaining. Long-standing peer review programs in Toledo, Ohio; Cincinnati; Rochester, New York; and elsewhere have shown various degrees of success. A study of PAR programs in two California districts found that they not only linked evaluation and support in constructive ways, they also fostered collaborative, problem-solving approaches in other areas of union-management concern.[7]

Just as with student assessment, evaluation can be a tool for improving teaching and learning or an instrument of bad policy and external control. The key in both cases is to make sure that people, not tests, are the point of departure and that real collaboration among all parties shapes the process. ✳

ENDNOTES

[1] Winerip, Michael. June 5, 2011. "Helping Teachers Help Themselves." *New York Times.*

[2] *MCPS Schools at a Glance*, 2010–2011, Office of Shared Accountability Montgomery County Public Schools. Webinar presentation, MCPS Consulting Teacher Team, Office of Human Resources and Development, July 25, 2011.

[3] MCPS Teacher Professional Growth System Handbook, p. 3.

[4] MCPS webinar presentation, July 25, 2011.

[5] Cullison, Bonnie (former MCEA president). "Union Leadership: How Teacher Professional Growth Systems Can Help Transform Schools, The Union Role in Systemic Change." Presentation, Coalition for Educational Justice. Sept. 24, 2011.

[6] MCPS Teacher Professional Growth System Handbook, p. 1.

[7] Koppich, Julia E. & Daniel C. Humphrey. Oct. 12, 2011. "Getting Serious About Teacher Evaluation: A fresh look at peer assistance and review." *Education Week.*

ADDITIONAL RESOURCES

Performance Test for New Teachers: A Forum on the EdTPA
Rethinking Schools Vol. 27, No. 4 (Summer 2013)
rethinkingschools.org/issues/volume-27-no-4-summer-2013

- "The Role of Performance Assessment in Developing Teaching as a Profession"
  By Linda Darling-Hammond and Maria E. Hyler
- "Wrong Answer to the Wrong Question: Why we need critical teacher education, not standardization"
  By Barbara Madeloni and Julie Gorlewski
- "What's a Nice Test Like You Doing in a Place Like This? EdTPA and corporate education 'reform'"
  By Wayne Au

Beyond Test Scores

Introducing the MCIEA School Quality Measures

BY JAMES NOONAN

Ask anyone who loves a school what exactly makes it special, and you are liable to hear a wide range of opinions: competent and caring teachers, a diverse and appropriately challenging curriculum, access to cutting-edge technology, a variety of extracurricular activities, availability of special education support services, an established track record of academic performance; the list goes on. And yet, measures of school quality — largely based on student standardized test scores — have long remained disappointingly narrow, unable to capture the full complexity of school quality.

Beginning in 2014, in an effort to move school quality "beyond test scores," a team led by Dr. Jack Schneider from the College of the Holy Cross worked with district and city leaders in Somerville to produce a more holistic picture of school quality. Together, they developed a framework now being revised and piloted by a consortium of six school districts across the state of Massachusetts (Attleboro, Boston, Lowell, Revere, Somerville, and Winchester).

Convened by the Center for Collaborative Education, the Massachusetts Consortium for Innovative Education Assessment (MCIEA) is committed to more authentic ways of assessing student learning and school quality, addressing the shortcomings of current measurement systems by collecting data that is both broader in scope and deeper in substance. In so doing, MCIEA hopes to demonstrate that collecting better data can produce better outcomes for schools, students, and families.

Broadly speaking, the work of MCIEA is happening across two strands. At the classroom level, teacher-designed and curriculum-embedded performance assessments offer teachers a more nuanced and authentic way to assessing student learning, one that could over time replace standardized testing. At the school and district levels, the School Quality Measures (SQM) project aims to better model the diverse perspectives and experiences of a range of school stakeholders when assessing school quality.

At the classroom level, teacher-designed and curriculum-embedded performance assessments offer teachers a more nuanced and authentic way to assess student learning, that could over time replace standardized testing.

The School Quality Measures project aims to describe the full measure of what makes a good school. Drawing on a close reading of public polling research and empirical research on factors related to school quality, and engaging in conversations with teachers, students, families, principals, and district administrators, we have identified five categories — the first three being essential inputs and the last two being key outcomes — and more than 30 unique measures to capture the nuances of schools:

- **Teachers and the Teaching Environment.** This category measures the relevant abilities of a school's teachers and the degree to which they are receiving the support they need to grow as professionals. It considers factors like teacher professional qualifications, effective classroom practices, and schoolwide support for teaching development and growth.

- **School Culture.** This category measures the degree to which the school environment is safe, caring, and academically oriented. It considers factors like bullying, student/teacher relationships, and regular attendance.

- **Resources.** This category measures the adequacy of a school's facility, personnel, and curriculum, as well as the degree to which it is supported by the community. It considers factors like physical spaces and materials, class size, and family/ school relationships.

- **Indicators of Academic Learning.** This category measures how much students are learning core academic content, developing their own academic identities, and progressing along positive trajectories. It considers factors like test score growth, performance assessments, engagement in school, problem-solving, and college-going rates.

- **Citizenship and Well-Being.** This category measures the development of traits relevant for students to lead full and rewarding lives — in society, the workplace, and their private lives. It considers factors like perseverance and determination, participation in arts and literature, and social and emotional health.

Importantly, the information collected using this school quality framework will not be used to rank schools. Rather, the information will be used to more precisely communicate the work of schools and to allow district and school leaders to better allocate energy and resources toward improvement.

Importantly, the information collected using this school quality framework will not be used to rank schools. Rather, the information will be used to more precisely communicate the work of schools and to allow district and school leaders to better allocate energy and resources toward improvement, support teachers to advocate for the working conditions and resources they need to do their work well, and empower parents to make informed choices when selecting schools for their children.

One of the implicit assumptions of the current accountability system is that, when it comes to the measured outcomes, it is not possible for all schools to excel. Some schools win, while other schools lose, even if they are all doing well, even if the differences between them are so slight as to be inconsequential.

In contrast, the MCIEA framework accounts for the possibility that all schools may be doing things well, and if so, they ought to be duly recognized. This does not mean that there is not always room for improvement, but it is an acknowledgment that school quality — like education writ large — is not a zero-sum game. It's time for it to be measured accordingly. *

ADDITIONAL RESOURCE

Massachusetts Consortium for Innovative Education Assessment (MCIEA)
MCIEA is a partnership of Massachusetts public school districts and their local teacher unions, joined together to create a fair and effective accountability system that is guided by a set of principles and offers a more dynamic picture of student learning and school quality than a single standardized test. MCIEA seeks to increase achievement for all students, close prevailing achievement gaps among subgroups, and prepare a diversity of students for college, career, and life.
mciea.org

Beyond the Classroom

The critical scholar Jean Anyon once wrote that trying to improve schools without improving the communities they are in "is like trying to clean the air on one side of a screen door." More than ever, our classrooms are tied to the communities around them. How we learn from and engage with those communities is a key to our success or failure.

In this closing chapter Stan Karp urges those entering education to see critical teaching not as an "academic formula for classroom 'experimentation,'" but as "a strategy for educational organizing that changes lives, including our own."

This means creating curriculum using our students' lives as a central point of departure and building connections with the families and communities our schools serve. It also means being aware of the larger landscape of education politics at the district, state, and national levels.

Schools have always been the target of competing social visions about what the curriculum should include, the role of teachers, even the very purposes of schooling. Today schools are also the object of fierce fights over social policy with implications far beyond our classrooms. The privatization of public education — through

charters, vouchers, and disinvestment —
poses a fundamental threat to the hope of
sustaining a multicultural democracy. For all
their problems, public schools remain one of
the few places where an increasingly diverse
and divided population still comes together
for a common purpose. Whether we invest in
and nurture our system of public education, or
starve and dismantle it in the name of reform,
is one of the most defining public policy
issues we face.

This chapter addresses some basic
dividing lines in public policy with respect to
school funding, privatization, and education
reform. It gives special attention to the role
teacher unions must play in advancing the
democratic side of these debates and in
linking the struggle for an improved public
education system to the larger fight for social
and racial justice. It also suggests ways that
educators can build ties with parents and
communities to form the broader coalitions
we need to create the schools and society we
imagine.

Together, these threads tie our
classrooms to the world and to the future we
hope to win.

Moving Beyond the Classroom

BY STAN KARP

S chool power comes in many pieces.

Teachers committed to social justice have daily opportunities to project a vision of democracy and equality in their classrooms. Whether it's developing curriculum that includes the real lives of our students, encouraging young people to examine issues of race, class, and gender as they build academic ability, or organizing activities that promote cooperative skills and spirit, teachers can often find ways to create social justice classrooms despite the institutional agendas and bureaucratic practices imposed upon us.

But what if our vision of social justice stops at the classroom door? Is the job of critical teachers primarily to create "safe spaces" inside an often ineffective and oppressive educational system? Can we sustain ourselves as social justice educators by focusing solely on the 30, 60, or 150 students for whom we assume direct responsibility each September? What about the many factors that shape the space in which students and teachers meet: schoolwide policy, community and district education politics, state and national education reform debates, larger social and political dynamics? What do these have to do with next week's lesson plans?

One answer is that teachers will never really succeed until the conditions of teaching and learning improve dramatically. We need more resources, better preparation and support, smaller classes, more effective partnerships with the communities we serve, and, especially in struggling communities, a vision of social change that can replace poverty and despair with progress and hope. Our schools need effective responses to violence, racism, drug abuse, family crises, and the many other problems that surface daily in our classrooms. We need to make our classrooms safer spaces for children facing hate speech, sexual abuse, and the immigration police. None of this can be won without activism and advocacy beyond our classroom walls.

Schools Are Social Battlegrounds

Adding extracurricular activism to a teacher's workload can seem overwhelming, especially for new teachers. But it is also a way to find the allies, support, and knowledge we need to become fully effective educators. It is naive, even arrogant, to believe we can transform our schools and our students' lives by ourselves. Critical teachers need to move beyond the classroom because to do otherwise would undercut the efforts we make every day. If we recognize that effective education requires students to bring their real lives into the classroom and take what they learn back to their homes and neighborhoods in the form of new understanding and new behavior, how can we not do the same? Critical teaching should not be merely an abstraction or academic formula for classroom "experimentation." It should be a strategy for educational organizing that changes lives, including our own.

But what if our vision of social justice stops at the classroom door? Is the job of critical teachers primarily to create "safe spaces" inside an often ineffective and oppressive educational system?

Although there is much to learn from teachers who create powerful classroom communities through hard work and commitment, the real hope for educational transformation lies in the reconstruction of school life. We need better, more collaborative relations with our colleagues and the space to nurture those possibilities. We need better, more cooperative relations with parents and communities, particularly across cultural and racial divides. And we need more democratic practices in our schools, our unions, and our districts, which can only come with activism beyond classroom boundaries.

More than ever, schools have become public battlegrounds for competing social and political agendas. "School reform" itself has become a deeply polarizing issue, with many proposals making matters worse under the banner of "reform." If educational change is going to make schools more effective, more equitable, and more democratic institutions, the grassroots voices of teachers, parents, and students are essential. If we don't help to change our schools from the bottom up, we will have them changed for us from the top down.

Today's new teachers are entering a political landscape that has dramatically altered both the teaching profession and attitudes toward public education. Several decades of "corporate education reform" have eroded the support public education needs to thrive.

"Corporate education reform" is a shorthand for a specific set of policy proposals that have driven more than a decade of education policy at the state and federal level. These proposals include:

- Chronic underfunding of public education.
- Increased test-based evaluation of students, teachers, and schools.
- Standardized, scripted curriculum that de-skills teachers and fails to engage students.
- Erosion of job security, due process rights, and teacher union power.
- Closing schools deemed low performing and replacing them with publicly funded, but privately run charters.
- Vouchers and tax credit subsidies for private school tuition.
- Replacing governance by elected local school boards with various forms of mayoral and state takeover or private management.
- Increases in class size, often tied to reductions in teaching staff.
- The privatization of school services, including cutbacks for aides, custodians, and food service workers who often form an important layer of community-based staff in schools.

At the same time there has been a dramatic change in federal education policy — away from its historic role as a promoter of access and equity through support for things like school integration, extra funding for high-poverty schools, and services for students with special needs, to a much less equitable set of mandates around standards and testing, promoting charters, closing or "reconstituting" schools, and replacing school staff.

Testing has been the engine of this corporate reform movement, and privatization its ultimate goal. In fact, almost everything public, from the schoolhouse to the post office, is under attack from the forces of privatization. Unless we change direction, the combined impact of these proposals will do for public schooling what market reform has done for housing, healthcare, and the economy: produce fabulous profits for a few and unequal access and outcomes for the many. This is a global phenomenon that poses a universal threat to democratic social institutions, including public education.

> **Critical teaching should not be merely an abstraction or academic formula for classroom "experimentation." It should be a strategy for educational organizing that changes lives, including our own.**

The good news is that the current ferment around education has broadened the space for all sorts of activism. The Black Lives Matter and immigrant rights movements reflect the increasing diversity seen in public school classrooms. The women's, #metoo, and LGBTQ movements reflect concerns shared by public school educators who are overwhelmingly female. Grassroots, parent-led movements are turning the tide against the misuse and overuse of standardized testing. Youth are demanding climate justice, an end to gun violence, and alternatives to an economic future of debt and austerity.

In different ways, demands for the radical improvement and revitalization of public education echo through each of these social movements. Similarly, the expansion and reinvestment in public education that we urgently need depends on strengthening our ties with such movements and bringing their insights and lessons into our schools and classrooms. Education justice must ultimately be part of these larger social struggles for democracy and equality.

Educators have been responding in many positive ways: forming activist teacher groups, creating social justice curriculum models, mounting campaigns against tracking and punitive discipline polices, building stronger ties with communities and other labor organizations. The wave of grassroots teacher walkouts in the spring of 2018 showed how powerful teacher voices can be when they speak on behalf of themselves, their students, and their communities.

In the final analysis, what's important is not that classroom teachers assume an impossible burden of individual responsibility for solving all the social and educational problems that affect their classrooms. What matters is that they see and understand the connections between those classrooms and the society around them, and realize that efforts to apply critical teaching are part of broader efforts to promote the multicultural democracy upon which our future depends. If teachers can find ways to link the two, they will strengthen both. ✳

ADDITIONAL RESOURCES

Rethinking Schools
This independent quarterly magazine is written by teachers, parents, and education activists — people who understand the day-to-day realities of today's schools. Every issue is filled with innovative teaching ideas, analyses of important policy issues, and listings of valuable resources. For information on these and other special issues, see rethinking-schools.org.

Rethinking School Reform: Views from the Classroom
Edited by Linda Christensen and Stan Karp
Rethinking School Reform puts classrooms and teaching at the center of the debate over how to improve public schools. Drawing on some of the best writing from *Rethinking Schools*, this new collection offers a primer on a broad range of pressing issues, including school vouchers and funding, multiculturalism, standards and testing, teacher unions, bilingual education, and federal education policy.
rethinkingschools.org/books/title/rethinking-school-reform

"The Problems with the Common Core"
By Stan Karp
The rollout of the Common Core was more like a marketing campaign than an educational plan. This look at the funders, origins, and uses of the new standards outlines some of the basic strategies of corporate school reform.
Rethinking Schools Vol. 28, No. 2
rethinkingschools.org/issues/volume-28-no-2-winter-2013-2014

As a new educator, why should I be concerned about school privatization?

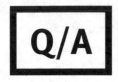

Privatization threatens the very existence of public education and its role as a foundation of our democracy. Every state constitution guarantees the right to a free public education for all children. Public school districts are required to serve all children, regardless of their abilities, special needs, home languages, or immigration status. Historically, public schools have been locally controlled within a broad policy framework set at the state level. In most districts, public schools are overseen by an elected school board.

That's not the case with most voucher and the overwhelming majority of charter schools, which are publicly funded but privately run. After Hurricane Katrina devastated New Orleans in 2005, pro-privatization forces moved in and now there are no truly public schools left in the city — they were all converted to privately run charter or voucher schools. Writer Naomi Klein calls this process of privatization the "Shock Doctrine." A similar attempt is now underway in Puerto Rico in the wake of Hurricane Maria.

Other major cities like Detroit; San Diego; Cleveland; Milwaukee; Gary, Indiana; Newark, New Jersey; and many others have a third to more than half of their students going to privately run charter schools or receiving publicly subsidized vouchers. The growing transfer of funds and students from public to privatized schools in these locales is contributing to massive underfunding of public schools that serve all children.

Voucher Schools

Voucher schools are private schools that enroll students receiving publicly funded "vouchers" that pay partial or full tuition. Most are religious schools, including Catholic, evangelical, Jewish, and Muslim institutions. Voucher schools do not have the same legal responsibilities as public schools and operate with minimal oversight or transparency. Private schools, for instance, do not have to provide the same level of special education services as public schools. They can sidestep basic constitutional protections such as freedom of speech or due process when students are expelled. They generally do not have to follow requirements for open meetings and records. Religious voucher schools can teach church doctrine that is at odds with public policy, for instance basing their science classes on creationism or teaching that homosexuality is a sin or women should be obedient to men.

The longest-running and largest voucher program is in Milwaukee, siphoning off more than $250 million each year from the public schools. Other programs exist in Cleveland, New Orleans, and Washington, D.C. As of 2016 there were 61 voucher and voucher-like programs in 28 states and Washington, D.C. Scores of similar proposals are currently pending in legislatures across the country. They vary in detail and go by various names, such as "parental choice scholarships," "opportunity scholarships," "education savings accounts," and "tax credit savings accounts."

Charter Schools

Charters are often described as "public" schools because they are authorized and funded by state law, but they are overwhelmingly privately run. They may not charge tuition and cannot teach religion. Typically, charter schools are granted a "charter" that exempts them from many regulations governing traditional public schools. In exchange, they are supposed to "experiment," improve academic achievement, and share the lessons learned. Charters first appeared, often with community and teacher union support, in urban districts in the late 1980s and early 1990s.

Over time, however, charters have become part of a charter "movement" — a national and well-funded campaign organized by investors, foundations, and educational management companies to create a parallel, more privatized school system with less public accountability and less democratic oversight. The Walton Foundation, perhaps the most aggressive funder of this movement, has given money to a quarter of all charter schools.

Oversight of charters is based on state law and can vary significantly. Some states allow for-profit charter schools and/or cyberschools. Unlike traditional public schools, most charter schools are governed by appointed boards not subject to public oversight or approval. Board members of privately run charters are not required to live in the community the school serves. They can limit their enrollment and may not have to admit students after the school year begins. Students usually must apply.

Charter schools are in virtually all states. From 2006 to 2016, charter school enrollment nearly tripled — from 1.2 million students to an estimated 3.1 million — while more than 4,000 traditional public schools were closed. Charters and public school closings are mainly concentrated in urban areas with high numbers of Black and Latina/o students.

What can teachers and other supporters of public education do to stop school privatization?

All children deserve good schools and no one questions the desire of parents to find the best options they can for their children. But the central question for public policy is whether expanding charters is an effective strategy for improving public education as a whole. Experience shows it is not. Nowhere have charters produced a model for equitable districtwide reform, and in many places charters have weakened support and funding for public education while increasing new forms of inequality. It's time to stop charter expansion and refocus public policy on providing excellent public schools for all.

To accomplish this, we educators and our unions, working in alliance with parents, community groups, and students, need to build broad alliances, coalitions, and social movements that are politically strong enough to shift policy. We must work with parents and communities to ensure that public schools are adequately and fairly funded. Affordable housing, healthcare for all, and living wage jobs are necessary so that our students and their families have the quality of life they deserve. As educators we should insist that our unions, the single largest organized voice for working people in this nation, take up social justice issues and make them a reality. It's up to us the take the next steps. See the resources in Action Education (p. 302) for local, state, and national efforts to defend and improve public education and the democracy that depends on it.

ADDITIONAL RESOURCES

For more information and sources, see "Backpack Full of Cash Discussion Guide" at rethinkingschools.org/backpack-full-of-cash

Keeping the Promise? The Debate over Charter Schools
Edited by Leigh Dingerson, Barbara Miner, Bob Peterson, and Stephanie Walters
An examination of one of the most complex reforms in education: charter schools. This wide-ranging and thought-provoking collection of essays examines the charter school movement's founding visions, on-the-ground realities, and untapped potential — within the context of an unswerving commitment to democratic, equitable public schools. Essays include policy overviews from educators such as Ted Sizer and Linda Darling-Hammond, interviews with leaders of community-based charter schools, and analyses of how charters have developed in cities such as New Orleans and Washington, D.C.

School Funding Basics

BY STAN KARP

"This is not a money problem, this is a values issue."
—Helen Gym, member, Philadelphia City Council

T he details of school funding are complicated, but the heart of the matter is simple. Our schools don't get enough money, and the money they do get is not distributed fairly. Chronic underfunding of public education is a fundamental — and appalling — fact of school life in the United States. Here are some basics worth knowing when the topic comes up at your school:

- State and local sources provide about 90 percent of school funding. Federal funding provides only about 10 percent of the total.

- This mix of funding sources typically does not provide a solid foundation for quality education for all children. "Is School Funding Fair? A National Report Card," released annually by New Jersey's Education Law Center, says "that public school funding in most states continues to be unfair and inequitable, depriving millions of U.S. students of the opportunity for success in school."

- Gaps in wealth across regions, states, and local districts are starkly reflected in school funding differences. The gap between the highest (New York) and lowest (Idaho) funded states is *more than $12,400 per pupil and growing.*

- In 1973, the U.S. Supreme Court ruled in *San Antonio v. Rodriguez* that education was not a fundamental right guaranteed in the U.S. Constitution, but a responsibility of the states. Since then 45 of the 50 states have faced legal challenges to their school funding systems. Most of these challenges begin with parents advocating for their children. The landmark cases in school funding equity bear their names: *Rodriguez v. San Antonio*, *Serrano v. Priest*, and *Abbott v. Burke.*

- School funding legal challenges fall broadly into two categories:
  - "Equity" suits that challenge the disparities in educational programs, services, and outcomes across school districts, especially urban and suburban districts.
  - "Adequacy" suits that document gaps between the resources schools receive and the resources actually needed to meet mandated levels of performance (e.g., those set by state standards or the language of state constitutions).

- About half these cases have led to court findings that funding systems were so unfair that they violated the law. But it remains mostly up to state legislatures to fix them. In most states, the per-pupil amounts schools receive are not based on reliable estimates of the staff, programs, and resources actually needed to provide a quality education for all children. Instead, they are political decisions made by state and local officials based on budgetary pressures and spending priorities. The over-reliance on local property taxes to fund schools also contributes to funding inequities across urban, suburban, and rural districts, and communities with different tax bases.

- "Equitable" funding does not mean the same amount for each student. All students should receive "adequate" funding for a quality education. But equity requires additional needs-based funding for bilingual students, students facing poverty, and other special needs.

- Many states, including Pennsylvania, North Dakota, New York, and Illinois, have "regressive" school funding. They provide less funding to school districts with higher concentrations of students in poverty.

- As the Center on Budget and Policy Priorities (CBPP) reported, "Most states cut school funding after the deep recession of 2009, and it took years for states to restore their funding to pre-recession levels. In 2015, 29 states were still providing less total school funding per student than they were in 2008."

- Deep funding cuts lead to increases in class size and declines in program quality. For example, according to the CBPP, "while the number of public K–12 teachers and other school workers has fallen by 135,000 since 2008, the number of students has risen by 1,419,000."

- Privatization policies compound these funding problems. Privatization thrives by starving public services of needed resources. As services erode, those who rely on them grow more frustrated and more receptive to privatization policies. It's no surprise that school privatization is strongest in urban areas, and charter schools are infrequent in wealthy suburban communities.

- The wave of teacher strikes and walkouts in spring 2018 helped put the focus back on the underfunding of public education. Instead of emphasizing tests and charters, the focus of education coverage and debate became the need to address inadequate funding and low teacher salaries. Led by teachers in alliance with local communities, these broadly supported protests point the way to the kind of sustained mobilization it will take to win the funding our students and educators need and deserve.

In the end two questions persist: Will we provide schools with the resources they need to make high-quality education possible, and will we provide those resources to all children or only some children? The answers we give will go a long way toward determining whether our society's educational future will be one of democratic promise or growing division. *

Why Teacher Unions Matter

BY BOB PETERSON

Many new teachers arrive at their first jobs without really knowing what a union is or what purpose a union serves. Unions are not something covered in most teacher education programs. Rarely are they mentioned in new teacher orientations. And more often than not, unions are portrayed negatively in mainstream media.

And yet teacher unions have been around for more than a century and continue to play an important role in education — from influencing policy to winning more funding for schools to assisting individual teachers when they have concerns.

The landscape and history of teacher unions is complex and shifting. There are heroic chapters and shameful ones. At times, labor unions have practiced segregation and discrimination against people of color and women. At other times, they've led struggles for social justice.

Today there are sharp differences over strategy and tactics within teacher unions, and legal and political attacks from outside enemies. The 2018 *Janus* decision, which limited public sector union rights, is one such attack.

New teacher involvement and leadership are critical to the future of our unions and schools. The more teachers get involved in our unions, the more democratic they will be, and the more they will reflect the values we stand for as educators.

Some Basics About Unionism

The bumper sticker slogan "The Labor Movement: The folks that brought you the weekend" is just one example of the power of unions and the benefits they bring to both union and non-union members alike.

Unions started in the United States in the mid 1800s when working people had few economic rights and little organized political power. Most unions formed as organizations that advocated for better wages, benefits, and working conditions. Some also campaigned for broader social change. By the early 1900s, unions had become a force to reckon with, raising broad social issues as well as specific economic ones. Bloody struggles were fought for the right to organize and to compel employers to enter into legally binding collective bargaining agreements about the terms and conditions of employment.

Initially unions formed in private industries, but they expanded to the public sector in the mid 1900s when the American Federation of State, County, and Municipal Employees and the two national teacher unions — the National Education Association (NEA) and the American Federation of Teachers (AFT) — emerged as strong forces. Each of the national teacher unions has state associations and local affiliates in school districts. In several states the NEA and AFT have unified. Together the NEA and AFT have a membership of 4.6 million active teachers and other school employees, college staff, retirees, and college students preparing to become teachers.

Membership in either of these organizations helps protect workers in education from the arbitrary whims of administrators, false accusations, and even unfair layoff or termination. Many local, state, and national teacher unions offer a range of educational opportunities in the form of committees, workshops, conferences, and special projects. More importantly, union members are a part of a collective organization that, while not perfect, plays an essential role in protecting the rights of educators, defending public education, and providing a democratic voice in the formation of public policy.

In many states, unions are able to collectively bargain and negotiate single or multiyear contracts. Depending on state laws and the local school board, these can include not only salaries, benefits, and working conditions, but other educational matters as well, such as preparation time and class size. Collective bargaining rights are frequently under political and legal attack, and in some states are limited or non-existent.

Teachers who join their union are entitled to individual representation and support from the union staff and leadership. Together unions strengthen the collective voice of educators at local, state, and national levels.

Social Justice Unionism

In recent years there has been a growing interest by teacher union activists in what has come to be known as social justice unionism. Social justice unionism is an organizing model that calls for the expansion of internal union democracy and increased member participation.

It contrasts with a business model that is narrowly focused on a limited range of contractual issues to the exclusion of broader issues of social, racial, and educational justice. Bureaucratic models of business unionism often disempower members and concentrate power in the hands of a small group of elected leaders and/or paid staff. In contrast, an organizing model, while still providing services to members and engaging in collective bargaining, focuses on building union power at the school level in alliance with parents, community groups, and other social movements.

The three components of social justice unionism are like the legs of a stool. Unions need all three to be balanced and strong:

- Social justice unionists organize around bread-and-butter issues.
- Social justice unionists organize around teaching and learning issues to reclaim our profession and our classrooms.
- Social justice unionists organize for social justice in our community, our schools, and in our curriculum.

More and more union locals and state and national union leaders are adopting a social justice union perspective. In some cities and states, rank-and-file caucuses are pushing their unions to adopt these more progressive policies and practices. In Seattle, for example, a caucus called Social Equity Educators (SEE) successfully organized against the imposition of harmful standardized tests and also mobilized teachers to support the Black Lives Matter at School movement, both of which the union participated in.

Grassroots union organizing also played an important role in the wave of statewide teacher strikes in the spring of 2018. Teachers in several states started rank-and-file actions using social media. In North Carolina, a statewide rank-and-file caucus, Organize 2020, initiated a rally at the state capitol that ultimately closed 42 of the state's 115 school districts, transforming a traditional "lobby day" into a forceful showing of political power by educators.

This social justice approach to unionism comes partially in response to the concerted efforts by well-financed right-wing and corporate forces to limit the influence of and ultimately destroy public sector unions. These efforts accelerated in 2011 in Wisconsin when the Republican-controlled state government banned collective bargaining, ended payroll deduction for union dues, and stopped "agency fees" (payments by non-union members who directly benefit from the work of the union). Other state legislatures have passed similar legislation. Then in 2018, the U.S. Supreme Court overturned previous pro-labor decisions and in its *Janus* decision undermined unions by preventing them from collecting agency fees.

> **The more teachers get involved in our unions, the more democratic they will be, and the more they will the reflect the values we stand for as educators.**

These attacks, along with decades of decline in the unionized U.S. manufacturing sector — principally due to corporations moving operations abroad in search of low-wage workers and fewer environmental regulations — have led to a precipitous decline in the percentage of unionized workers, which now hovers around just 7 percent in private industry and 35 percent in the public sector.

Still, unions reflect a powerful democratic impulse despite these repeated efforts to undermine and eliminate them. During the same months that the U.S. Supreme Court was deliberating over the *Janus* decision, an unprecedented wave of teacher strikes and walkouts swept across the United States. Starting in West Virginia and spreading to Kentucky, Oklahoma, Colorado, Arizona, and North Carolina, teacher and educational support personnel left their jobs and marched on state capitols demanding better salaries and benefits and more money for public schooling.

Teacher unions in other cities and states supported these walkouts. Locals have adopted various tactics, including "wear red for ed" days, "walk-ins," and mass pickets and demonstrations to advocate for educators and our students and to defend public education against privatization efforts. Some unions such as those in St. Paul, Chicago, and Los Angeles have embraced the practice of "bargaining for the common good," in which parents, communities, and students participate directly in the bargaining process. "Bargaining for the common good" extends the demands of the teacher unions beyond traditional bread-and-butter issues to broader issues such as increasing art, music, physical education, nurses, guidance counselors, and programs like restorative practices and community schools.

Such efforts to encourage strong membership participation, along with genuine coalitions with community, parent, civic, student, and religious organizations, have been winning significant gains for their members and communities.

To see what your union has to offer, check out its national website and your local and state union websites as well. And attend a union meeting. You might discover that in addition to representing you, unions provide great benefits and resources that you might never have imagined. ✳

ADDITIONAL RESOURCES

On local, state, and national levels, these teacher unions work to improve and promote public schools and to stop privatization:

American Federation of Teachers (AFT)
aft.org

National Education Association (NEA)
nea.org

Other groups active in the teacher union movement:

Caucus of Rank-and-File Educators (CORE)
The caucus that helped bring new leadership into the Chicago Teachers Union (CTU) in 2010 continues to fight for equitable public education and to improve the CTU so that it fights both on behalf of its members and on behalf of Chicago's students.
coreteachers.org

Labor Notes
A media and organizing project that since 1979 has been the voice of union activists who want to put the movement back in the labor movement. It promotes organizing and social justice through its monthly magazine, website, books, conferences, and workshops.
labornotes.org

Rethinking Schools

Nonprofit publisher and activist organization that has promoted social justice teacher unions for more than 25 years. Go to its special collection on social justice teacher unionism (rethinkingschools.org/magazine/special-collections/the-role-of-teacher-unions). Also check out the book *Transforming Teacher Unions: Fighting for Better Schools and Social Justice* (rethinkingschools.org/books/title/transforming-teacher-unions).

Social Equity Educators (SEE)

SEE is a rank-and-file caucus of Seattle Education Association educators that focuses on democratic, anti-racist, and anti-oppression policies and practices in their classrooms, schools, and communities. A monthly newsletter is available at their website. socialequityeducators.org

United Caucuses of Rank and File Educators (U-CORE)

A network of social justice educators and union activists working together to advance economic and racial justice and democracy, U-CORE works to transform unions at the local, state, and national levels into militant, democratic organizations capable of leading the fight against corporate control and for equitable, fully funded public schools. ucore.org

Union locals of note:

Also check out the activities and websites of the growing number of teacher union locals embracing social justice teacher unionism in various and creative ways: Boston Teachers Union, Chicago Teachers Union, Milwaukee Teachers' Education Association, Portland Association of Teachers, Saint Paul Federation of Teachers, Seattle Education Association, and United Teachers Los Angeles.

New Teachers Energize Their Union

BY GABRIEL A. TANGLAO

As a child, I looked forward to visiting my mother's workplace. Like many Filipinos, her pathway to U.S. citizenship was as a professional nurse. One winter day at the hospital, we pulled up to a spectacle that left me in awe: A large group of people marching in circles along the sidewalk. We were greeted by my mother's co-workers with warm hugs, and the sounds from the crowd were rhythmic and up-lifting as everyone raised their voices in unison. "What are they saying?" I asked. Mom replied, "Our chant lets people know that we are powerful together." This experience marching with my mother at this union rally planted the seeds of collective joy in action that later grew into a deep passion.

Years later when I started teaching in Bergenfield, New Jersey, my first impressions of the local union were less inspiring. The hurricane of paperwork, meetings, lesson plans, and dozens of new colleagues con-verged into an overwhelming stream of information. It felt like drink-ing water from a firehose. I remembered sitting uncomfortably in the dense August air of the auditorium for orientation. A captive audience of new and returning teachers was enduring a long lineup of white, male, suit-wearing, authority figures. "What a waste of time! These are the same PowerPoints they used last year," complained a veteran teacher loudly from the back row.

The local Bergenfield Education Association (BEA) president was the final speaker for that day. He made a mostly dry presentation about legal rights, contract language, grievance procedures, and evaluation processes. In retrospect, the union president's placement at the end of a long boring program left him with an impatient audience anxious to be set free. "Ugh! We could have just read through the PowerPoints ourselves. Don't they know how much work we have to do to prepare our classrooms?" proclaimed a frustrated teacher in the hallway. Her honesty felt like a breath of fresh air cutting through the humidity. We became instant friends.

Jasmin had a quick wit and a wealth of knowledge that made her an engaging person and a great teacher. We shared a classroom and taught different sections of the same Financial Literacy course. I remember being motivated by her relentless commitment. Jasmin spent countless hours planning, preparing, and modifying lessons for her Modern World History class. She also served as advisor to the Genders & Sexualities Alliance, Academic Decathlon, and rarely missed an after-school game. As we grew close, I learned about how influential Jasmin's family was in shaping her character. Her mother, like mine, was also a proud union member.

Jay, a close colleague of ours, taught U.S. History Honors two doors down from our classroom. He was highly respected by students, despite his reputation as the "hardest history teacher." Ironically, we had grown up in the same hometown, but only later became friends through teaching. One day during lunch, Jay pitched a game-changing question: "What are your thoughts on our contract?" I admitted, "I haven't carefully read the contract." Then I asked, "How do contract negotiations even work?" This moment eating lunch in the workroom sparked a conversation that lit a flame.

For the next few weeks, we started exploring the contours of our district that led to the current contract. Since we are in a state that recognizes collective bargaining rights, our local union reps negotiate on behalf of all teachers, including teachers at every grade level and all education support professionals. The salary guide is a complex grid that allocates pay scales based on years of experience and level of education. This often leads to thorny decisions that sometimes encourage union leaders to prioritize increased pay for senior teachers over new teachers or vice versa. We also looked into how our pension payments and healthcare costs added nuance to the calculations. It took time to understand the

"Our chant lets people know that we are powerful together."

complex process of contract negotiations, but the trail of breadcrumbs made us hungry to learn more.

We checked in with each other regularly to share our discoveries. Jay had a methodical nature that gave us important context for the bread-and-butter issues that impacted our take-home pay. Jasmin had great instincts and people skills that helped uncover personal accounts of how contentious elements of the contract played out. I started to identify key players and assess power dynamics through a social justice lens. With a 40 percent Latinx, 30 percent white, 20 percent Asian, and 10 percent Black student population, Bergenfield was one of the most diverse communities in New Jersey. But the administrative staff and school board were dominated mostly by white men.

We reached out to the local union officers and asked how we could get involved. After we received no response, I followed up in person. "Hello," I said to our union president during a break at an inservice. "I'm Gabriel. I just wanted to follow up on an email we sent last week asking about how Jasmin, Jay, and I could get involved with the union, and help out." His confused face confirmed that he did not read the email or take us seriously. "Help out?" he repeated. His implication was clear. I was viewed with suspicion as an eager, young, educator of color — a rarity in this longtime union officer's circle I imagined. Our exchange felt a long way from the warm hug that I remember the day of my mother's union rally. Still, we persisted.

Jasmin encountered a more patronizing, but equally dismissive attitude. Jay was up next. It may have been his powers of persuasion, or his position as a white, heterosexual, cisgender man, but he was our most effective messenger — evident by the result. Soon we were all nominated to serve as "building reps" and asked to attend "just one monthly meeting." Each meeting started with an opening monologue by the local president who spent an exhaustive amount of time disseminating information. The central message was clear: He speaks, we listen. The occasional daydream would cross my mind of those rally chants: "We are powerful together."

We began to exercise our voices to ask questions. "Should we use Robert's Rules of Order during meetings?" I asked. "Where can we find copies of our constitution and bylaws?" Jasmin followed up. "Will we receive an agenda in advance of the next meeting?" Jay asked. This volley of questions was not meant to be disruptive, but rather to help us move business forward and make our union processes more transparent. I was soon nominated by a veteran building rep to serve as "sergeant-at-arms" and help enforce the rules of parliamentary procedure. These rules can be bureaucratic and confusing, but it was also an opportunity to open up discussion and include more voices. I did my job, perhaps too well.

One of my responsibilities was to keep time during meetings. This sometimes meant calling "time" on people who spoke too long, including officers. "Sorry, that was three minutes," I would say respectfully. The president bristled at any attempt to check his control of discussions. Having been in power for more than a decade, the local president seemed used to unquestioned authority. This tension grew into hostility at my first winter leadership conference, a regional union event that offered leadership training for members.

As I made my way through the hotel lobby, I walked over toward familiar faces expecting to be welcomed with some friendly greeting. My local president took a swig of his drink and slammed his glass on the countertop. He turned to me and said, "You're not going to tell me I have three minutes to speak in my meeting!" He then launched into a verbal barrage. At first I tried to deescalate the situation, but I eventually raised my voice to demand some respect. Flanked by the vice president to my side, the president was able to slip away without a clear resolution. His message could be summed up as "know your place, and stay in it." In that moment, I realized changing that dynamic would require more than an individual confrontation; it would take collective action. It was time to squad up.

I texted Jasmin to ask if we could meet up after our first training session. We found a quiet table near the lobby to speak privately. She listened intently as I told her about the encounter. Rather than react, we decided to take time to think about our next steps. The following week, Jasmin invited a few trusted co-workers to her house for an informal meeting. I shared my experience with the group, uncertain of how it would be received. I felt affirmed when people shared similar experiences. "This leaves us no choice. How can we continue to work with these people?" one person said. The purpose of the meeting quickly shifted into a strategy session and thus started "A New Day for the BEA."

The confrontation with the local president was a turning point in our union journey. It prompted us to organize a slate of candidates and challenge the incumbent officers in the upcoming elections. Our team of five candidates for union office was majority women, and one person of color. Jay ran for president, Jasmin ran for vice president, and I ran for treasurer. We asked Phyllis, the person who had nominated me for sergeant-at-arms, to run for corresponding secretary. She was a veteran middle school teacher with union experience. An elementary school teacher decided to run for recording secretary. The attitudes of the incumbent officers grew increasingly hostile, but there was no turning back.

In an effort to learn about issues that impacted our members, we organized a districtwide listening tour. Within three weeks, we visited seven out of eight schools, and connected with nearly a quarter of our 450 members. Representatives who were loyal to the old regime attempted to put up roadblocks, but rank-and-file members showed up. Teachers, librarians, secretaries, counselors, custodians, and paraprofessionals shared stories of their struggles, frustrations, and hopes. "This is the first time I can remember candidates running for union office having ever visited our school," one woman said with gratitude. The common theme was a desire for greater communication.

It became clear that democratic process had not been exercised regularly in the local for many years. Most people were hard-pressed to remember the last time there were any challengers, let alone a slate of candidates. In fact, it took weeks to even receive a copy of the constitution and bylaws that outlined the election rules, procedures, and timeline. One event that we were encouraged to attend was a meet-the-candidates debate. "They are going to frame us as weak and inexperienced. That will be our advantage," Jay said with a cool resolve. As coach of the debate team, he was ready to go toe-to-toe with anyone. The outcome of that event was as clear as the outcome on the ballots. We won a resounding victory for all five union officer positions.

Having successfully campaigned for office, we hoped to transform the culture of our union to be more inclusive and transparent. Our team shared a sense of urgency about the need to engage members from our generation. We were acutely aware from our recent experiences that fresh blood in the ranks of active membership meant a healthier union. It was also visibly apparent that we did not reflect the rich diversity of the Bergenfield student body or local community. "I should not be the only person of color at the leadership table," I affirmed. But we were moving in the right direction.

We kept the concerns of members from our listening tour at the forefront of our minds. We centered organization, communication, and engagement as our main priorities. Internally, we focused on the empowerment of building reps with opportunities for training, support, and resources that we wished we would have had. That summer, about one-third of our building reps attended the statewide summer leadership conference to participate in trainings on a variety of issues. As I walked into the crowded dining room on the first night, I had a flashback of the previous winter's confrontation. I heard my name, and started walking over toward the familiar faces waving me over.

One of our new building reps had thoughtfully saved us all seats at a table in the conference dining room. We sat together and shared our excitement about the weekend. This was a new experience for most of our team, and it felt good to have other people to share in the journey. We checked in with each other at each meal to share discoveries. "Do we use any funding from the PRIDE community organizing grant?" one person inquired. "Is there an Evaluation Committee?" added the new building rep. "Who serves on our Legislative Action team?" another person asked. This was a very different experience from the last conference. It felt like that collective joy in action.

This wave of momentum carried our growing team into the following school year. Starting with small teams of people, we revived the committee structures including the Legislative Action Team, "PRIDE" Community Organizing Committee, Evaluation Committee, and others. In an effort to strengthen face-to-face relationships, we mapped the buildings to connect building reps with clusters of members located in their respective hallways. This effort paid dividends when we invited people to the social events that Jasmin would plan. From happy hours for new members to retirement celebrations, we tried to attract educators to take collective ownership of our union.

In an effort to strengthen face-to-face relationships, we mapped the buildings to connect building reps with clusters of members located in their respective hallways.

We grew into each leadership role with every experience. Jay was our contract guru who mastered the grievance procedures, organized the negotiations team, and was the lead defender of members' rights. Jasmin's dynamic personality and thoughtful nature was an incredible asset as she led, planned, and launched a series of membership engagement events throughout the year. I discovered the radical possibilities of this union work in and beyond the district. I represented our local to the Parents Association, community groups, political organizations, and our state and national affiliates. We each discovered our own leadership style, and added to the collective vision in different ways.

I admit that the work was fun and challenging, but also frustrating at times. As chair of our Legislative Action Team, I wanted our union to have a real impact in our larger community. As we acknowledged the lack of diverse representation in our administrative staff and faculty, we set our sights on the local school board elections. It took months to identify worthy candidates, and navigate the complexities of local politics. We spread the word throughout our membership. We partnered with the Parents Association who hosted a meet-the-candidates night. We even organized a community door-knocking to turn out the vote with Bergenfield residents who were also union members.

Despite all of the time and effort, we were able to help elect only one candidate of color. This did not shift the balance of power, or change the racial dynamic in a substantive way. This "L" was not a loss, but a lesson: The strategic vision of transformational change takes time, and could take years of sustained collective action. We were also reminded that the power is in the people, not in the position. Organizing to support the campaigns of school board candidates of color led to deeper connections with the community.

At the swearing-in ceremony of the newly elected school board members, I was greeted by Andres, a board candidate who had lost the election. Andres, who had migrated from the Dominican Republic to earn his doctorate and planted his family roots in Bergenfield, was a parent of my former student and board president of the Bergenfield Public Library. "Welcome, my friend," he said. "We would like to invite the Bergenfield Education Association to partner with us on our annual Multicultural Celebration." That was the beginning of a partnership between our organizations that has allowed us to collaborate for more sustainable change in the community.

From our core team to our rep council, from local membership to community spaces, we used our union as a vehicle to drive change forward. It took time and effort, but we reshaped our local to be more intergenerational and inclusive for educators, students, and families of color. In three years, we reached a contract agreement in record time, established community partnerships, and started to shift the political landscape of our district. None of this was easy, and it could not be done alone. It was a collective effort and truly a labor of love. We learned some simple, yet important lessons: (1) show up; (2) step up; (3) squad up; (4) build community; and (5) enjoy the journey. ✴

From Outrage to Organizing

*Building community ties through
education activism*

BY IKECHUKWU ONYEMA

❝Freedom Schools" have taken many forms over the years, but
all evoke the legacy and militancy of the Civil Rights Movement. In their earliest iterations, they functioned as liber-
ated spaces for political education and literacy interventions inside of
churches or in community centers over the summer. This was certainly
our inspiration when our group of educators and activists embarked on
an organizing mission in response to a confrontation between police and
student youth that transpired on July 5, 2016, in our community of Ma-
plewood/South Orange, New Jersey.

On that day several African American teenagers experienced the
violence and disrespect from police officers that is a pervasive fact of life
for young people of color. After Fourth of July festivities in a local park,
police were summoned to clear the area. As the crowd dispersed, a group
of African American teenagers sought to return home to their families in
this diverse and affluent suburb. Yet, police prevented them from doing
so. Assuming that they must be residents of a working-class urban town
nearby, the police herded the youth in that direction. The pleas and protests from the local teenagers fell on deaf ears, while the police proceeded
to scream obscenities as if to provoke the students into behavior that
might "justify" escalated police force. The confrontation reflected the
pattern of disproportionately harsh treatment of Black youth by police
that gave rise to the Black Lives Matter movement.

This incident touched a nerve in this multiracial community of about 40,000 people. T. J. Whitaker, a local veteran high school English teacher and African American activist in the community, had an established reputation and students believed they could confide in him. Upon hearing student testimony, T. J. quickly reached out to other activists and educators to assist with a meaningful response.

The South Orange/Maplewood Community Coalition on Race had a reputation for meekly addressing these kinds of instances of racism. In response to the assault, the group convened a "conversation" at a local school. At this event, some student voices were heard, but the overall thrust was to extol the virtues of the police for their role in protecting community safety. T. J. was outraged by the narrative reversal of blame and responsibility. The need for a stronger response was deeply felt. Thus, when Okaikor Aryee-Price, my friend and fellow educator, suggested a "Freedom School" as an effective response, it resonated with many educators in the audience who silently nodded at each other in approval.

Fortunately, for the majority of educators who decided to get involved, this transpired in the summer and we had time to dedicate to regular meetings. We met in T. J.'s living room to plan out our first event: a day of activities that we hoped would deepen the "conversation" on race and invoke the activist, participatory spirit of the Freedom Schools. Students, parents, and educators planned the event together.

We met to plan our first event: a day of activities that we hoped would deepen the "conversation" on race and invoke the activist, participatory spirit of the Freedom Schools.

For one session, I co-taught a "Know Your Rights" workshop with a rising senior high school student, Xavier. I learned a lot from Xavier as we planned.

"What's a great way for us to engage our workshop participants when they first walk in?" I asked.

"Something that my history teachers often use are political cartoons," Xavier replied. As a science teacher, I wasn't accustomed to incorporating these into my lessons. He emailed me some samples later on that evening. When we implemented them in the workshop, the results were incredible. The students and parents who attended enjoyed parsing the implied and layered messages in the cartoons. In one cartoon titled "The Talk," there were two images of a father conversing with his son about the most critical issue they may encounter as adolescents. In one image, the father and son were Black, in the other, they were white. The white parent was speaking to his son about "the birds and the bees" while the Black parent was speaking to his son about how to interact with the police.

During the workshop Xavier and I used Kahoot!, a game-based learning app that participants could access on cell phones, to highlight a variety of protocols and procedures that one must be aware of when interacting with the police. Examples of multiple questions we asked were: "When pulled over by a cop, a cop may do all of the following except _____." (Answer: Search your car without probable cause.); "If an officer knocks on your door saying that they have an arrest warrant, what do you do?" (Answer: Ask to see the warrant.) We held brief discussions for further clarification after each question.

"THE TALK"

WHiTe AMeRiCANS   AFRiCAN-AMeRiCANS

U.S. JUSTICE SYSTEM

STEVE SACK/CAGLE CARTOONS, INC.

This day of activist education inaugurated the Maplewood South Orange (MAPSO) Freedom School. After this event, we joined the voices of other local activists and organizations, including the Black Parents Workshop, an organization of Black parents in Maplewood/South Orange, to demand the release of the video and audio recordings of what transpired on July 5. We also pressed for the removal of the police chief. Eventually both happened and the tapes confirmed complaints by residents about the incident. They documented unnecessary use of pepper spray against children. Several officers were seen punching and kicking one of the students whom they later arrested. This prompted additional marches, protests, and attendance at town council meetings.

The community organizing with MAPSO Freedom School continued to grow. Consistent with our organizing principle of participatory action, we looked for ways to engage the community and to link community concerns with educators' concerns and school-based issues.

Throughout this period, and as a result of my community activism,

I also became more active in my union. During the fall, I became a fellow in the New Jersey Education Association (NJEA) Apprentice Program. This was a decades-old program that sought to create a pathway for more teachers from disenfranchised demographics, including women and Black educators, to learn more about the organization and ascend into positions of leadership. In addition to getting trained in collective bargaining, I attended conferences dedicated to urban education, "minority" leadership, and educational support professionals.

Being inside of the union had advantages for professional growth and leadership skills. Yet, there were times when I felt unsatisfied with the union's inability to organize communities around deeper issues of social justice that were especially central to communities of color. Although I appreciated the union's solid commitment to addressing teachers' issues, I felt they too often overlooked the communities in which teachers taught. Through organizing with MAPSO Freedom School, I began to see ways to bridge this gap and to support and encourage movements on the ground. By working inside the union and outside in the community, MAPSO helped to strengthen both.

By working inside the union and outside in the community, MAPSO helped to strengthen both.

Later in the school year, MAPSO Freedom School planned an "unconference" modeled after a series of flexible, "open space" events called EdCamps. Often, EdCamps were technology-centered, teacher-led conferences for best practices among mostly white educators. We wanted to merge these participatory conversations about pedagogy and "innovation" with urgent political discourses around race, gender, and poverty. We titled our event "EdCamp Revolution." The NJEA agreed to assist us with funding for refreshments and promotion. The event was a tremendous success as about 100 educators from New York, New Jersey, and elsewhere came to learn and present their expertise under the banner of "revolution."

One session that received significant parent, teacher, and student attendance centered on the unfolding events and activism in the wake of the previous summer's clash with police. Yet, the conversation expanded beyond that incident to contextualize the pattern of Black disenfranchisement inside the community's schools. In particular, parents from the Black Parents Workshop raised civil rights concerns about district tracking, discipline, and equity policies. Although the high school is mixed demographically — approximately 50 percent Black and white — one need only glance through the door of each classroom to gauge the leveling of instruction. If the racial makeup is predominantly white, then you're looking at an advanced-level course offering. On the other hand, if that class is predominantly Black, then you're likely encountering a lower-level course offering. Whether you were observing an AP Calculus course or a basic-level math course appeared more evident by the racial makeup of the class than the notes on the board. Such concerns eventually led to a lawsuit by the Black Parents Workshop.

Some of the most powerful ways that this "inside/outside" strategy has worked for MAPSO Freedom School were reflected in local efforts to connect with national campaigns. In August 2017, we helped organize a summer conference in the wake of the racist mobilization in Charlottesville, Virginia. Clashes with counter-protesters turned deadly and sparked a national debate about the resurgence of white supremacist groups and organizing. Since this event transpired shortly before the beginning of the school year, MAPSO sought to transform this into an organizing opportunity for educators to ensure that the school year began on a critical note. The conference provided resources, strategies, and encouragement for teachers to address these issues as the school year opened.

Similarly, MAPSO Freedom School embraced the call for a Black Lives Matter Week of Action in Schools in February 2018. The planning for BLM Week was extensive. Our calendar of events featured the following themes: The importance of Black educators, Assata Shakur

We wanted to merge conversations about pedagogy and "innovation" with urgent political discourses around race, gender, and poverty.

and the freedom struggle, integration, gender/sexuality, and education policy. Each day of this organizing week had a different emphasis, engaging the community, students, and educators.

In the midst of this activity, the group raised the idea of pushing the NJEA, the NEA's second largest state organization, to formally recognize the Black Lives Matter Week of Action and affirm its demands. We thought this level of institutional backing could extend the critical content of our organizing to educators statewide. Through the coordinated efforts of activists across the state, we succeeded in winning NJEA endorsement of the BLM Week of Action in Schools.

In each of our organizing endeavors, T. J. managed to arrange professional development certificates from the local teacher union so teachers' time spent would be recognized by the local school district. This created a powerful incentive for teachers to attend and strengthened ties with the union.

My organizing with MAPSO Freedom School has been largely the result of committed teacher organizers working for social change in partnership with students and parents. Our collective dedication to realizing this vision has been tireless and joyful. In the process of doing this work, we've found tremendous opportunities to link our efforts with the teacher union at the local, state, and national levels. This collaboration holds important lessons, especially in the face of new impediments to public sector union organizing that arrived to the Supreme Court in 2018. As legal and political efforts to erode union power accelerate, teachers will need to build on examples of teacher unions collaborating with community organizations in order to enhance community trust and advance social change. *

Why Community Schools?

Public schools as greenhouses of democracy

I n response to privatization and other damaging "school reform" initiatives, growing numbers of educators, community activists, and teacher unions have promoted a vision of "community schools" that incorporates key values and components that speak to what all children deserve. Such schools promote democratic practices and engagement in the broader community, the school, classrooms, and the curriculum.

Some schools label themselves as community schools because they provide some "wraparound" social, health, and recreational services. Although such services are important, they alone won't transform a school and are only one part of a successful community school. Such schools must also have engaging curriculum, high-quality teaching, inclusive leadership, community support services, positive discipline practices, and significant parent and community engagement.

These additional characteristics have been described in various ways. The National Education Association speaks of "the six pillars of community schools" — all of which promote equity and democratic practices. The description below is based on the NEA's six pillars.

1. Strong and Culturally Relevant Curriculum. Educators engage students with challenging, culturally relevant curriculum using teaching strategies that provide active, project-based learning with critical reading, writing, speaking, and thinking skills in all subject areas. Students learn to value all people and how to stand up and act to promote democracy and justice. Curriculum includes the students' lives and heritages as well as additional languages, fine arts, physical education, and before- and after-school programs.

2. High-Quality Teaching. Community schools are places of inspiration and freedom. Educators have adequate time to plan collaboratively and analyze student work to improve their teaching skills and pedagogical approaches. Creating student-centered classrooms, teaching problem-solving and critical thinking, and engaging students with rich, challenging curricula are a central schoolwide focus.

3. Inclusive/Shared Leadership. Leadership is a responsibility shared by the school principal with a community school coordinator and the community school committee that includes parents, community partners, school staff, youth, and other stakeholders.

4. Community Support Services. Community schools are hubs of their community. They provide a host of services, often in conjunction with community partners, including meals, healthcare, mental health counseling, and other services before, during, and after school.

5. Positive Discipline Practices. Community schools foster positive school climates and healthy relationships among students and between students and staff. Zero-tolerance policies that promote suspension and expulsion are replaced with restorative practices that build relationships and improve school climate. Discipline issues are dealt with in proactive ways. For example, restorative justice practices may be used to address conflict within a positive school climate that values and respects all members of the school community.

6. Family and Community Engagement. Parents and community members are full partners in community schools. They have substantive roles in school governance and setting school policies. Educators' expertise and experience are valued and respected, but all partners have a seat at the table and a voice in the learning community.

Past practice shows that in order to successfully implement these six pillars, schools need to hire a full-time community school coordinator, conduct regular needs and asset assessments, develop strategic plans, and create school-based problem-solving teams. Schools that do these things in collaboration with community stakeholders have become sustainable and show dramatic improvements. For example, community schools in Austin and Cincinnati have demonstrated success through various measures such as attendance, graduation rates, student engagement, academic achievement, and teacher satisfaction.

When people hear of the six pillars, they often say "that's what all schools should be like." That's true. But to achieve that goal requires resources, enlightened leadership, and the support of broad sections of a community.

It also requires intentional organizing and advocacy on many peoples' parts, particularly educators. Encourage your colleagues to ask your local union and parent and community organizations to help build the kinds of schools that all children deserve. ✳

ADDITIONAL RESOURCES

American Federation of Teachers
Resources on community schools.
aft.org/position/community-schools/resources

Coalition for Community Schools
Sponsors biannual national conferences and has many resources on their website, including *Community Schools Playbook: A Practical Guide to Advancing Community School Strategies* by the Partnership for Future Learning.
communityschools.org

Community Schools: Transforming Struggling Schools into Thriving Schools
Published by the Center for Popular Democracy, the Coalition for Community Schools, and the Southern Education Foundation.
populardemocracy.org

Journey for Justice Alliance
A network of more than two dozen community organizations that organize to improve public schools, stop school privatization, and promote transformative community schools.
j4jalliance.com

The Six Pillars of Community Schools Toolkit: NEA Resource Guide for Educators, Families & Communities
National Education Association
nea.org

How can I decide if a school reform project is worth supporting?

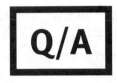

Unfortunately, school reform is a notoriously top-down process and teachers, especially new teachers, don't always have a choice about whether to participate. Counterfeit "stakeholder buy-in" and ceremonial "seats at the table" without real input are all too common.

But most schools do need change, and cynicism is rarely the path to progress. So it helps to have some guidelines for evaluating calls for reform in your school or district.

A useful first step is to speak with colleagues and fellow union members about the history of reform efforts in your school. This can provide important context and background.

Whether or not a particular district or school-based reform project is worth your investment of time and energy usually depends on the answers to a number of related questions. Has the project been created in response to a top-down directive or is it the product of teacher, student, or community initiative? Does the project have the political/administrative support and resources it needs to be successful? Is the timeline realistic? Will the project provide opportunities for participants to build trust across lines of race, gender, and constituency? Is the group leading the reform representative of the whole school community? Is there agreement about how such reform will affect the roles and responsibilities of staff, parents, and students? Will the reform lead to sustainable new arrangements or is it being grafted onto existing structures?

Even where the answers to such questions are mixed, asking them will help gauge the potential of a reform project and prepare teachers for critical participation in the process.

As educator Deborah Meier has written, "A democratic school culture is the best professional development." Ultimately, whether a particular reform effort is worth a teacher's time and effort depends on whether it will contribute to a more just and democratic school culture or simply rearrange the furniture.

"Aren't You on the Parent Listserv?"

Working for equitable family involvement in a dual-immersion elementary school

BY GRACE CORNELL GONZALES

When I first visited what would become my new school in San Francisco, I was excited by the diversity that I saw. There were Latina/o students, African American students, white students, all chattering away in Spanish. I was elated.

Then, in September, after starting my new job as a kindergarten teacher, I went to a PTA meeting. The parents at the meeting were excited to be there and dedicated to making the school a place that would serve their children. They were also almost entirely white, and almost entirely middle- or upper-middle-class native English speakers. On paper, our dual-immersion bilingual school was about 50 percent Latina/o and 20 percent African American. Yet, in that first PTA meeting, with about 40 people in attendance, I saw only a handful of Latina/o parents. There were no African American families present. Later in the year, one African American family did frequently attend, but the number of Latina/o parents who came and used the interpretation services quickly dropped to zero. In addition, most of the parents involved came from the Spanish immersion track. The general education track, composed largely of students of color, was essentially unrepresented.

As I watched the PTA set fundraising goals, choose art enrichment programs, fund teaching positions, allocate money for books, determine what technology would be purchased, and select what types of paraprofessionals to hire, I became more and more concerned about whose voices were being heard and whose children were being advocated for.

I quickly began to see these inequities play out in my own classroom. The three mothers who signed up to be room parents were middle-class professionals, all white native English speakers. They all knew each other because their children had gone to the same bilingual preschool. The majority of families at Back to School Night were also white and English speaking. In the first two weeks, emails were sent, Google Docs created, and listservs were joined, all in English. One half of the classroom parent community got to work, humming right along on rails that missed the other half by miles.

I became more and more concerned about whose voices were being heard and whose children were being advocated for.

I was also concerned about this pattern for another reason: As teachers we see the direct impact of parent involvement on our students — families who feel comfortable with and included in the school community can advocate for their children's needs, check in about their progress, get tips on how to help them at home, and stay informed about programs and opportunities that will be beneficial to their family. Attendance goes up and children benefit from seeing their parents as involved in their school community. When parents and teachers talk, children's behavior and motivation improves as they begin to understand the ways their home and school worlds are connected. I was going to have to do something quickly or risk losing those benefits for many of my students, and instead see my classroom duplicate the same sort of inequitable parent involvement that I saw at that first PTA meeting. The story of how I attempted to shift those dynamics is one of tiny victories, but it also shows how what we do in our own classrooms to address equity in parent participation can ripple out to affect the school as a whole.

Overcoming Communication Barriers

From the first week, when emails began to fly around in English asking parents to volunteer for important school roles, it became clear that communication was the key. Only about half of my families regularly used email and at least one family did not have an email address at all, yet nearly all parent communication was happening via electronic means.

I asked the advice of other teachers and talked to my room parents, and we started to negotiate some guidelines:

All communication must be bilingual, and Spanish always goes first. This applied to emails, letters home, handouts, homework packets, and sign-up sheets. Putting Spanish first was of symbolic as well as practical significance — it served to remind us all that we are committed to a bilingual environment, and that means that native English speakers have to get used to not having their language always come first. Also, it helped to elevate the status of Spanish in our school community, which is essential because children are sensitive to issues of language and power and will sometimes be resistant to learning and speaking languages that they perceive to be low status.

Important communication cannot just be through email. As convenient as email may be, important communication must also go home in paper form in the weekly homework folders. This included invitations to classroom events, field trip notifications, notices about school or class policies, and invitations to volunteer. I also usually printed these out and taped them to the classroom door.

Sign-up opportunities have to be fair. This is especially important because there are usually limitations on how many parents can go on the bus or enter a field trip location for free. I had to think a bit about the best way to give parents equal chances to sign up for those spots. I settled on this routine: I would create a paper sign-up sheet and hang it on the door of the classroom. The sign-up sheet would have spots for parents who needed to ride on the school bus and spots for parents who volunteered to drive and pay for themselves. I also approached families I thought might not see the sign-up sheet on the door (because they didn't pick up their kids in the afternoon) and who I knew didn't use email. If they wanted to go, I signed them up on the sheet myself. I also told parents that the spots that guaranteed free transport and entrance were reserved for families who needed them.

Teacher-to-parent communication needs to fit the family. For some families, email really did work best. For others, the best way to get a hold of them was a call home. For still more parents, text messages were the most effective. By creating a profile in my mind of how to communicate best with each family, I was able to reach out in appropriate ways and ultimately get more families involved.

Determine which families require more concerted effort. Over the course of the year, I identified a couple of families who were trickier to loop into classroom communication in traditional ways, either because of work schedules or because home language literacy levels made reading print notices a challenge. So I tried to catch up with these families frequently in person — snagging them at any opportunity to just check in about how things were going, to personally invite them to important events, and to help, if necessary, with filling out forms and permission slips.

These strategies paid off in visible ways. Some of my native Spanish-speaking parents were the most involved, chaperoning all of the field trips and consistently coming to classroom events like writers' celebrations, birthdays, and family reading parties. This was also the case for my three African American families. In fact, one of those families never missed a classroom event all year, and four generations showed up for our promotion ceremony.

However, when it came to the room parents, the parents who participated in the PTA or SSC, and the parents who came in weekly to volunteer in class, the majority were still from the same affluent group who dominated the schoolwide parent committees. Although that represented significant missed opportunities, it did fuel some interesting interactions that helped begin to shift the tone of parent dialogue.

Building Awareness

Throughout the year, I tried to be as explicit as possible about the reasons why I communicated with parents the way I did. As I worked through issues of equitable parent participation myself, I tried whenever possible to include parents in those conversations, even when I myself was not sure I was doing the right thing.

Near the end of the year, something interesting started happening. The parents in my class who were most explicitly involved in the operations of the school — the ones who were room parents, PTA members, and committee leads — started to bring up issues of equity themselves.

One mom who was a fluent Spanish speaker approached me, wondering how she could help get more Spanish-speaking parents in to volunteer in the classroom. One of my room parents asked about how I thought she could best utilize phone trees and texting to reach the parents who were hard to get by email. Several parents who were active in the PTA wanted to talk about recruitment and retention of Latina/o families in the immersion program.

These conversations extended out into interactions with other parents as well. Parents who hadn't thought twice about communicating entirely through English emails at the beginning of the year began advocating for the diverse communication needs of the families in our class.

The conversations that we had in my classroom were a step, albeit a small one, toward opening up wider dialogues about these issues at the school level.

Missed Opportunities, New Beginnings

Looking back on the year, I wanted to celebrate the victories without losing sight of the things that I would do differently in the future.

But, most importantly, I was acutely aware that the majority of those vital conversations I had with parents about equity happened with my room parents and a few other regular classroom volunteers, most of whom were from white middle-class families. Here I realized I was swayed by my own issues. As a white teacher, I felt more comfortable bringing up equity issues with the more privileged parents, particularly white parents, and those parents felt more comfortable bringing them up with me. If real changes were going to take place, however, everyone would need to be involved in the conversation.

Instead of waiting for parents to volunteer, I approached a couple of Spanish-speaking parents individually before Back to School Night and asked if they would be room parents.

Armed with the knowledge of what had gone well and what had gone wrong during that first school year, I entered the next school year with a different set of priorities. My first priority was to find room parents who were native Spanish speakers. My second priority was to begin to have the conversations that I had avoided the previous year.

Instead of waiting for parents to volunteer for the room parent slots, I approached a couple of Spanish-speaking parents individually before Back to School Night and asked if they would be room parents. One accepted; the other politely declined and offered to volunteer in another way. At Back to School Night, I asked for volunteers and got one native Spanish speaker and one English-speaking parent. Thus, I had my team of three: one mother from Argentina and one from Mexico, both bilingual native Spanish speakers, and one white parent who spoke some Spanish.

I also sent around a list asking parents to specify how they wanted to be contacted — phone, text, or email. Then, my room parents and I set up contact lists and divided them up. One room mother would send bilingual emails, one would text, and the third would call the families who requested to be contacted by phone, all of whom happened to be Spanish speaking.

Partnering with bilingual parents is even more crucial for teachers who are not bilingual themselves but work in communities where many families speak other languages.

Mercedes, my room parent from Mexico, was an extraordinary resource. Because she was willing to call the Spanish-speaking families to ask for volunteers, I ended up with many Spanish-speaking volunteers doing classroom work — three who read with children during reading workshop and two who helped out during art class. Thus, my students had Spanish language models from their community during the school day, and the Latina/o parents in my classroom got to know my room parents and each other through phone calls and working alongside each other in the classroom.

This system — that of divvying up the task of contacting families among my room parents — led not only to increased involvement but also to a model of family engagement that is more sustainable for me as a teacher. Partnering with bilingual room parents is even more crucial for teachers who are not bilingual themselves but work in communities where many families speak other languages.

Ripples of Change

Although we have a long way to go, these conversations with parents across our school community seem to be bearing some fruit. At the end of the first year, a parent from my classroom volunteered to head a committee focused on recruiting and maintaining Latina/o families at our school. Another made a presentation in Spanish at our new kindergarten family orientation appealing to Spanish-speaking families to volunteer in classrooms and join the PTA.

Parents started talking about holding some PTA meetings in Spanish with English translation, and about changing the structure of the PTA meetings to allow for small-group breakout sessions to foster more participation.

There is still a lot to be done, both in my classroom and at the school level, to rectify exclusive patterns of parent involvement. It's not easy, but I think that substantive change is possible if we begin to talk about these issues instead of leaving them unexplored. If we want equitable schools, we need to be as intentional about how we involve parents as we are about how we educate their children. ✳

Blood on the Tracks

*Why are there so few Black students
in our science classes?*

BY AMY LINDAHL

O ne day, while table groups read through a lab activity, Maya, my lab assistant, came over to me with papers in her hands. "Ms. Lindahl, I found these graphs on your desk. What are they?"

"Those are graphs showing who takes science classes here, broken down by race. Ms. Pilgrim, Mr. Medley, and I are going to a conference to talk about it as a problem we are trying to solve. Some students are going to present, too."

"I'm shocked. I had no idea that our classes were so segregated; I mean, I did, but I just didn't think about it. It's crazy."

Maya, who is South Asian American, was looking at a demographic graph from spring semester 2011, the year I started teaching at Grant High School in Portland, Oregon. In Biology, a class taken by all 9th graders, classes averaged 65 percent white, 15 percent African American, 7 percent multiracial, 7 percent Latina/o, 5 percent Asian, and less than 1 percent Native American and Pacific Islander students, a close match to our overall school demographics. But other classes, especially when comparing African American and white students, were wildly different. Most significantly, Chemistry, which was a prerequisite for upper-level science classes, including Advanced Placement (AP) classes, was 78 percent white and only 7 percent African American. (It was 6 percent Latina/o and 3 percent Asian.) Foundations of Physics and Chemistry, a survey course that was not accepted as a prerequisite for advanced upper-level science classes, was 49 percent white and 37 percent African

American. What was going on here? This is the question my science teaching colleagues and I are trying to figure out.

I could have shown Maya data from the entire country as well. For 2009, white high school students earned an average of 2.0 high school science credits; African American students earned an average of 1.6 credits.

And these patterns continue beyond high school. In 2009, African Americans were 12 percent of the U.S. population, yet Black students earned only 7 percent of all bachelor's degrees in science, technology, engineering, and math (STEM) fields. In that same year, African Americans earned 4 percent of all STEM master's degrees, and 2 percent of STEM PhDs. The problems we observed at Grant were clearly part of a much bigger national story.

Maya was right to be both intrigued and appalled. Yet it was her shock about the racial disparities in our science classes that has stayed with me. How could she, and so much of our school community, be immersed in something so apparent and yet be surprised to see the data? As a white teacher, I knew this was something that I and we needed to work on. This blindness lies at the core of why societal inequities are so persistent and seemingly unchangeable. When we grow up surrounded by a particular cultural landscape, we rarely question its origins or the right for it to exist.

"Don't You Want to Be an Athlete?"

At the conference I mentioned to Maya, we started our presentation with a video of Neil deGrasse Tyson, director of the Hayden Planetarium in New York City and host of *Cosmos*, talking about his experience as an African American boy obsessed with becoming an astrophysicist.

Viewers hear an audience member ask deGrasse Tyson why there are so few prominent female scientists. He responds:

> I have never been female. But I have been Black my whole life. And so let me perhaps offer some insight from that perspective. . . .
>
> I've known that I wanted to do astrophysics since I was 9 years old. . . . Any time I expressed this interest teachers would say, "Don't you want to be an athlete?" I looked to become something that was outside the paradigms of expectation of the people in power.
>
> Now here I am, one of the most visible scientists in the

land, and I look behind me and say, "Where are the others who might have been this?" And they're not there. And I wonder . . . what is the blood on the tracks that I happened to survive that others did not?

DeGrasse Tyson was able, for whatever reason, to persist despite teacher discouragement and societal unease. But how many of my own students would not recover when they faced these same forces? The expectations about who becomes a scientist are so overwhelming and widespread, we shouldn't be surprised when our own classrooms perpetuate crimes of assumption and exclusion. We need to acknowledge how these pressures have impacted our classrooms. In particular, we need to encourage and support students whose ambitions and interests are at odds with societal comfort and expectation.

Enrollment Disparities

When I started working at Grant, I was struck by the enrollment disparities in my upper-level classes. Although my AP Biology classes were 69 percent white students and 9 percent Black students, my Ecology class was 54 percent white students and 38 percent Black students. Ecology, as I knew from my time in research, should be a challenging course, requiring complex experimental design and analysis, along with the ability to draw ideas from all fields of biology. However, I saw a distressing trend: This class was viewed as the easy option for juniors and seniors needing a science credit. I raised concerns about this with other members of the science department. They were well aware of the patterns, but were convinced they were unavoidable. They explained to me that our juniors and seniors expected to have a course menu of "easy" and "hard" options, and parents demanded this as well. "Student choice" was named repeatedly as the driving force behind our course offerings.

But when adolescents are allowed to enroll in classes based entirely on their level of comfort or degree of fear, unsurprising patterns emerge. White students with college-educated parents of higher socioeconomic status often "choose" the most demanding classes. Students who vary from this demographic often fear these classes and sign up for lower-track options. We say this is student choice, but it is much more about students repeating the patterns of our broader society. When we cite student choice, we remove adult culpability and responsibility when classes enroll along racial lines. When our classrooms become segregated environments, we send dangerous messages to students about who is welcome and who is capable of succeeding in advanced classes.

I knew there were better options. I told my department that science classes at my previous school were untracked, although this was because we were so small that we couldn't staff many science classes. Despite this, I had developed an Advanced Biology class that worked for nearly all my students. I saw huge benefits to all students having similar science experiences as they progressed through high school, especially because I saw students who blossomed after a year or two of struggling in science. Most importantly, I argued, was the moral imperative to keep opportunities open to as many students as possible. Is it really the job of a high school teacher to decide which of our students have a future in science? We began a series of regular discussions about the broader patterns in science course enrollment at Grant.

When our classrooms become segregated environments, we send dangerous messages to students about who is welcome and who is capable of succeeding in advanced classes.

As these discussions about access and equity progressed, more teachers became open to reforming our course offerings. Two other members of our department and I wrote a successful grant for laptops in our science classrooms that included a commitment to demonstrate increased enrollment of under-represented racial groups in advanced science classes.

With the approval of our principal, we ended AP Biology and replaced it with an Advanced Biology class that earns community college credit. And we eliminated the tracked chemistry classes: Instead of two classes — high-tracked Chemistry and low-tracked Foundations of Physics and Chemistry — now all sophomores take Chemistry. Two years into our efforts, we added college-credit Anatomy and Physiology, a course that we hoped would draw a wide swath of the school interested in careers in medicine.

Some of our efforts have paid off: Upper-level courses like Advanced Biology and Anatomy and Physiology approach overall school enrollment by race. However, enrollment disparities in other advanced classes, including AP Chemistry, Physics, and AP Physics, persist. African American students enrolled in our newly untracked Chemistry class have had higher failure rates than their white peers.

African American Students Speak Up

We realized our reform efforts required more information than enrollment statistics could provide. Several science teachers volunteered to survey African American students about their experiences in science classes. We needed to find out when these students felt supported and encouraged, but also when they felt excluded, hurt, or underestimated.

We started with informal surveys after class. Keri Pilgrim, an African American teacher, reported that Black students told her they felt isolated and that their voices or communication styles were ignored. Kelly Allen, a white teacher, reported that students feared some advanced classes because of the workload and expressed a desire to be in classes with other African American students. These students particularly felt isolated and intimidated in the new, untracked sophomore Chemistry classes.

We decided to invite African American students from each grade level to a lunch to discuss their experiences in more detail. Three of us attended a meeting of the Black Student Union (BSU) and explained our project. Keri talked to the BSU staff and student leaders, and several students promised to attend. The rest of us approached African American students in our classes. We hoped that personal and printed invitations, along with the promise of a catered lunch and our partnership with the BSU, would convince students to take a chance and meet with us. Despite our recruitment efforts, only seven students showed up to our lunch meeting. Although our turnout was a small percentage of invitees, we were glad to see that we had a good balance of male and female students, and representatives from all grade levels.

We asked two BSU student leaders to lead the discussion; we thought this would help the participants feel more comfortable about speaking up. The facilitators started things off by asking why some of the students decided to enroll in advanced science classes like Physics or Advanced Biology.

James answered first, his voice clear and confident: "I'm going to study engineering in college. I need to take advanced classes in high school so I'm ready for college classes, when I'm more on my own."

Shawn said: "I want to go into the medical field. . . . I think taking Anatomy will help me get into college and do better later on. Plus a friend told me the class wasn't too hard, and that Ms. Pilgrim would help me."

Michelle added: "My freshman Biology class was good. . . . My teacher was nice. It was a hands-on class and it was fun. . . . I had a good experience, so I wanted to try more science."

Then the facilitators asked about negative experiences.

Lia spoke quickly and intensely: "It was all group work in Chemistry and I didn't like that. I'd say something and then a white student in my group would repeat it but with advanced vocabulary, and everyone praised them. I said the same thing! But everyone ignored me when I said it."

"Chemistry was bad," Monique agreed. "The other students in my group, they didn't include me. I would ask a question and it was like I hadn't said anything. Then I would ask the teacher and he would tell me to just go ask my team. I didn't feel like I could get help from anybody. I felt isolated. I was isolated. Then I shut down. And the worst part is I had been excited about this class when it started."

Shawn nodded. "When you have someone else in the room who looks like you, it's almost like you have double the confidence. But when you are the only one, it's really hard."

Jacqui pointed out a pattern she saw. "In some groups, we like to work together, but sometimes teachers don't like to put us together because of fear of segregation. It's like, 'Hello, we can see that you're never letting the two Black kids in class sit together.'"

Facilitators moved toward wrapping up the discussion by asking students what needed to change in our science classes.

Some classes were essentially "busy work and packets," Jacqui said. "It should be more hands-on." She added: "Chemistry needs tutoring, during and after class. That would have helped so much."

Shawn said: "I would have liked more than just me in there. You know, other Black students to work with. Maybe they could schedule us so we're in the same class together."

Deanna told the group: "I need one-on-one time with my teacher. I need to know my teacher."

During the discussion, students' faces lit up when they heard their own experiences echoed by one another. The conversation moved quickly, and the fear of talking freely in front of adults quickly fell away. At the end, we thanked the students for their work and time and asked if they would want to come back together before school was over. We hoped to start a science club for African American students the next year and wanted to talk to them about how it might work. They were eager to meet again and wanted to keep the conversation going.

What I realized that day, and continue to realize, is that my African American students need a place to talk about the frustrations and disappointments they've experienced in their classes. They need to see that their feelings of isolation are part of broader patterns of discrimination and stereotyping. As teachers hearing these stories, we must listen, willing to be deeply critical of our own practices. When students trust us with their stories, we must move toward action. Our classes need to welcome all students, and then we need to imagine what it feels like to be in our classes. I began to look at my own classroom with new eyes. What am I doing to make student voices equally shared and appreciated? How do I make group work a positive experience? Do I frame content in ways that give an entry point for all of my students? What can I do to narrow the confidence gap between those students who expect to excel and those who expect to struggle?

What am I doing to make student voices equally shared and appreciated?

Changing Curriculum, Changing Pedagogy

It was an important first step to untrack Chemistry classes, but our conversations made it clear that having all students take the same Chemistry class wasn't enough. We needed to change what we were teaching and how we were teaching to make it accessible and supportive for all our students.

We are still struggling to figure out new course designs. I am pushing for a redesign centered on themed units. High schools in California and New York have been experimenting with this model. At these schools, students explore questions about how molecules produce a scent and how fireworks work. Based on labs I've done with students, I know that experiments that monitor water, air, and soil quality can be compelling, ground science concepts in students' experiences, and link to social justice discussions.

Rooting science in student lives also applies to improving our Biology curriculum. I started a recent Advanced Biology class by asking student groups to discuss and record their answers to the question "What have you heard about genetically modified organisms?" I then asked each table to share out something from their conversations. Students who rarely contribute during a more traditional prompt spoke up.

Bringing controversies and real-life problems into our classrooms is one of the most powerful tools we have when designing inclusive courses.

When Keri developed Anatomy and Physiology, she sought out hands-on experiences for a class that is traditionally reliant on rote memorization. She uses the "Anatomy in Clay" curriculum, in which students construct muscles out of clay and apply them to skeletons. She also has students do three-dimensional modeling of proteins to better understand why human hair varies in texture.

As a department, we have looked at our junior- and senior-level classes and asked ourselves: Does this class put students in the role of scientist as often as possible? Is the class structured in ways that promote scientific discussion and risk-taking? Are students with multiple skill sets and backgrounds going to find avenues toward success?

Bringing controversies and real-life problems into our classrooms is one of the most powerful tools we have when designing inclusive courses.

This work is complex and time-consuming. Changes in course offerings and elimination of low-track offerings can decrease racial segregation. But ultimately, achieving equity demands extensive experimentation with pedagogical strategies and curriculum.

Our work is unfinished. But we all must face, head-on and with humility, the many ways racial inequities persist in our schools. And then we must counter these forces with everything we've got. Our students deserve nothing less. ✳

Author's note: This article, originally published in 2015, incorporated deGrasse Tyson's thoughts on why people of color are under-represented in scientific fields. In 2018, multiple sexual misconduct stories about deGrasse Tyson came to light. At least one accuser, a woman of color, stated that his actions drove her away from her scientific career goals. These accusations highlight a deep hypocrisy between deGrasse Tyson's words and actions: He used his own power in ways that hurt female scientists and students. Although the quote used in this article still holds truth and provides an important lens for teachers, deGrasse Tyson's damaging actions and tone-deaf apology serve as a reminder: We are often blind to how our own behaviors are part of a larger problem. Dismantling the systems of oppression requires that we each put our own actions and assumptions under the microscope, keeping our minds, hearts, and ears open to the experiences and needs of others.

Little Kids, Big Ideas

Teaching social issues and global conflicts with young children

BY THE EDITORS OF RETHINKING SCHOOLS

Recently, a Rethinking Schools editor was a chaperone on a field trip when he overheard a 2nd-grade student talking about how he wanted to "nuke the world."

Taken aback, he asked the child what he meant.

"Everything is just so bad. We should just nuke the world and start over."

When pressed further, the student mentioned Donald Trump and Kim Jong-un. The editor was left wondering how an 8-year-old even knew the name of the leader of North Korea. And he not only knew the names of these world leaders, but also knew enough about the current climate to feel hopeless, and to channel that hopelessness into a broad and dramatic wish for destruction.

We live in an increasingly turbulent time, and it can feel intimidating or inappropriate to discuss the world's crises with young children. How can you explain climate change, tensions with North Korea, or the war in Syria to an 8-year-old? After all, most adults don't even fully understand many of the complex issues affecting our world. Is it responsible to even try?

Yet this story about the 8-year-old who wanted to "nuke the world" reminds us that we aren't protecting children by not engaging them in conversation around these topics. If done in a developmentally appropriate manner, even the youngest children deserve to learn about and discuss such questions.

Young children live in the world, just like we do. They listen to snippets of news reports on the radio; they catch clips of news broadcasts on the television; they hear things from their siblings, parents, and classmates. They watch movies and play video games that encode social tensions and global conflicts. And most importantly, in this time of intense political upheaval, they feel the stress and anger that adults around them are feeling. For many children, poverty, racism, and anti-immigrant hysteria have a daily impact on their lives. When we choose not to deal with these issues explicitly and sensitively, we effectively leave children alone with their misunderstandings and fears.

So what is the alternative? We need to listen to children's questions and respect them, even if our responses are imperfect. Can a kindergartener fully grasp the science behind climate change? No, but they can understand in broad strokes that human action — our use of cars and planes and big machines — is causing our world to heat up and is threatening the homes and well-being of animals, plants, and people. Can a 3rd grader fully comprehend the politics behind calls for a border wall and mass deportations, and the groundswell of anti-immigrant sentiment backing them? Eight-year-olds won't be able to draw the same historical parallels that high schoolers or adults might, but they can understand how fear and racism can cause people to lash out at those who are different from them — and to selfishly guard what they think of as their own.

Sometimes we may not feel like we understand something well enough to explain it to our students. What if our students ask questions that we ourselves don't know the answers to? What if we stumble when we try to explain the tangled web of conflict that has resulted in the flood of refugees in unfamiliar parts of the world? We have to do our research and provide students with the most accurate explanations possible, but we shouldn't be afraid to explore these topics ourselves and invite our students to explore with us. We can recognize imperfect and incomplete explanations and understandings as a necessary part of teaching and learning.

Of course we can and should use discretion about the resources we show to children; certain pictures, videos, and stories can clearly be too graphic and too disturbing. It's up to teachers to know their students and make judgments about how much is too much. It's also up to teachers to inform and involve parents in this process, without allowing individual parents to dictate what should be taught in school based on personal biases or prejudices. This is a delicate balance. Teachers have used homework assignments in which students ask parents what they think of some of these issues as a way to inform and connect with parents about the curriculum and to encourage multiple perspectives on such topics. The more we as teachers build strong ties to our families and communities — and reach out to and collaborate with colleagues — the more able we are to provide our students with a safe, respectful environment to tackle these challenging subjects. Children also need to learn how to discuss, question, respect, and at times challenge differing points of view.

Our job also goes beyond providing summary explanations to students. Simply telling children "how things are" can lean toward indoctrination, imposing on them our worked-out conclusions about the world. Young children learn best by acting out the world around them, by putting themselves in other people's shoes. We see this, for example, when teachers give students the chance to understand the roots of the refugee crisis through personal stories of unfairness and hardship. We also see it when students take on roles and present a wide variety of perspectives on climate change. As teachers, we choose whose voices we privilege, whose stories we put center stage. We can repeat the narratives of the powerful, or we can give students the chance to see the world through the eyes of the people who are most vulnerable, and those who are trying to work for justice.

We can recognize imperfect and incomplete explanations and understandings as a necessary part of teaching and learning.

Students deserve the opportunity to try to look at the world through the eyes of a refugee, at the border wall through the eyes of an undocumented child, at climate change through the eyes of a person in the Marshall Islands watching their home disappear — and also from the perspective of those who spend their lives advocating for their communities and trying to make things better. Children need — and deserve — both truth and hope.

This kind of teaching, where children explore the world through multiple eyes, is developmentally appropriate and engaging. It also lays the foundation for a pattern of inquiry that we hope they will continue to return to throughout their lives. When confronted with a complex and contentious issue, we hope students will ask: Whose story is not being told? What does this look like from a different perspective? What is fair? How can everyone's needs be met? What can I do?

When we teach in this way, we cultivate empathy, especially for those who are different from us. To paraphrase writer Alfie Kohn, educators should help children locate themselves in widening circles of empathy that extend beyond self, beyond country, to all humanity. Today that is more important than ever. In the time of Trump, we are told that America should come first, implying that the lives of U.S. citizens are more valuable than the lives of others. We are told that we should want to build walls and enforce immigration bans to block off people who are not like us. And if we lose sight of empathy, we can end up feeling just like the 2nd grader who wants to "nuke the world" — that there is no hope for humans, that

We owe it to our students, perhaps especially the youngest among them, to resurrect the culture of empathy.

there is no way back from this dark place we find ourselves in. We owe it to our students, perhaps especially the youngest among them, to resurrect the culture of empathy. We do this by listening to their concerns, trying our best to respond to their questions with respect and compassion, and teaching them to push for a world where everyone's life is valued. ✱

ADDITIONAL RESOURCES

Rethinking Early Childhood Education
Edited by Ann Pelo
rethinkingschools.org/books/title/rethinking-early-childhood-education

Rethinking Elementary Education
Edited by Elizabeth Barbian, Linda Christensen, Mark Hansen, Bob Peterson, and Dyan Watson
rethinkingschools.org/books/title/rethinking-elementary-education

Teaching Big Ideas with Little Kids
Rethinking Schools Vol. 31, No. 4 (Summer 2017)
rethinkingschools.org/issues/volume-31-no-4-summer-2017
- "The (Young) People's Climate Conference: Teaching global warming to 3rd graders"
  By Rowan Shafer
- "Love for Syria: Tackling world crises with small children"
  By Cami Touloukian

Action Education

Education organizers worth connecting with

Years of top-down corporate school reform, massive over-testing, and accelerating privatization have sparked an unprecedented upsurge in organizing by educators, parents, students, and community members that continues to grow. Activists have formed new organizations, committees, networks, and coalitions not only to defend public education from repeated rounds of privatization and austerity, but also to address a host of important social issues that directly affect students, families, and educators.

These issues include Black Lives Matter, gun violence, immigrant rights, ethnic studies, LGBTQ+ rights, the fight for $15, climate justice, and the defense and transformation of public schools.

The following is a partial listing of educator and education-related groups. In addition to organizing and activism, many of these groups produce valuable curriculum resources for social justice teaching.

Check out our website rethinkingschools.org/NTB for updated listings or to suggest additional groups to be listed.

Educator Groups

Association of Raza Educators (ARE)

The Association of Raza Educators is a group of public and charter school educators, university professors, students, and community allies committed to using education as a tool for the liberation of our community. ARE holds conferences and have conducted successful campaigns for ethnic studies and in defense of undocumented people. razaeducators.org

Badass Teachers Association (BATs)
A network of more than 65,000 teachers and education activists throughout the United States who fight for communities to have strong, sustainable, and well-funded public schools. badassteacher.org

Critical Educators Collective (CEC) – Portland, Oregon
The Critical Educators Collective is committed to teaching for social justice and advocating for social justice throughout our education system. CEC believes that for a more democratic, just, and equitable education system, we must critically examine and refine our teaching praxis within the classroom as well as organize in our wider communities. It holds accessible and regular meetings and workshops, and also uses a variety of online resources to share and collaborate. facebook.com/criticaleducatorscollective

Defending the Early Years (DEY)
Defending the Early Years is a nonprofit organization working for a just, equitable, and quality early childhood education for every young child. DEY publishes reports, makes mini-documentaries, issues position statements, advocates on policy, and has an active website full of resources, blogs, and activist steps for early childhood educators. deyproject.org

Educators for Social Justice (ESJ) – St. Louis
ESJ is a grassroots, teacher-led professional development group that believes educators are public intellectuals. Its mission is to support socially just, equitable, and sustainable practices in schools and communities. ESJ sponsors a teacher grant, a racial equity curriculum partnership, teach-ins, an annual Educating for Change Curriculum Conference, and a social justice podcast for teachers across the life span. educatorsforsocialjustice.org

EduColor
EduColor is an activist collective founded by people of color, with people of color, for people of color that strives to build a new, better,

more effective way of reaching equity and justice in public education.
educolor.org

Morningside Center for Teaching Social Responsibility
Morningside Center works hand in hand with educators to build
students' social and emotional skills, strengthen the classroom and school
community, and increase racial equity through restorative practices and
brave conversations on race. It provides training and coaching to help
educators teach their research-based curricula and plan for schoolwide
change.
morningsidecenter.org

New York Collective of Radical Educators (NYCoRE)
NYCoRE is a group of current and former public school educators and
their allies committed to fighting for social justice in our school system
and society at large, by organizing and mobilizing teachers, developing
curriculum, and working with community, parent, and student
organizations. The struggle for justice does not end when the school
bell rings.
nycore.org

Northwest Teaching for Social Justice Conference
Launched in 2007, the Northwest Teaching for Social Justice
Conference is an annual gathering that rotates between Portland and
Seattle. The conference, held in October, is sponsored by local unions,
social justice education organizations, and *Rethinking Schools* magazine,
and features more than 75 teacher- and activist-led workshops that
demonstrate exemplary classroom practice, and explore critical social
and educational issues.
nwtsj.org

Rethinking Schools
Rethinking Schools, started in Milwaukee in 1986, is a nonprofit
publisher and advocacy organization dedicated to sustaining and
strengthening public education through social justice teaching and
education activism. Its magazine, books, and other resources promote
equity and racial justice in the classroom. Rethinking Schools
encourages grassroots efforts in our schools and communities to
enhance the learning and well-being of our children and to build broad
democratic movements for social and environmental justice. Please buy

our books and subscribe to the magazine in order to help sustain the education justice movement.
rethinkingschools.org

Teacher Action Group (TAG) Philadelphia
TAG Philadelphia works to strengthen the influence of educators within schools and over policy decisions. Partnering with parent, student, and community groups, TAG is committed to fostering positive school transformation, environments where students and teachers can thrive, and community ownership and influence within education. The majority of TAG members are full-time public, charter, and independent school teachers, but also include nurses, counselors, after-school educators, and allies of public education.
tagphilly.org

Teachers 4 Social Justice (T4SJ) Bay Area
A grassroots teacher support and development organization in the San Francisco Bay Area, the T4SJ mission is to provide opportunities for self-transformation, community building, and leadership to educators in order to effect meaningful change in the classroom, school, community, and society. They conduct many events, including study groups and book clubs, and sponsor their annual Teaching for Social Justice conference.
t4sj.org

Teachers for Social Justice (TSJ) Chicago
TSJ is a 20-year-old organization of teachers and other education workers/organizers in the Chicago area. TSJ supports teachers in classrooms preparing young people to understand/change the world, while collaborating with others in education justice movements fighting education privatization, school closings, and charter proliferation. TSJ stands for public education, justice for excluded and marginalized communities, and for a new, reimagined Chicago/world.
teachersforjustice.org

Teacher Activist Groups
A coalition of 10 social justice teacher groups that holds conferences and organizes for educational justice in major cities.
t4sj.org/about/gallery/t-a-g-teacher-activist-groups

Teaching for Change
Teaching for Change provides teachers and parents with the tools
to create schools where students learn to read, write, and change the
world. It co-coordinates the Zinn Education Project with Rethinking
Schools.
teachingforchange.org

Teaching Tolerance
Teaching Tolerance provides free resources to educators — teachers,
administrators, counselors, and other practitioners — who work
with K–12 students. Educators use these materials to supplement
their curriculum, to inform their practices, and to create civil school
communities where children are respected, valued, and welcomed
participants. Teaching Tolerance's mission is to help teachers and
schools educate children and youth to be active participants in a diverse
democracy.
splcenter.org/teaching-tolerance

Teaching While Muslim
Teaching While Muslim describes itself as "Muslim American teachers
thinking aloud about our experiences, our students, and the need for
a more socially just education system." Their website shares stories of
teachers, students, and families dealing with issues of representation,
cultural identity, and Islamophobia. TWM offers a variety of
workshops and training sessions, including "Supporting Refugee
Students" and "Public School Outreach to Muslim Communities."
teachingwhilemuslim.org

Zinn Education Project (ZEP)
The Zinn Education Project promotes teaching of people's history
in classrooms across the country. Founded in 2008 by Teaching for
Change and Rethinking Schools, ZEP offers workshops for educators
and community groups as well as free, downloadable lessons and
articles. Based on the approach to history highlighted in Howard Zinn's
best-selling book *A People's History of the United States*, ZEP's teaching
materials and workshops emphasize the role of working people, women,
people of color, and organized social movements in shaping history.
zinnedproject.org

Parent/Community Groups

The Alliance to Reclaim Our Schools (AROS)
An alliance of parent, youth, community, and labor organizations that represent more than 7 million people. AROS organizes nationwide days of action to reclaim the promise of public education as our nation's gateway to a strong democracy and racial and economic justice. reclaimourschools.org

Education for Liberation Network
National coalition of teachers, community activists, researchers, youth, and parents who believe a good education should teach people — particularly low-income youth and youth of color — how to understand and challenge the injustices their communities face. Education for Liberation Network organizes a "Free Minds, Free People" conference and, with Rethinking Schools, publishes *Planning to Change the World: A Plan Book for Social Justice Teachers*. edliberation.org

Journey for Justice (J4J)
An alliance of grassroots community, youth, and parent-led organizations in 21 cities across the country pushing back on school closings and racism in education, and demanding community-driven alternatives to the privatization of public school systems. j4jalliance.com

MAPSO Freedom School
MAPSO was formed by activist educators in Maplewood/South Orange, New Jersey, who were inspired by the legacy of Freedom Schools of the Civil Rights Movement. It seeks to build on the original concept while understanding that the freedom struggle has evolved with new challenges to overcome. facebook.com/MAPSOFREEDOMSCHOOL

The Network for Public Education (NPE)
An advocacy group whose mission is to preserve, promote, improve, and strengthen public schools. Check out their "NPE Toolkit: School Privatization Explained." networkforpubliceducation.org

New York Coalition for Educational Justice (CEJ)
A parent-led movement for educational equity and excellence in New York City's public schools. CEJ has successfully mobilized citywide for culturally responsive curriculum and pedagogy initiatives and to ensure that every child in NYC receives a high quality and well-rounded education.
nyccej.org

Opportunity to Learn Network
A national network working to secure a high-quality public education for all students.
schottfoundation.org/our-work/otl-network

Parents Across America
A grassroots organization that connects parents from around the United States to strengthen and support public schools.
parentsacrossamerica.org

Parents for Public Schools
A nonprofit organization of parent leaders who work to improve public schools by educating, engaging, and mobilizing parents across the country.
parents4publicschools.org

Contributors

Hiwot Adilow is an Ethiopian American poet from Philadelphia. She received her BA from the University of Wisconsin–Madison, where she was a First Wave Urban Arts Scholar. Hiwot is one of the 2018 recipients of the Brunel International African Poetry Prize and author of the chapbook *In the House of My Father* (Two Sylvias Press, 2018).

Katy Alexander is a special education teacher in Portland, Oregon.

Camila Arze Torres Goitia teaches social studies, equity, and leadership at Madison High School in Portland, Oregon. She is an Oregon Writing Project coach.

Bill Bigelow taught high school social studies in Portland, Oregon, for almost 30 years. He is the curriculum editor of *Rethinking Schools* magazine and co-director of the Zinn Education Project.

Lynsey Burkins has been an early childhood educator for the past 15 years. She contributes to the Classroom Communities blog and serves on a national committee for National Council of Teachers of English (NCTE).

Linda Christensen (lchristensen51@gmail.com) is author of *Reading, Writing, and Rising Up: Teaching for Social Justice and the Power of the Written Word (2nd Edition)* and *Teaching for Joy and Justice*, and co-editor of several books, including *Rhythm and Resistance: Teaching Poetry for Social Justice* and *Rethinking Elementary Education*. She taught high school language arts for more than 30 years in Portland, Oregon. She is currently the director of the Oregon Writing Project at Lewis & Clark College. She is a Rethinking Schools editor.

Zanovia Clark is a queer elementary educator of color living in the Pacific Northwest who is always looking for ways to improve, educate, and seek justice.

Rachel Cloues is a middle school teacher-librarian in the San Francisco Unified School District.

Grace Cornell Gonzales worked as a bilingual elementary school teacher in California and Guatemala, and is now the submissions editor for *Rethinking Schools* magazine. She is co-editor of *Rethinking Bilingual Education*.

Mykhiel Deych is a high school English language arts teacher and Queer Straight Alliance advisor. They work with the Oregon Writing Project.

Kara Hinderlie Stroman teaches at Irvington School in Portland, Oregon. She works with the Oregon Writing Project.

Alejandro Jimenez is a formerly undocumented immigrant, educator, TEDx speaker, and Emmy-nominated spoken word artist/poet living in Denver, where he is a restorative justice coordinator in a public high school.

Jaydra Johnson teaches high school language arts and Leading for Social Justice in Portland, Oregon. She is an active member of the Oregon Writing Project.

Kim Kanof teaches high school social studies at Madison High School in Portland, Oregon. Some of her students have just moved to the United States and are beginning to learn English. Kim is also a certified reading specialist and Oregon Writing Project coach.

Stan Karp (stan.karp@gmail.com) taught high school English and journalism for 30 years in Paterson, New Jersey. He is a Rethinking Schools editor and co-editor of *Rethinking Our Classrooms: Teaching for Equity and Justice* and *Rethinking School Reform: Views from the Classroom*. He is currently director of the Secondary Reform Project for New Jersey's Education Law Center.

Gretchen Kraig-Turner teaches science at Burlington-Edison High School in Burlington, Washington. She previously taught at Jefferson High School in Portland, Oregon. She is also on the Rethinking Schools Science Editorial Committee.

Chrysanthius Lathan is an instructional coach at Harriet Tubman Middle School in Portland, Oregon. She was a middle school language arts/social studies teacher, is an Oregon Writing Project coach, and has written other articles for *Rethinking Schools*.

Amy Lindahl is working as a STEM coach in Centennial School District in Oregon. She previously taught high school science in Portland Public Schools in Portland, Oregon. She is an Oregon Writing Project coach and has written other articles for *Rethinking Schools*.

Cauldierre McKay was a senior at Classical High School in Providence, Rhode Island, and a member and youth organizer with Providence Student Union when "Testing Assumptions" was written. He is currently studying computer science at the Rochester Institute of Technology.

Tom McKenna has been a teacher for the past 44 years and currently is an adjunct professor at the University of Portland in Portland, Oregon.

Lyn Mikel Brown is professor of education at Colby College and co-founder of three girl-fueled social change organizations. Her most recent book is *Powered by Girl: A Field Guide for Supporting Youth Activists*.

Larry Miller was elected to the school board of Milwaukee Public Schools in April of 2009 after teaching high school social studies in MPS for nearly two decades. Previously he'd been a community organizer and factory worker. Larry is an editor of Rethinking Schools and an adjunct at Marquette's College of Education.

James Noonan is project director for School Quality Measures at the Center for Collaborative Education in Boston.

Ikechukwu Onyema is a teacher, organizer, teacher union representative, and writer in New Jersey.

Bob Peterson (bob.e.peterson@gmail.com) is an editor of Rethinking Schools and former president of the Milwaukee Teachers' Education Association. He is co-editor of several books, including *Rethinking Columbus*, *Rethinking Mathematics*, *Rethinking Elementary Education*, *Rethinking Globalization*, and *Transforming Teacher Unions*. He is a co-founder of La Escuela Fratney, Wisconsin's first two-way bilingual school. He taught 5th grade in Milwaukee Public Schools for 30 years.

Aaron Regunberg is an organizer in Rhode Island, and was executive director of Providence Student Union when "Testing Assumptions" was first published.

Tim Shea was a senior at Classical High School in Providence, Rhode Island, and youth organizer with Providence Student Union when "Testing Assumptions" was written. He recently graduated Harvard College and is completing a one-year postgraduate fellowship in Ireland and Scotland.

Michelle Strater Gunderson is a 31-year teaching veteran who teaches 1st grade in the Chicago Public Schools. She is the chair of the Early Childhood Committee for the Chicago Teachers Union, where she also serves on the board of trustees.

Anita Stratton is an elementary school teacher in Ohio. She a teacher leader with the Columbus Area Writing Project and National Writing Project.

Gabriel A. Tanglao is a former social studies teacher in Bergen County, New Jersey. He now works in the Professional Development and Instructional Issues division for the New Jersey Education Association.

Rita Tenorio is a retired bilingual early childhood teacher. She is one of the founding editors of Rethinking Schools and taught at La Escuela Fratney for 24 years.

John Terry teaches at Wayne Hills High School in Wayne, New Jersey. He works with Human Rights Educators USA.

Chelsea Vaught is an artist, writer, and art educator currently living in Seattle. Originally from the Chicago area, she has taught general education and visual art with an emphasis on student-directed work in elementary classrooms in both the United States and United Kingdom.

Dyan Watson is an editor for Rethinking Schools and an associate professor in teacher education at the Lewis & Clark Graduate School of

Education and Counseling. She is also a co-editor of *Teaching for Black Lives, Rhythm and Resistance: Teaching Poetry for Social Justice*, and *Rethinking Elementary Education*.

Moé Yonamine (yonaminemoe@gmail.com) teaches at Roosevelt High School in Portland, Oregon. She is a Rethinking Schools editor.

Index

peer assistance and review (PAR), 237–40

A People's Curriculum for the Earth, 134

A People's History for the Classroom (Bigelow), 137

A People's History of the United States (Zinn), 124

performance assessments, 214, 227–28, 243

personal space, 151–53

Peterson, Bob
    on classroom organization, 33–39
    on presidents who owned slaves, 74–83
    on restorative practices, 182–83
    on teacher unions, 260–65

PGS (Professional Growth Systems), 237–40

Phi Delta Kappan, 209

PHS (Public Health Service), 88

Pierce, Franklin, 78

Pilgrim, Keri, 294, 297

Pine, Gerald, 55

planning books, 47–48

Planning to Change the World, 307

poetry
    as activism, 161–62
    forgiveness poems, 7
    metaphors in, 70–71
    name poems, 36
    praise poems, 52, 161–64
    resources for teaching, 134
    "Why am I so?" poems, 65–73

Polk, James K., 78

Pollard, Charles, 86–87

portfolio-based assessment, 214

Portland Area Rethinking Schools, 45

Portland Public Schools, 176–77

Portland Youth Builders, 26

praise poems, 52, 161–64

PRIDE community organizing grants, 271

privatization of schools. *See also* charter
    schools; voucher schools
    and corporate education reform, 252
    democracy threatened by, 247–48, 252, 254
    efforts to stop, 256
    and funding, 255, 259
    test results as rationale for, 208, 252
    voucher schools, 254–55

Professional Growth Systems (PGS), 237–40

PSU (Providence Student Union), 205–6, 223–28

PTA meetings, 283–84, 289

Public Health Service (PHS), 88

Q

QSA (Queer Straight Alliance), 198–204

R

racism. *See also* white supremacy
    Black disenfranchisement in schools, 276–77
    and Black students in science classes, 290–97
    in Charlottesville (2017), 277
    definitions of, 157–59
    ignored in textbooks, 47
    toward immigrants, 146–48, 299
    medical apartheid, 84–91
    "Mexican Education," 18–19, 139, 141–45
    and police violence/disrespect, 273–75, *275*
    resources for teaching about, 133
    reverse, 157–58
    rise in incidents, 35–36
    textbooks as ignoring, 80–81
    white teachers' fear of students of color, 168–75

Rain in a Dry Land, 95–96

Ramadan, 190–91

rape culture/sexual harassment, 149–56, 181, 187

read-arounds, 52, 119–20

Reading, Writing, and Rising Up (Christensen), 133

re-entry circles, 183

refugees, 94–101

Regunberg, Aaron, 223–28

repairing harm circles, 182–83

resources from Rethinking Schools

U

V

W

Y

Z

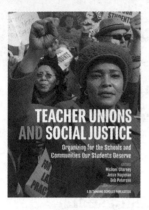

Teacher Unions and Social Justice
Organizing for the schools and communities our students deserve

Edited by Michael Charney, Jesse Hagopian, and Bob Peterson

An anthology of over 60 articles documenting the history and the how-tos of social justice unionism. Together, they describe the growing movement to forge multiracial alliances with communities to defend and transform public education.

2021 • Paperback • 448 pages • ISBN: 978-0-942961-09-6
$29.95*

Teaching for Black Lives
Edited by Dyan Watson, Jesse Hagopian, Wayne Au

Teaching for Black Lives grows directly out of the movement for Black lives. We recognize that anti-Black racism constructs Black people, and Blackness generally, as not counting as human life. Throughout this book, we provide resources and demonstrate how teachers can connect curriculum to young people's lives and root their concerns and daily experiences in what is taught and how classrooms are set up. We also highlight the hope and beauty of student activism and collective action.

Paperback • 368 pages • ISBN: 978-0-942961-04-1
Print: $29.95*

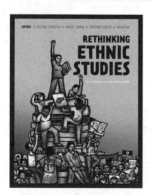

Rethinking Ethnic Studies
Edited by R. Tolteka Cuauhtin, Miguel Zavala, Christine Sleeter, and Wayne Au

Built around core themes of indigeneity, colonization, anti-racism, and activism, *Rethinking Ethnic Studies* offers vital resources for educators committed to the ongoing struggle for racial justice in our schools.

Paperback • 368 pages • ISBN: 978-0-942961-02-7
Print: $24.95*

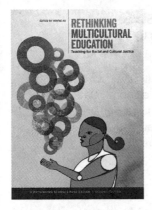

Rethinking Multicultural Education
Teaching for Racial and Cultural Justice

Edited by Wayne Au

This expanded second edition demonstrates a powerful vision of anti-racist social justice education. Practical, rich in story, and analytically sharp, *Rethinking Multicultural Education* reclaims multicultural education as part of a larger struggle for justice and against racism, colonization, and cultural oppression—in schools and society.

Paperback • 418 pages • ISBN: 978-0-942961-53-9
Print $24.95!*

Reading, Writing, and Rising Up
SECOND EDITION
Teaching About Social Justice and the Power of the Written Word

By Linda Christensen

Essays, lesson plans, and a remarkable collection of student writing, with an unwavering focus on language arts teaching for justice.

Paperback • 196 pages • ISBN: 978-0-942961-69-0
Print: $24.95*

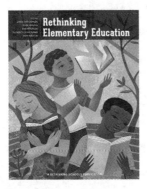

Rethinking Elementary Education
Edited by Linda Christensen, Mark Hansen, Bob Peterson, Elizabeth Barbian, and Dyan Watson

Offers practical insights about how to integrate the teaching of content with social justice, seek wisdom from students and their families, and navigate stifling tests and mandates. Some of the finest writing about elementary school life and learning.

Paperback • 320 pages • ISBN: 978-0-942961-52-2
Print $24.95!*

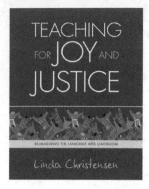

Teaching for Joy and Justice
Re-Imagining the Language Arts Classroom

By Linda Christensen

Demonstrates how to draw on students' lives and the world to teach poetry, essays, narratives, and critical literacy skills. Part autobiography, part curriculum guide, part critique of today's numbing standardized mandates, this book sings with hope—born of Christensen's more than 40 years as a classroom teacher, language arts specialist, and teacher educator.

Paperback • 287 pages • ISBN: 978-0-942961-43-0
Print: $19.95* | PDF: $14.95

Rhythm and Resistance
Teaching Poetry for Social Justice

Edited by Linda Christensen and Dyan Watson

Practical lessons about how to teach poetry to build community, understand literature and history, talk back to injustice, and construct stronger literacy skills across content areas—from elementary school to graduate school.

Paperback • 272 pages • ISBN: 978-0-942961-61-4
Print: $24.95*

A People's Curriculum for the Earth
Teaching Climate Change and the Environmental Crisis

Edited by Bill Bigelow and Tim Swinehart

Engaging environmental teaching activities from *Rethinking Schools* magazine alongside classroom-friendly readings on climate change, energy, water, food, pollution—and the people who are working to make things better.

Paperback • 433 pages • ISBN: 978-0-942961-57-7
Print $24.95*

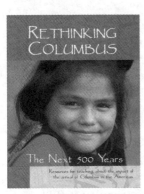

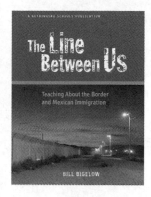

The Line Between Us
Teaching About the Border and Mexican Immigration

By Bill Bigelow

Using stories, historical narrative, role plays, poetry, and video, veteran teacher Bill Bigelow shows how he approaches immigration and border issues in his classroom.

Paperback • 160 pages • ISBN: 978-0-942961-31-7

PDF: $11.95

Rethinking Popular Culture and Media
SECOND EDITION

Edited by Elizabeth Marshall and Özlem Sensoy

Beginning with the idea that the "popular" in the everyday lives of teachers and students is fundamentally political, this provocative collection of articles examines how and what popular toys, books, films, music, and other media "teach." The second edition includes revised articles, nine new articles, and an updated list of resources.

Paperback • 340 pages • ISBN: 978-0-942961-63-8

Print $24.95*

Open Minds to Equality
A Sourcebook of Learning Activities to Affirm Diversity and Promote Equity

By Nancy Schniedewind and Ellen Davidson

Activities to help students understand and change inequalities based on race, gender, class, age, language, sexual orientation, physical/mental ability, and religion.

Paperback • 408 pages • ISBN: 978-0-942961-60-7

Print $24.95*

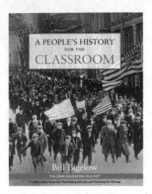
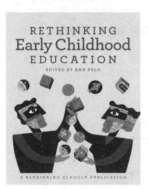
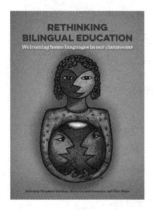